MW00743990

NIGHT+DAY
LOS ANGELES

By Paul Zemanek

PULSE GUIDES

Distributed in the United States and Canada by National Book Network (NBN). First Edition. Printed in the United States. 30% postconsumer content. Copyright © 2006 ASDavis Media Group, Inc. All rights reserved. ISBN-10:0-9766013-5-4; ISBN-13:978-0-9766013-5-7

Credits

Executive Editor	Alan S. Davis
Editor	Anita Chabria
Contributing Editor	Marlene Goldman
Author	Paul Zemanek
Nightlife Contributor	Patrick Green
Copy Editors	Gail Nelson-Bonebrake, Kelly Borgeson, Elizabeth Stroud
Maps	Chris Gillis
Production	Jo Farrell, Samia Afra

Photo Credits: (Front cover, left to right) Les Byerley (martini), courtesy of Nadine Johnson, Inc. (Rooftop Bar at the Standard Downtown), courtesy of Laphil.org (Walt Disney Concert Hall); (Back cover, left to right) courtesy of Aaron Cook (AOC), Hollywood Roosevelt Hotel (Hollywood Roosevelt Hotel Pool), Richard Ross/J. Paul Getty Trust (Getty Villa), courtesy of Ole Henriksen; (Inside cover, top to bottom) Mario Anzuoni (Spider), 25 Degrees, Randall Michelson (Egyptian Theatre); (p.4) Mary Lou D'Auray.

Special Sales

For information about bulk purchases of Pulse Guides (ten copies or more), email us at bookorders@pulseguides.com. Special bulk rates are available for charities, corporations, institutions, and online and mail-order catalogs, and our books can be customized to suit your company's needs.

NIGHT+DAY
the Cool Cities series from **PULSE**GUIDES

P.O. Box 590780, San Francisco, CA 94159
pulseguides.com

Pulse Guides is an imprint of ASDavis Media Group, Inc.

The Night+Day Difference

The Pulse of the City

Our job is to point you to all of the city's peak experiences: amazing museums, unique spas, and spectacular views. But the complete *urbanista* experience is more than just impressions—it is grownup fun, the kind that thrives by night as well as by day. Urban fun is a hip nightclub or a trendy restaurant. It is people-watching and people-meeting. Lonely planet? We don't think so. **Night+Day** celebrates our lively planet.

The Right Place. The Right Time. It Matters.

A **Night+Day** city must have exemplary restaurants, a vibrant nightlife scene, and enough attractions to keep a visitor busy for six days without having to do the same thing twice. In selecting restaurants, food is important, but so is the scene. Our hotels, most of which are 4- and 5-star properties, are rated for the quality of the concierge staff (can they get you into a hot restaurant?) as well as the rooms. You won't find kids with fake IDs at our nightlife choices. And the attractions must be truly worthy of your time. But experienced travelers know that timing is almost everything. Going to a restaurant at 7pm can be a very different experience (and probably less fun) than at 9pm; a champagne boat cruise might be ordinary in the morning but spectacular at sunset. We believe providing the reader with this level of detail makes the difference between a good experience and a great one.

The Bottom Line

Your time is precious. Our guide must be easy to use and dead-on accurate. That is why our executive editor, editors, and writers (locals who are in touch with what is great—and what is not) spend hundreds of hours researching, writing, and debating selections for each guide. The results are presented in four unique ways: The *99 Best* with our top three choices in 33 categories that highlight what is great about the city; the *Experience* chapters, in which our selections are organized by distinct themes or personalities (Hot & Cool, Hip, and Classic); a *Perfect Plan* (3 Nights and Days) for each theme, showing how to get the most out of the city in a short period of time; and the *Los Angeles Black Book*, listing all the hotels, restaurants, nightlife, and attractions, with key details, contact information, and page references.

Our bottom line is this: If you find our guide easy to use and enjoyable to read, and with our help you have an extraordinary time, we have succeeded. We review and value all feedback from our readers, so please contact us at **feedback@pulseguides.com**.

From the Publisher

Retirement for me ten years ago meant setting out on a journey to find the 100 most fun places to be in the world at the right time—from experiencing Fantasy Fest in Key West, Florida, to participating in the Songkran Water Festival in Changmai, Thailand. Retirement ended because these travels compelled me to create two extraordinary guidebooks—one for North America, and one for Europe, Latin America, and Asia—named *The Fun Also Rises* after Ernest Hemingway's *The Sun Also Rises*. His book, by the way, helped popularize what has become perhaps the most thrilling party on earth, Pamplona's Fiesta de San Fermín, also known as the Running of the Bulls.

Those two guides morphed into an entirely new series called the **Night+Day** guides, the first travel series from Pulse Guides. They share with *The Fun Also Rises* the same underlying principle: *Never settle for the ordinary*. Created for Gen-Xers to Zoomers (Boomers with a zest for life), **Night+Day** provides the kind of detail, in a unique and easy-to-access format, that is key to unlocking what is great about Los Angeles. Unlike guidebooks that are neither informative nor exciting enough to capture peak experiences—whether for world-class events or a night on the town—**Night+Day** presents the best that a city has to offer—hotels, restaurants, nightlife, and attractions that are exciting without being stuffy.

More than 35 years ago I attended college in L.A.—and so as not to upset those who attended our crosstown rival, including our senior editor, let's just say I attended the Harvard of the West. At that time, L.A. could have been fairly described as a cultural and social wasteland. It wasn't a cool city. Now even we San Franciscans have to admit that L.A. is fun, world-class, and something to behold.

I hope that our willingness to explore new approaches to guidebooks, combined with meticulous research, provides you with unique and significant experiences.

Wishing you extraordinary times,

[signature]

Alan S. Davis, Publisher and Executive Editor

Pulse Guides

P.S. To contact me, or for updated information on all of our **Night+Day** guides, please visit our website at **pulseguides.com**.

TOC

About the Authors

Paul Zemanek is a Santa Monica–based freelance writer who has contributed to Reuters, *Maxim*, Travelocity, and *Southwest Spirit*, and has written about museum restaurants, vintage hot spots in San Francisco and Chicago, downtown development, and many other travel trends. He is working on his first novel, a murder-mystery satire, not to mention the requisite screenplay.

Patrick Green is a Hollywood-based writer who channels his inner Bukowski to document the L.A. nightlife scene. His nightlife reviews appear in citysearch, shecky's, la.com, and **Night+Day** Los Angeles and Las Vegas, but check out his current myspace page's blog, myspace.com/patrickgreen_la, for his latest tales, lies, and exaggerations on everything from the legacy of Dolemite to the brilliance of Sergio Leone, the many uses of peanut butter, and the resurgence of spandex.

Acknowledgments

A special thanks to those who helped guide me to the very best that Los Angeles has to offer: Paul Davis; Jeff and Didi Fine; Dennis, Florence, and Lisa Forst; Jim and Gloria Hassan; and John and Holly Nuckols.

Alan S. Davis, Executive Editor

Introduction

Welcome to Los Angeles. By that, we mean welcome to that vast county in Southern California comprised of a half-dozen area codes, 21 freeways, 75 miles of coastline, 88 independent cities, 300 museums, a half-million strip malls, and a gazillion straight days of sunshine per year (give or take).

Los Angeles: What It Was

It all started humbly enough when a small, racially mixed band of farmers was dispatched by Spanish missionaries to settle a piece of land by a river about ten miles south of the Mission San Gabriel Archangel. On September 4, 1781, what was surely the longest-named small city in the world was founded in the area that is now Downtown L.A.—El Pueblo de Nuestra Señora la Reina de los Angeles del Río Porciúncula (population 44). In time, the city would come to be known simply as Los Angeles.

Over the next century of change, a combination of booms, bumper crops, land grabs, and engineering feats would transform this isolated farming pueblo into a Big American City. Among the first to stake their claim in the early 1800s were the rancheros, a prosperous group of newly independent Mexican landowners shipping cattle hides to the eastern U.S. and selling beef to a soaring population of gold miners in Northern California. Their fortunes would change radically after the U.S.-Mexican War (1846–48), when land rights were reviewed and land was largely expropriated by the U.S. government. The arrival of a railroad connecting Los Angeles to the East Coast coincided with the planting of some orange trees in the area. Soon Southern California's sagging economy was back in business, the area swiftly becoming the nation's top orange producer. In the 50 years leading up to 1900, Los Angeles' population would balloon from barely 1,000 to more than 100,000. L.A. soared into twentieth-century prosperity with the discovery of oil and a burgeoning industry led by L.A.'s first oil baron, Edward L. Doheny. The opening of the Panama Canal would turn young San Pedro Harbor (now part of the nation's busiest cargo terminal) into a bustling port. Of course, none of this desert basin's wild success could have been sustained without the biggest civic coup in L.A. history. In 1904, Los Angeles water bureau superintendent William Mulholland found

> **El Pueblo de Nuestra Señora la Reina de los Angeles del Río Porciúncula was founded on September 4, 1781. In time, the city would be known simply as Los Angeles.**

the city's badly needed solution to its water supply woes, 250 miles north in the snowmelt-rich Owens Valley. Land was snatched up on false pretenses (ostensibly for a cattle farm), and soon an enormous aqueduct project was under way. Nine years, $24.5 million, and one con job later, water from the Owens Valley was being siphoned into the thirsty jaws of its metropolis neighbor to the south. Problem solved. Case closed.

Hollywood's pioneers were ragtag peddlers churning out silent shorts and dodging Thomas Edison's patent royalty collectors. The world's most glamorous industry had arrived.

Nice weather, easy filming conditions, and safe distance from Thomas Edison's patent wars back east fostered L.A.'s first fledgling movie business around the same time the water started flowing. Edison and a team of companies held many patents over the filmmaking process, and routinely went after independent filmmakers who failed to pay their dues. Many of those fledgling auteurs headed west, reasoning that putting a few thousand miles between themselves and Edison's patent enforcers was no bad thing. The pioneers of this trade were ragtag peddlers cranking out silent shorts, taking only the occasional bullet in the lens—a tactic of Edison's collection agents. A bona fide movie industry of studio moguls, directors, and celebrities soon followed, churning out the first flicks, turning the name of its small community headquarters—Hollywood—into a major brand, and selling tickets to watch scenes being shot on the Universal lot (long before the *Back to the Future* ride was installed). The world's most glamorous industry—The Industry, as it would come to be called—had arrived, and its original location has been L.A.'s biggest marketing banner ever since. These days, you can't drive the streets of Los Angeles without seeing the star trailers, grip trucks, and other paraphernalia along some well-lit sidewalk, telling you something is being shot. Of course, it's a city that makes a perfect movie set, owing to all the drama that takes place around here.

What hasn't Los Angeles seen over the last century? Earthquakes, brush fires, mudslides, and race riots have periodically shaken this city to its roots. And what roots they are. Huge territorial expansions and an influx of people from some 140 countries have turned greater L.A. into a sprawling microcosm of the world. The Summer Olympics have been here twice. The Dodgers and Lakers have come, the Rams and Raiders have gone (along with O.J. and Shaq). The Queen Mary has parked herself in Long Beach Harbor and opened three restaurants and a hotel. Disneyland is just down the road.

Los Angeles: What It Is

Everyone has an opinion about Los Angeles, especially those who've never actually been here. If L.A. were Chicago, Des Moines, or Tampa, it might care what people have to say about it. But L.A. is too wrapped up in itself to return those calls. It's too busy being the entertainment capital of the world, speaking in 86 different tongues, making fashion statements, fusing Vietnamese and Salvadoran cuisines, erecting famous art galleries and music halls, sipping iced lattes in the dead of winter and cocktails from plastic cups at Skybar, talking about the Lakers or the Clippers, reserving a patio table in Beverly Hills, reading bad spec scripts on the treadmill, cruising Sunset Boulevard, hanging out at the Playboy Mansion, wobbling through Venice Beach on rollerblades, roaming the tide pools of Malibu, hiking in the Santa Monica Mountains, watching car chases narrated by breathless local newscasters, and welcoming about 25 million satisfied visitors each year. Los Angeles isn't trying to be rude. There's just no time to respond to all the jealous hate mail. Plus, life is way too short, especially with the Big One still out there.

Four million people inhabit the city of Los Angeles, with its crazy-legs borders running in various directions from the tip of the San Fernando Valley to the cliffs of San Pedro. Ten million people fill out Los Angeles County, which stretches from Malibu and Santa Monica (at its western borders) through Beverly Hills and Hollywood to Burbank and Pasadena (in the Valley), and as far south as Long Beach, and includes a patchwork quilt of several dozen other cities you'll probably never visit. Four neighboring counties belong to the greater Los Angeles area, which in itself constitutes the world's tenth

Key Dates

1781 El Pueblo de Nuestra Senora la Reina de los Angeles del Río Porciúncula (Los Angeles) is founded (population 44).

1876 Southern Pacific finishes its line to Los Angeles.

1913 William Mulholland builds a 233-mile aqueduct, bringing water to Los Angeles.

1965 The racially-motivated Watts Riots last six days, killing 34 and causing $35 million in damage.

1992 The Rodney King uprising sparks arson and looting and causes 50 to 60 deaths.

1994 A 6.7 trembler, known as the Northridge Earthquake, hits Los Angeles hard.

1994 The televised O.J. Simpson car chase is just the start of the renowned murder trial.

2002 Hollywood's proposed secession from L.A. is defeated.

Night+Day's Los Angeles Urbie

Night+Day cities are chosen because they have a vibrant nightlife scene, standard-setting and innovative restaurants, cutting-edge hotels, and enough attractions to keep one busy for six days without doing the same thing twice. In short, they are fun. They represent the quintessential *urbanista* experience. This experience wouldn't exist but for the creativity and talents of many people and organizations. In honor of all who have played a role in making Los Angeles one of the world's coolest cities, Pulse Guides is pleased to give special recognition, and our Urbie Award, to an individual or organization whose contribution is exemplary.

THE URBIE AWARD: Dodd Mitchell

If you're sitting in the latest Los Angeles restaurant, hotel, or nightclub, and you're feeling hip, sexy, and peaceful at the same time, the chances are pretty good that Dodd Mitchell did the interior design. The man who heads Dodd Mitchell Design, the firm responsible for the look of more than 20 sleek L.A. hot spots (Katana, Dolce, Sushi Roku, and the Roosevelt Hotel are a few of our favorites), is known for indulgent textures—black-leather tablecloths, red-velvet drapes, alligator-covered chairs, and mood-enhancing lighting (flattering light being a must in camera-ready Los Angeles).

Mitchell, a high school dropout who started as a floor sweeper at a design company, doesn't limit himself. "I don't have a formal education in this," he has said, "so I don't have any rules." In the case of the Hollywood Roosevelt Hotel redesign, he was able to pay homage to the original '20s architecture without being handcuffed by it. The attitude of the city often influences how Mitchell goes about his aesthetic decisions. He uses natural materials whenever possible to combat the superficial vibe that permeates the land that humility forgot. He also makes sure the space takes into account the stressful nature of life in the big city. "It's always helpful for those with chaotic schedules to feel as if they are somewhere else," Mitchell has said, "away from their troubles, escaping from daily stress while relaxing in the privacy of their own home."

Until now, Dodd Mitchell has focused his creativity mostly on Los Angeles destinations. But his services are in demand elsewhere (Las Vegas, New York, Mexico, and Europe beckon—his schedule is booked years in advance), so L.A.'s residents and visitors alike should enjoy him while they can.

largest economy and has a higher population than that of the 21 smallest states combined.

If you've come to L.A. to see Mötley Crüe's or Kermit the Frog's star on the Hollywood Walk of Fame, well, that's just fine, because they're both here. The entertainment industry is L.A.'s best known and most fluid backdrop, moving with

> **Welcome to the six area codes, 21 freeways, 75 miles of coastline, 88 independent cities, 300 museums, and half-million strip malls that make up the Los Angeles area.**

effortless ease between the silver screen, the patio at Spago, and the lobby at Shutters. But the rest of Los Angeles—a goliath among the world's major cities and perhaps the most culturally significant for good or bad—is out there too, under the same warm sun and twinkling satellites, using the same pinched water supply, resisting anything close to a cohesive definition.

Los Angeles loves the term "reinvention," but a city this size can change only about as fast as a big ship turns—slowly and significantly. If you haven't been here in a while, places like Hollywood and Venice Beach will look brighter and cleaner; if it's your first time, they may look like they could use a good scrubbing.

Undeniably, the place is changing, most recently from multimillion-dollar revitalization efforts that have given us the Hollywood & Highland complex (which, appropriately enough, has already had its first face-lift), the Kodak Theatre, the Grove at the Farmers Market, and the renovated Getty Villa. Downtown Los Angeles is now grander, hipper, and more inviting with the Walt Disney Concert Hall, the Staples Center, the Rooftop Bar at The Standard Hotel, and the upcoming $2 billion sports and entertainment center, L.A. Live, scheduled to open in 2008. First-timers may still see it as an eerily sequestered place, but Downtown is filled with history and with history in the making.

There are myriad other "centers" in Los Angeles to satisfy any personality. If you're looking for the beach, there's upscale Malibu, trendy Santa Monica, gritty Venice, nautical Marina del Rey, or the very small-townish South Bay. For the retro vibe, Hollywood is where it's at. If you want to live the high life, try Beverly Hills. If you want to live the alternative high life, head to the gay capital of Los Angeles, West Hollywood. If you like your world a little rougher around the edges, Echo Park is the place for cutting-edge art and fashion. In other words, let your mood dictate your geography.

This city-within-a-county-within-an-area offers an inexhaustible number of experiences for visitors (or locals who can pretend to be visitors in a place this large and varied). Challenges await you, like braving the monstrous line at Pink's Hot Dogs, learning to surf, or sitting in the same restaurant as Jack Nicholson and trying not to stare. But most experiences will leave you craving more, and the best are here between these covers. Have fun.

Welcome to fabulous Los Angeles ...

THE 99 BEST of LOS ANGELES

Who needs another "Best" list? You do—if it comes with details and insider tips that make the difference between a good experience and a great one. We've pinpointed the 33 categories that make Los Angeles exciting, magnetic, and unforgettable, and picked the absolute three best places to go for each. Check out the next few pages of our favorite ways to play in this invigorating city—the glamorous lounges, happening cultural scenes, stellar clubs, don't-miss museums, and liveliest places to see and be seen.

Beaches

#1–3: With so much sun-baked coast, the question is, where do you dive into the big blue? L.A.'s 75-mile stretch of surf has it all, from secluded coves and lonely tide pools to beach towns full of longboarder dudes and volleyball babes. You can pedal for 20 miles along Santa Monica Bay or park on a towel in Malibu.

Manhattan Beach

End of Manhattan Beach Blvd., Manhattan Beach • Classic

The Draw: Hard-to-please visitors cheer up when taken to this swell yuppie backyard in the South Bay. "Now, this is California ..."

The Scene: Former squatters like the Beach Boys would gasp at the rents down here these days, but otherwise it's still *Endless Summer*, a mecca for surfers, volleyball exhibitionists, rollerbladers, and bikini chasers. If you wove together all the blond hair on this sunny strand, it would reach Jupiter.

Hot Tip: For a lively happy hour, head one beach community south and take your pick of the bars on the Hermosa Strand.

Venice Beach/Ocean Front Walk

Ocean Front Walk at 27th St., Venice Beach • Hip

The Draw: At least once in your life, you have to visit Ocean Front Walk—a carnival of sun-damaged artists and performers, palm readers, homeless chiropractors, open-air weight lifters, incense hucksters, circle drummers, hoop dreamers, freaks, exhibitionists, voyeurs, and people on various wheeled contraptions.

The Scene: See above. If you were here ten years ago, you'll be impressed by the ace clean-up job. If not, the place may seem like it could use a cleaning.

Hot Tip: Tourists and locals alike seem too preoccupied with the Walk to notice Venice's excellent three-mile beach sitting wide open beyond it. Stretch out and pretend you're alone in Cancún.

Zuma Beach

30050 Pacific Coast Highway, Malibu • Classic

The Draw: Malibu seems a bit disappointing until you reach Zuma, its best full-service beach. Even Santa Monica residents gladly drive 20 miles to this patch of cleaner water and whiter sand.

The Scene: Families, surfers, biceps, and bikinis can find three miles of towel space with excellent facilities, lifeguards, volleyball courts, and some good wave activity—lots of fun for everyone.

Hot Tip: Lose the weekend crowds by following the surfers to Zuma's quieter north end or heading south to Westward Beach, near Point Dume (which is even quieter). Save six bucks by parking for free on Pacific Coast Highway (that's PCH in local parlance).

Celebrity Hangouts

#4–6: Celebrity sightings are as common in this town as a good freeway chase. But stars have to get their party on too, so where do they go to let loose? Why not go see for yourself at these paparazzi "stalk" yards? Just don't forget to bring your wallet, blue-steel stare, and A-list attitude.

Holly's

1651 Wilcox Ave., Hollywood, 323-461-1400 • Hot & Cool

The Draw: More hot young things pack into this Parisian party playpen than attend the half-yearly sale at Fred Segal.

The Scene: This Hollywood clubhouse caters to the likes of Scarlett Johansson and Hilary Duff by keeping the scene controlled (no cameras allowed). Exclusivity comes at a price—scenester Rick Calamaro's club dishes out Hollywood A- and B-list one night and an empty house the next. *Thu-Sat 10pm-2am.* C B ≡

Hot Tip: Come early to check out if it's worth the time and money (greasing the doorman). If not, try Calamaro's more democratic club next door, Nacional.

LAX

1714 N. Las Palmas Ave., Hollywood, 323-464-0171 • Hot & Cool

The Draw: Fly high among a constellation of stars (Ashton Kutcher, Britney Spears, Mischa Barton) at this airport-inspired first-class club.

The Scene: Celebrity wax wizard DJ AM has teamed up with club owner Loyal Pennings to try for L.A. nightlife's top gun title. Their spot is a cliquey scene set against a kitschy backdrop. This is where *Simple Lifers*–turned–mortal combatants Paris Hilton and Nicole Richie clawed it out. *Wed-Sat 10pm-2am.* C ≡

Hot Tip: DJ AM isn't the only famous face manning the wheels of steel. Benji Madden (Good Charlotte), Adam 12 (She Wants Revenge), and Steve Aoki (actress-model Devon's brother) are also known to stop by and spin tunes.

Tropicana Bar at the Roosevelt Hotel

7000 Hollywood Blvd., Hollywood, 323-769-7260 • Hip

The Draw: New staff means less drama at this Amanda Demme–less celebrity center where scene whores and starry-eyed cubicle creatures come together.

The Scene: Courtney Love's (alleged) overdose and Lindsay Lohan's underage dehydration antics were just two of the controversies surrounding this revived Hollywood landmark under nightlife guru Demme's reign. Now, the stuffy air has been let out, making this "it" spot less exclusive, while still catering to an industry crowd. Designer Dodd Mitchell's vintage Palm Springs look is ideal for lounging or late-night carousing. *Pool daily 9am-7pm, bar Thu-Sat 9pm-2am.* ≡

Hot Tip: Roosevelt guests are now given pool priority—sounds reasonable, but it wasn't always so. In the beginning, inexplicable rules put more weight on Hollywood status than the hotel's own guest list.

Celebrity-Owned Restaurants

#7–9: Any restaurant worth its sea salt in L.A. has some kind of celebrity connection, no matter how remote (George Clooney ordered the lavender crème brûlée, Cameron Diaz loves the chicken mole, Sean Connery used the restroom), but only a handful of hot restaurants actually have big star investors.

Ago
8478 Melrose Ave., West Hollywood, 323-655-6333 • Hot & Cool

The Draw: Robert De Niro and the brothers Weinstein, previously of Miramax, own a piece of this happening West Hollywood trattoria, run by executive chef Agostino Sciandri.

The Scene: Warm up at the front bar, abuzz with movie-biz types and dressed-to-kill industry fawns. Graduate to the perfectly lit split-level dining room or the heated outdoor patio for upscale classic Tuscan fare, priced for its clientele. *Mon-Fri noon-2:30pm, 6-11:30pm, Sat 6-11:30pm, Sun 6-10:30pm.* $$ B≡

Hot Tip: Sunday is the slowest night and easiest to get in, but Thursday is the hottest. If you can't score a reservation, it is possible to eat in the small bar.

Geisha House*
6633 Hollywood Blvd., Hollywood, 323-460-6300 • Hot & Cool

The Draw: Pan-Asian food and sushi are served in a social, sexy environment that can only be described as a fun-loving caricature of a Tokyo whorehouse.

The Scene: Adjust yourself in the full-length mirror before entering the restaurant, where seeing and being seen takes on a whole new dimension, even for L.A. A tall red fireplace dominates the main room, which is filled with well-dressed Hollywood hotshots, hangers-on, and anyone else hoping to be associated, however remotely, with co-owner Ashton Kutcher. *Nightly 6-11pm, bar until 2am.* $$$ B≡

Hot Tip: The Moon Bar upstairs, where smokers congregate, has a retractable roof. It sounds cool, but if you're not a big fan of cigarette smoke, avoid it.

Ortolan (G)
8338 W. Third St., Los Angeles, 323-653-3300 • Hot & Cool

The Draw: One of the hottest restaurants on Third Street is partly owned by actress Jeri Ryan and serves French cuisine in dramatic, creative ways.

The Scene: Sumptuous furnishings and dramatic archways set the tone for a special dining experience that attracts the cream of Los Angeles. Lighting is dim, giving the space a warmth further heightened by a fireplace and an herb garden wall. *Tue-Sat 6-10pm.* $$$ B❶≡

Hot Tip: If it's late and you're in the mood for a gourmet meal, the restaurant's bar is one of the few in L.A. that serves a full menu until midnight.

Celebrity-Spotting Restaurants

#10–12: There are visitors to Los Angeles who claim they don't care about seeing celebrities. And no one believes them. We can't promise that Gwyneth Paltrow will be at The Ivy having lunch the day you decide to dine there, but we can promise that if she isn't, there's a distinct possibility you'll spot someone else of a similar caliber. Or at least William Shatner.

The Ivy

113 N. Robertson Blvd., Beverly Hills, 310-274-8303 • Classic

The Draw: The chance of a Brad Pitt or Julia Roberts sighting, better-than-you-think American and Cajun cuisine, incredible desserts, and just the prestige of eating at this legendary restaurant draw in crowds every day, every meal.

The Scene: Agents come here to be seen making deals, and celebrity couples quash rumors of marital trouble by being photographed together on the rose-filled brick patio. Many people actually come for the food, particularly the crab cakes and the black-pepper shrimp. You can't go wrong with the pecan brownies for dessert. *Mon-Thu 11:30am-10:30pm, Fri 11:30am-11pm, Sat 11am-11pm, Sun 10:30am-10pm.* $$$ ≣

Hot Tip: The snappier your casual wardrobe, the better your chances of getting a table on the patio—the see-and-be-seen seats.

Mr. Chow

344 N. Camden Dr., Beverly Hills, 310-278-9911 • Classic

The Draw: Noodles are made by hand and Peking Duck is prepared the old-fashioned way. But the real draw here isn't the food—it's who is at the next table.

The Scene: Paparazzi stand out front while their prey sit elbow to elbow inside, eating scallion pancakes and wonton soup under the watchful eye of owner Michael Chow—or at least several images of him, including one painted by Andy Warhol. *Mon-Fri noon-2:30pm, 6-11:30pm, Sat-Sun 6-11:30pm.* $$$ ≣

Hot Tip: To blend in, let the waiter order for you—it's custom here.

Il Ristorante di Giorgio Baldi

114 W. Channel Rd., Santa Monica, 310-573-1660 • Classic

The Draw: Kick back for home-style Italian food and some serious star power combined with a bit of the Tuscan coast vibe in this wonderfully relaxed beach-shack of a place just off the Pacific Coast Highway.

The Scene: Friendly, efficient staff serve tables filled with casually dressed A-listers paying decidedly uncasual prices to enjoy the combination of a romantic setting and well-prepared food. *Tue-Sun 6-10pm.* $$$ ≣

Hot Tip: The patio here is a plastic-covered affair in the front—skip it in favor of the main room, where the buzz is better.

Best Cool Museums

#13–15: People are often surprised by the number of museums in this city, with its reputation for bottle-blonde superficiality. But look past the flaxen locks and silicone mountains and you'll find a vibrant art scene that fosters dozens of impressive venues from the Westside to Downtown.

Getty Villa

17985 Pacific Coast Hwy., Pacific Palisades, 310-440-7300 • Classic

The Draw: The newly renovated Getty has one of the world's greatest collections of ancient art, some 44,000 pieces, covering Greek, Roman, and Etruscan antiquities—all in a blow-your-mind beautiful setting.

The Scene: Since the Getty Villa hands out a limited number of tickets, you find yourself wandering through the main building, the long fountain courtyard, and the herb garden without bumping into masses of people. The audio for the self-guided tour means you can do so while in your own world. *Thu-Mon 10am-5pm.*

Hot Tip: Plan your visit around a performance in the Getty Villa amphitheater. And note: Day-of tickets are sometimes available on the website (getty.edu).

Los Angeles County Museum of Art (LACMA)

5905 Wilshire Blvd., Los Angeles, 323-857-6000 • Classic

The Draw: More than 100,000 works illustrate a fairly representative timeline of the art world from 3000 B.C. onward, including European masterpieces and impressive collections of Korean and Islamic art.

The Scene: The museum will open in stages over the next several years as the ambitious project to "expand, upgrade, and unify" its six-building campus continues. The redesign was developed by the Renzo Piano Building Workshop. *Mon, Tue, Thu noon-8pm, Fri noon-9pm, Sat-Sun 11am-8pm.* $

Hot Tip: Free evening concerts in summer are a lovely place for a cocktail.

Norton Simon Museum

411 W. Colorado Blvd., Pasadena, 626-449-6840 • Classic

The Draw: The austere museum holds a surprisingly vast collection of art—perhaps the best in the West—covering some 2,000 years, most notably European paintings, sculpture, and tapestry from the 14th century, first millennium statuary from India and Southeast Asia, and 20th-century paintings and prints by Western artists like Picasso and Warhol.

The Scene: You pass by sculptures of Rodin on the front lawn, a fitting introduction before heading into the galleries, where media tend to be mixed, with sculptures and paintings occupying the same room. *Sat-Mon and Wed-Thu noon-6pm, Fri noon-9pm.* $

Hot Tip: Who is Norton Simon? Find out at a screening of the museum's documentary on its founder, daily at 12:30, 2:30, and 4:30pm, and Friday at 6:30pm.

Date Spots

#16–18: Formal wining and dining is so passé in an informal MySpace, text-me social world. Chances are your date is more interested in his BlackBerry than the beurre blanc. So what's a 21st-century romantic to do? Order a good bottle, take in the scene, and remember—everything seems better after the second cork is popped.

The Bowery*
6268 Sunset Blvd., Hollywood, 323-465-3400 • Hip

The Draw: Trend-seeking urbanites slip into this cozy New York–style bar and bistro for comfort foods, quintessential cocktails, and an intimate neighborhood feel.

The Scene: More Lower East Side New York than Sunset Strip, the decor includes subway tile walls, a tin ceiling, and shoulder-to-shoulder seating. It's the perfect place to grab a bite (Bowery Burger, sweet potato fries) or buzz (imported beers, hand-picked wines, Ambrosia white martini) before heading to the Arclight Cinemas or going out to the clubs. *Mon-Fri noon-2am, Sat-Sun 6pm-2am.* $ ≣

Hot Tip: Metered street parking is practically nil on Sunset and the shared valet service is s-l-o-w. A much quicker alternative is the parking structure around the corner on Argyle across the street from the Hollywood Palladium.

Cinespace*
6356 Hollywood Blvd., 2nd Floor, Hollywood, 323-817-3456 • Hot & Cool

The Draw: The "dinner and a movie" date concept goes cutting-edge in a 21st-century supper club setting.

The Scene: Couples, clubbers, and cineastes find a one-stop, multipurpose, minimalist hangout to fit all their nightlife needs. Enjoy cult classics in an intimate screening room over dinner and drinks, before hitting the dance floor. *Dinner Thu-Sat 6-10pm, bar till 2am.* $$ ≣

Hot Tip: Check the cinespace.info.com website for upcoming movies. You can even make suggestions or set up a screening for your own film.

Citizen Smith*
1602 Cahuenga Blvd., Hollywood, 323-461-5001• Hot & Cool

The Draw: This self-proclaimed "everyman bistro" is guaranteed to satisfy the trend-seeking, people-watching "in-crowd."

The Scene: Stark urban contrasts define this low-lit restaurant/bar in the heart of the Cahuenga Corridor. A fashion-forward crowd of canoodling couples and posturing singles indulges in edgy twists (Jalapeno Mac) behind a gaucho-chic backdrop and classic rock beat. *Mon-Fri 11am-1:30am, Sat-Sun 6pm-1:30am.* $$ ≣

Hot Tip: The long hours make it a great place to start or end a night. There are plenty of options if you want to make the Cahuenga Corridor crawl, including The Beauty Bar, Burgundy Room, and Le Velvet Margarita.

Best

Daytime Drinking Spots

#19–21: If New York is the town that never sleeps, Los Angeles is the town that never works: This city dreads nine to five more than the avian flu. Add to that the fact that most industry folks get unemployment between gigs, and you have the perfect storm for a daytime drinking scene—cash and time.

Cabo Cantina*

8301 W. Sunset Blvd., Los Angeles, 323-822-7820 • Classic

The Draw: The daily two-for-one drink happy hour from 4pm to 8pm is the best in town. The moderately priced Mexican food menu is mundane, but underrated. Numerous flat-screen TVs also make it a great spot to catch a big game.

The Scene: Enjoy spring break revelry, all day, every day, in this Sunset Strip staple for Hollywood locals looking for some cheap, alcohol-fueled south-of-the-border fun. *Mon-Fri 4pm-midnight, Sat-Sun noon-midnight.*

Hot Tip: Park in the adjacent lot if you can't find a metered space on Sunset. You'll get back half of the parking fee ($10-$20) if you get your ticket validated inside the bar.

Lobby Lounge at the Standard Hollywood

8300 W. Sunset Blvd., West Hollywood, 323-650-9090 • Hot & Cool

The Draw: It offers a surreal life of leisure, marked by a picturesque poolside view, down-tempo DJ grooves, a lean and trim lunch menu, and a stylishly hip cosmopolitan crowd.

The Scene: It's a Diesel ad come to life. Think retro-futuristic community pool where trendy travelers and lounging locals chill and chat over drinks as cool as their designer shades. *Daily 9am-2am.*

Hot Tip: The magnificent minty-fresh mojitos are an insider favorite, while the fresh fruit sherbet dish is the perfect summer season accompaniment. And don't laugh, but the lobby barber shop (Rudy's) is a great spot for a trendy cut.

Saddle Ranch Chop House*

8371 W. Sunset Blvd., Los Angeles, 323-656-2007 • Hot & Cool

The Draw: *Animal House* antics, Texas-sized food and drink portions, and a good, bad, and ugly crowd make it a prime people-watching destination.

The Scene: The hungry, hip, and horny are satiated at this Wild West–themed restaurant/bar. Sticky floors, peer-pressuring bartenders, a mechanical bull, cute coeds, and obnoxious drunks give it a fun, if cheesy, frat house feel. *Daily 8am-2am.*

Hot Tip: The daily Ranch Brunch (8am to 3pm) is both filling and flavorful and includes bottomless champagne and Bloody Mary specials. It also offers the cheapest valet service on Sunset ($3.50), so park here and grab a bite or a beverage before heading out to the Strip.

Dive Bars

#22–24: The essential elements of a good dive are loud music, stiff drinks, no cover, and a word-of-mouth following. In L.A., even the most down-and-out, no-sign spots are often hipster hangouts—you just have to know which unmarked doors to enter, and which to avoid.

The Bar

5851 Sunset Blvd., Hollywood, 323-468-9154 • Hip

The Draw: This subtly named dive bar is a local favorite among indie-minded Eastsiders who come here to drink and drool at the vampish bartenders while rockin' out to guilty pleasures from the '80s.

The Scene: A modern makeover has given this longtime dingy dive a new lease on (night) life. The parlor-like interior and laid-back scene are dark and brooding, but warm up as drinks flow behind the backdrop of hits by the likes of Madonna and the Who. *Nightly 8pm-2am.* ≡

Hot Tip: The staff doesn't exactly discourage smoking, as evidenced by the ashtrays lying about, which makes it a good or bad draw depending on whether you light up or not.

The Burgundy Room

1621½ N. Cahuenga Blvd., Hollywood, 323-465-7530 • Classic

The Draw: It's a no-attitude, no-frills place where punk rock revelry and jackass antics go together like Sid and Nancy.

The Scene: Anarchy rules this spot in the bustling Cahuenga Corridor. The narrow, dingy, burgundy-tinted interior is more like a hallway than a room. Whiskey flows and three-chord classics blow, while a rough-and-tumble tattooed crowd only enhances a classic New York dive bar vibe. *Nightly 8pm-2am.* ≡

Hot Tip: If you play Johnny Cash's "Ring of Fire" on the jukebox, the bartenders will light the length of the bar on fire in tribute to the "Man in Black."

Tiki Ti

4427 W. Sunset Blvd., Los Feliz, 323-669-9381 • Classic

The Draw: A colorful, family-owned-and-operated landmark that's a tropical blend of exotic cocktails and Hawaiian-inspired inebriation.

The Scene: The very tiny, packed interior is cluttered with island ambience and strict family rules and regulations. The regular and random crowd is as eclectic as the 80-plus drink menu (no beer or wine). Come early or be prepared to wait in line outside. *Wed-Thu 6pm-1am, Fri-Sat 6pm-2am.* ≡

Hot Tip: Can't decide on which one of the crazy booze concoctions to order? In the back of the room is the Tiki Drink Wheel, created by the owners. Give it a spin and try something new—spinning it can turn into a social event for the whole bar.

Best Graveyards of the Stars

#25–27: It might seem like celebrities go to reality TV to die, but a few do choose the old-fashioned, down-in-the-ground departure. Thank goodness—visiting a celebrity boneyard is certainly less tiresome than waiting at the latest "it" spot for someone better than Delta Burke or Daniel Baldwin to show. Stargazing in these final resting grounds is a sure thing—unless you're after an autograph.

Hollywood Forever Cemetery

6000 Santa Monica Blvd., Hollywood, 323-469-1181 • Classic

The Draw: Formerly called Hollywood Memorial Park, interred stars include Cecil B. DeMille, Douglas Fairbanks (Sr. and Jr.), Alfalfa (Carl Switzer) and Darla (Hood) from *The Little Rascals*, and, in a mausoleum of his own, Rudolph Valentino.

The Scene: The grounds are more than a century old, and it shows. It's still the most respectable plot in workingman's Hollywood, with two giant mausoleums, an interesting assortment of moldering headstones, and a lake. Get oriented with a detailed map of the grounds, available in the flower shop by the front gate. *Mon-Fri 7am-7pm, Sat-Sun 7am-5pm.*

Hot Tip: Every other Saturday night in summer and on other special nights (like Halloween), Cinespia screens oldies on the marble outer wall of Valentino's mausoleum. BYO bottles, blankets, and picnic dinner (cinespia.org).

Holy Cross Cemetery

5835 W. Slauson Ave., Culver City, 310-670-7697 • Classic

The Draw: Bing Crosby, Rita Hayworth, Bela Lugosi, John Candy, John Ford, and Sharon Tate reside here, among others.

The Scene: Large, tasteful grounds hiding down in lower Culver City are dotted with waterfalls, ponds, and peaceful grottos. *Daily 8am-6pm.*

Hot Tip: If you haven't had your fill of famous headstones, check out Hillside Memorial, a few blocks south. Guests there include Al Jolson, Jack Benny, and Michael Landon (6001 Centinela Ave., 310-641-0707).

The Pierce Bros. Westwood Village Memorial Park

1218 Glendon Ave., Westwood, 310-474-1579 • Hot & Cool

The Draw: Marilyn Monroe.

The Scene: Norma Jean's headstone steals the show in this tiny two-acre cemetery hiding behind some office towers on Wilshire Blvd., but the impressive supporting cast includes Eva Gabor, Jack Lemmon, Walter Matthau, Carol O'Connor, Natalie Wood, and the unmarked graves of Roy Orbison and Frank Zappa. *Daily 8am-sundown.*

Hot Tip: To ensure that this tiny place stays public-friendly, park on the street or in the lot across the road, and leave the video camera in the trunk.

Guided Tours

#28–30: A good guided tour is an indispensable window on L.A. in its myriad shapes, forms, and fetishes. These tours have heart. They have soul. They have character. One of them even has drinks.

Los Angeles Conservancy Walking Tours
523 W. Sixth St., Suite 826, Downtown, 213-623-2489 • Classic

The Draw: L.A.'s most earnest walking tours are run by a nonprofit organization dedicated to preserving and restoring the city's historic architectural landmarks. Volunteer guides lead a variety of excellent Saturday morning Downtown walks for less than the price of a movie.

The Scene: The Broadway Theater tour is a runaway favorite, showcasing the ornate remains of Movietown's first Main Street (before Hollywood Boulevard took over in the '20s). Other walks include close-ups of Union Station, the Biltmore Hotel, and Little Tokyo, as well as tours focused on Art Deco and Downtown's Evolving Skyline. $

Hot Tip: Book in advance for Last Remaining Seats, a Conservancy-organized June festival of classic screenings in the old theaters along Broadway.

Los Angeles Neon Tour
Museum of Neon Art, 501 W. Olympic Blvd., Downtown, 213-489-9918 • Hip

The Draw: Board an open-air double-decker bus at the Museum of Neon Art (MONA) for an evening exploration of L.A.'s coolest, brightest neon signs.

The Scene: Three dozen people roll through Downtown, midtown, Chinatown, and Hollywood, questing for neon and picking up various cultural and historical tidbits along the way. Drinks and snacks are served at a reception at the museum. C–

Hot Tip: Book well ahead, and bring a sweater for those cool evenings. Tours run from April through October.

Red Line Tours
6773 Hollywood Blvd., Hollywood, 323-402-1074 • Classic

The Draw: This small outfit runs knowledgeable walking tours around Hollywood and Downtown, getting you inside places the buses can't. Miked guides equip guests with volume-controlled headsets, so you can walk, look, and listen at the same time.

The Scene: The 75-minute Inside Historic Hollywood Tour roams through the heart of Hollywood Boulevard, getting you up to speed on the area's multimillion-dollar revival and dipping into several historic theaters and hidden landmarks along the way. $

Hot Tip: Customized and extended walks can be arranged with advance notice.

Hikes

#31–33: Stretching from Malibu to Downtown, those hills out yonder comprise one of the world's largest urban recreation areas—a 150,000-acre swath of parkland that can transport you from concrete jungle to secluded canyon trail with the twist of a car key. And don't let all the dog walkers and jog bunnies fool you—it's still wild territory, with mountain lions and coyotes to prove it.

Point Mugu State Park

9000 Pacific Coast Hwy., Malibu, 818-880-0350 • Hot & Cool

> The Draw: La Jolla Valley Loop Trail at Point Mugu is one of the most rewarding ten-milers in the western Santa Monica Mountains, featuring secluded peaks, gorgeous ocean vistas, and rare indigenous grasslands.
>
> The Scene: From the Ray Miller trailhead, take the La Jolla Canyon Trail to the La Jolla Valley Loop Trail. Small seasonal waterfalls, oak groves, and bursts of sage, lavender, and spring wildflowers greet you along the way. It's moderately strenuous but crowd-free.
>
> Hot Tip: Near the junction of the two trails, La Jolla Valley Camp provides piped water, restrooms, and oak-shaded picnic tables. Bag a few more miles and higher vistas on this day hike by cutting west from the Valley Loop Trail to the Mugu Peak Trail.

Runyon Canyon Park

2000 N. Fuller Ave., Hollywood, 323-666-5046 • Hip

> The Draw: A quick and easy retreat in the Hollywood Hills, this is one of the more reliable spots in the city to run into stars walking their canines.
>
> The Scene: Early, before work, or late in the afternoon, the main entrance at Fuller is a convention of randy hounds waiting for the leashes to come off. From here, it's a two-mile loop up and down a chaparral-covered hill with a nice pay-off view of the entire city on a clear day. *Daily until sundown.*
>
> Hot Tip: Enter from the park's quieter north entrance at Mulholland Drive for a quick scramble up Indian Rock to Runyon's highest point.

Temescal Gateway Park

15601 Sunset Blvd., Pacific Palisades, 310-454-1395 • Classic

> The Draw: Westsiders actually turn off their cellphones and check out for a few hours at Temescal, a favorite spot in Topanga State Park.
>
> The Scene: Enter the parking lot from Sunset at Temescal Canyon Road. Follow either the Temescal Ridge Trail or the Temescal Canyon Trail (they form a five-mile loop up a moderate to steep grade) into an oasis of seasonal waterfalls, rocky outcrops, and sweeping coastal views.
>
> Hot Tip: Bring your own water, and watch out for poison oak and snakes—L.A. is rattler territory, and they like to sun themselves on the trails occasionally.

Hotel Bars

#34–36: Los Angeles has a host of transcendent hotel bars that are both bold and beautiful, offering trend-seeking tourists and savvy locals a great escape while also making them feel right at home. Although there are many chic choices, the best of the bunch happen to span the city from Downtown to the beach.

Cameo Bar at the Viceroy

The Viceroy, 1819 Ocean Ave., Santa Monica, 310-260-7500 • Hot & Cool

The Draw: Discover a chic Hollywood feel mixed with relaxing Santa Monica appeal in a space filled with high-class style and elegance.

The Scene: Privileged pampering makes this Westside cocktail and cabana lounge a favorite with seasoned travelers and de-suited, local socialites. Shades of vintage green and pristine white cover the classy, yet cramped indoor bar, but the breezy pool deck lounge is a breath of fresh air. *Daily 6:30am-10:30pm.* ⊟

Hot Tip: The much-desired cabanas can be rented out day or night ($250-$750). During the summer months (May 1 to September 15), they're strictly reserved for hotel guests during the day—but anyone is welcome to drink outside.

Rooftop Bar at the Standard Downtown*

The Standard, 550 S. Flower St., Downtown, 213-892-8080 • Hot & Cool

The Draw: Poolside lounging and skyline views dominate this Downtown rooftop retreat, where random revelers and jet-set travelers are ready to let loose.

The Scene: The sprawling, urban setting is a perfect big-city backdrop to a vacation getaway, afterwork hang, and after-dark hot spot all wrapped in one. Dance the night away under the stars, cozy up in a space pod cabana, or sip and dip poolside the next morning. *Daily noon-2am.* ⊡⊟

Hot Tip: Securing a required wristband is generally no problem during the week (it's also free), but you'll have to cough up $20 to get in on the weekends (Fri-Sun) unless you're a hotel guest. They also only give out a limited amount so come early or you'll have to wait for people to leave.

Skybar

The Mondrian, 8440 W. Sunset Blvd., West Hollywood, 323-848-6025 • Hot & Cool

The Draw: Californicate your way around the well-heeled and well-connected at this gorgeous and glamorous Sunset Strip institution.

The Scene: This plasticized poolside oasis is a caricature of the lifestyles of the rich and famous. Grab an overpriced cocktail from a MAW (model-actress-waitress) and filter the stunning view, industry braggadocio, and "what do you do for a living" interrogations, ahem, conversations. *Daily 11am-2am.* ⊟

Hot Tip: Fuggedabout getting past the velvet rope mafia without a room key or connections. Your best bet is to dine at the Mondrian's Asia de Cuba or show up before the doorman (around 8pm) and say you're dropping in for a drink.

Hotel Pools

#37–39: L.A. is full of hotel pools, but only a few of them are destinations unto themselves. Walk into these rarified spots and an undeniable feeling of "I have arrived" washes over you. Whether you can swim or not is irrelevant.

Beverly Hills Hotel & Bungalows

9641 Sunset Blvd., Beverly Hills, 310-276-2251 • Classic

The Draw: If you need a few names, Katharine Hepburn, Raquel Welch, Faye Dunaway, and Ringo Starr have all waded at this most exalted waterfront in Beverly Hills.

The Scene: Surrounded by palms and manicured grounds, the competition-size outdoor pool comes with a Jacuzzi, pool cafe, neat rows of traditional green-and-white striped lounge chairs, and those storied cabanas—21 of them in all.

Hot Tip: All cabanas are not created equal here. Spring the extra $125 for the lower cabanas, which are larger and offer poolside convenience. They're available to registered guests for the bargain price of $225 during the high season.

Hollywood Roosevelt Hotel

7000 Hollywood Blvd., Hollywood, 323-466-7000 • Hip

The Draw: The hippest celebrity bodies bronze in the sun here. Also check out the recently restored mural on the bottom of the pool, painted by David Hockney. Oh, and Marilyn Monroe is said to still haunt the suite named after her, which means her ghost probably heads to the pool during the day.

The Scene: Stars along the lines of Eva Longoria, Jake Gyllenhaal, and the ubiquitous Lindsay Lohan lay out amongst the palms. You can too, except it might require actually getting a room. Pony up $450-plus for a poolside cabana and your chances of gaining entry to the pool and its nightclub, Tropicana Bar, will increase exponentially.

Hot Tip: The cabanas aren't just day scenes—keep yours for cocktails well into the evening.

Mondrian

8440 W. Sunset Blvd., West Hollywood, 323-650-8999 • Hip

The Draw: It's the holy grail of pools on the Sunset Strip and the centerpiece of the Mondrian's chic club, Skybar.

The Scene: A stunning infinity pool surrounded by teak decking, a bevy of cozy lounge beds, and a sweet panoramic view of the city. The demographic is usually a mix of bikini-clad Eurotrash, power-lunchers from nearby Asia de Cuba, and gawkers like yourself.

Hot Tip: Only 14 of the standard rooms have a balcony and pool view.

Late-Night Eats

#40–42: When it seems like every place serving decent grub in L.A. must've closed about four hours ago, a closer look reveals an amazing assortment of kitchens working the after-last-call shift with gusto. In a pinch, there's always the 24-hour Hollywood Denny's (7373 Sunset Blvd.), but these late-night shrines hit the spot in an only-in-L.A. way.

Canter's
419 N. Fairfax Ave., Los Angeles, 323-651-2030 • Classic

The Draw: Come to this Fairfax district landmark for an around-the-clock bowl of matzo-ball soup and a thick pile of corned beef on rye, served by grandmas in Keds.

The Scene: Little has changed since the first bagels came out of the oven in 1931—old brown booths, seasoned staff, and a few odd personal touches like an autumnal scene on the ceiling. After midnight, there's a decent chance you'll see someone relatively famous here. *24/7.* $ ≡

Hot Tip: For dicey live music with your kishke (and the occasional surprise appearance by a famous rocker), head to the row of tables next door in the Kibitz Room.

Pink's
709 N. La Brea Blvd., Los Angeles, 323-931-4223 • Classic

The Draw: Hot dogs are smothered with chili and cheese. With a line like this, the food must be good.

The Scene: It seems like no matter what time of day or night you visit, there's always a crowd. And it's usually filled with a representative mix of locals and tourists. *Sun-Thu 9:30am-2am, Fri-Sat 9:30am-3am.* $ ≡

Hot Tip: First time at Pink's? Start with the classic chili-and-cheese hot dog.

Sanamluang Café
5176 Hollywood Blvd., Hollywood, 323-660-8006 • Hip

The Draw: Great noodle dishes and curries are served almost until sunrise at this savory Thai stop between the bars in Hollywood and Silver Lake.

The Scene: The bright, no-frills room and frantic cooking noises in the back are like a good shot of caffeine. Thai teens breaking curfew and tattooed musicians graze on curried noodles and sip Thai iced tea, like the rebels they are. *Daily 10:30am-2am.* $ ≡

Hot Tip: Two words: General's Noodles.

Best

Live Music Venues

#43–45: The infamous L.A. music scene reads like myth. Tragic tales of sex, drugs, and rock 'n' roll stretch from the lascivious '70s "Riot House" to the '80s, when metal bands ruled the Sunset Strip like Roman gods. Although the '90s saw a dip in decadence, the new millennium has ushered in a musical revolution thanks to the revitalization of L.A.'s classic concert venues.

The Music Box @ The Henry Fonda Theatre

6126 Hollywood Blvd., Hollywood, 323-464-0808 • Classic

The Draw: Intimate, eclectic entertainment options range from KCRW-sponsored concerts to burlesque shows and monthly boxing matches.

The Scene: Extensive renovations have given this elegant, vintage venue a new lease on life. Buzz-worthy artists like the Streets and Peaches now grace the same intimate stage where legends like Joan Crawford and Clark Gable once performed. *Hours vary.* C≡

Hot Tip: If the standing-room-only main floor gets to be too much, opt for the mezzanine level, where you can wander out to the rooftop patio bar for a drink and watch the show on live-circuit TV.

Troubadour

9081 Santa Monica Blvd., Hollywood, 310-276-6168 • Classic

The Draw: This storied WeHo rock 'n' roll shrine deserves its own VH-1 *Behind the Music* documentary. An old-school ethos stresses guitar-crunching tunes, and welcomes music fans of all ages.

The Scene: While everything in the nearby area has undergone a stylish "Queer Eye" makeover, this historic, hard-rocking jam joint rolls into a new ear-splitting era. It features an in-your-face stage, a perched VIP balcony, and a pair of beat-up bars plastered with 8-by-10s of famous past performers. *Nightly 8pm-2am.* C≡

Hot Tip: Be on the lookout for surprise shows from elite groups like the Red Hot Chili Peppers, who drop in to tune up before heading out on tour. Monday night's local band showcases are free, but are a hit-or-miss affair.

The Wiltern LG

3790 Wilshire Blvd., Koreatown, 213-380-5005 • Classic

The Draw: The likes of the Rolling Stones, Radiohead, and Thievery Corporation have graced the stage at this 1930s-era grandiose concert hall.

The Scene: A first-rate face-lift brings this L.A. landmark into the modern age. The breathtaking Art Deco interior, superior sound system, A-list talent, and a classy clientele make it one of the best live music venues on the West Coast. *Box office noon-6pm. Show times vary.* C≡

Hot Tip: The level in front of the stage is limited to the first 250 people. So come early and get a bracelet that allows you to come in and out of this spot.

Movie Theaters

#46–48: In the town that invented the whole movie-watching pastime, you can bet there are some fine places to drop ten bucks and sit in the dark for a few hours. L.A.'s top movie theaters range from Westwood premiere palaces and ornate Hollywood relics to indie landmarks that still host Saturday-at-midnight *Rocky Horror* screenings.

Arclight Cinemas

6360 Sunset Blvd., Hollywood, 323-464-4226 • Hip

The Draw: Your seats are assigned, and you're spared the annoying pre-movie commercials. For that you'll gladly pay a couple bucks more.

The Scene: The main room resembles a train station, with vaulted ceilings, a gift shop, and a large board showing movie times. This is film-fan central, even though it looks like the place where you catch the overnighter to Berlin. $$

Hot Tip: Theater number 8 is the only one where you're allowed to drink alcohol. A ticket to whatever is showing there gives you access to the adjacent bar.

Egyptian Theatre

6712 Hollywood Blvd., Hollywood, 323-466-3456 • Classic

The Draw: Hollywood's first major movie house doesn't draw mobs of tourists like its younger sister, Grauman's Chinese Theatre. But the eclectic range of screenings in this revived theater, the home of the American Cinematheque, is far more impressive.

The Scene: Hieroglyphics, sphinx-heads, and ancient Egypt–style columns line the forecourt. The main auditorium has sliding walls that reveal some of the theater's original structure. $

Hot Tip: For the full experience, book a guided afternoon tour of the theater. American Cinematheque's Aero Theatre in Santa Monica (1328 Montana Ave., 323-466-3456) has a similarly eclectic lineup of movies.

Mann's Village Theatre

961 Broxton Ave., Westwood, 310-248-6266 • Classic

The Draw: This huge movie premiere site is one of the few reasons people schlep out to Westwood Village these days. Of several excellent movie theaters in the neighborhood, it's the oldest, the largest, and the loudest.

The Scene: Outside is the historic FOX tower. Inside are polished marble floors, 1,400 cushy seats full of UCLA students, and a sound system to suit them. $

Hot Tip: Forget popcorn. Buy half a dozen warm cookies across the street at Diddy Riese (926 Broxton Ave.) and sneak 'em in under your trench coat.

Nightclubs

#49–51: In the fickle Los Angeles nightlife scene, new equals hot, while old equals not. Hot spots flicker out faster than you can say "Deep," "the Lounge," and "Concorde"—famous clubs that are now no more. The migratory night owls are constantly looking for something fresh, so join the hip herd as it makes its rounds of the trendiest spots in L.A.

Basque

1707 N. Vine St., Hollywood, 323-464-1654 • Hot & Cool

The Draw: Nightlife voyeurs and exhibitionists get down and dirty at this sexually charged supper club on the legendary corner of Sunset and Vine.

The Scene: Burlesque beauties press up against Red Light District windows, setting a dirty-dancing tone to this Spanish bordello–flavored hot spot. The new owners mix a bit of decadence with sensual sensibilities to create a unique nightlife experience. *Mon, Thu-Sat 10pm-2am.* C≡

Hot Tip: The cover doubles after 11pm.

Cabana Club

1439 N. Ivar Ave., Hollywood, 323-463-0005 • Hot & Cool

The Draw: Party under the sun and/or stars with L.A.'s bold and beautiful at this open-air oasis just off the Sunset Strip.

The Scene: Poolside fun, hip-hop tunes, private cabanas, lush palm trees, and splashing waterfalls produce a white-hot, pseudo–St. Tropez scene that's pure P-Diddy. *Thu-Sat 10pm-2am.* C≡

Hot Tip: The late-arriving crowd tends to show up after 11pm, so get there before to avoid the lengthy line. Avoid the club's expensive and time-consuming valet service by parking at the Arclight Cinemas parking structure across the street.

Privilege

8117 Sunset Blvd., West Hollywood, 323-654-0030 • Hot & Cool

The Draw: This Hollywood hot spot retains its A-list appeal by constantly changing its look and feel. Owner Sam Nazarian's makeover magic has kept the trendy club community coming back, but at a steep price for the common clubber.

The Scene: The 7,000-square-foot setup changes more often than Lindsay Lohan's hair color, staying ahead of the club curve. Like all things new and fresh, it lacks character and substance, but what do you expect in a town ruled by Paris Hilton? If you manage to get inside, live it up 'cause you'll be paying off that credit card bill for quite a while. *Tue, Thu, Fri 9pm-2am.* C≡

Hot Tip: Without connections or cleavage you have little chance of getting past the embezzling doormen and their elitist tactics unless you throw down some serious cash and reserve a VIP bottle service table—low end during the week starts at $300, and can go up to $2,400 for champagne on the weekends.

Patio Dining

#52–54: This is Southern California, home of year-round al fresco dining (except for those three days we actually get rain). Of course, some of those tables sit on crowded sidewalks, where city buses rattle the water glasses as they roar by. Save yourself the extra smog inhalation and check out one of these scenic spots instead.

Hotel Bel-Air Restaurant (G)

701 Stone Canyon Rd., Bel-Air, 310-472-5234 • Classic

The Draw: This is one of the most beautiful places on the planet to eat a meal.

The Scene: A huge pergola, cascading bougainvillaea, and heated tiles in winter are among the many advantages of dining out on the Hotel Bel-Air Restaurant's terrace, where the city's movers and shakers—make that the world's movers and shakers—enjoy plenty of elbow room amidst the flowering flora of this Eden-like setting. *Daily 7am-9:30pm.* $$$ ▤

Hot Tip: You'll have to call well in advance to even dream of getting a dinner table al fresco—so consider the lovely afternoon tea (seatings Monday-Friday 3-4pm, Sat 3:30-4pm).

Katana

8439 W. Sunset Blvd., West Hollywood, 323-650-8585 • Hot & Cool

The Draw: A dramatic, über-trendy space overlooking Sunset Boulevard makes for some prime people-watching.

The Scene: Well-dressed trendsters congregate for sushi and industry gossip on a laid-back patio overlooking the Sunset Strip. When they're not checking each other out, Katana patrons are eyeing the limos and lines of people across the street at the entrance to Skybar. On Sundays during the summer, a DJ from NPR-affiliated KCRW radio station spins tunes. *Sun-Mon 6-11pm, Tue-Wed 6-11:30pm, Thu-Sat 6pm-12:30am.* $$ ▤

Hot Tip: Robata—grilled meats—are the specialty here, set off by the house beer, Red Sun. But portions are small, so order accordingly.

Michael's (G)

1147 Third St., Santa Monica, 310-451-0843 • Classic

The Draw: It may be the only garden setting in Los Angeles that rivals the Bel-Air Restaurant terrace for beauty.

The Scene: An adjustable canvas roof helps protect diners in inclement weather, but when it's warm and sunny, is there a better place to be in L.A. than out in the middle of this wild garden with statuary peeking from the foliage? *Mon-Fri noon-2:30pm; Mon-Thu 6-10pm, Fri-Sat 6-10:30pm.* $$$ ▤

Hot Tip: Make the reservation at least two weeks ahead of time and you're guaranteed a table outdoors.

Places to Rent Wheels

#55–57: There's always a white midsize with your name on it, but in L.A. it's only natural to crave a more rousing ride, partly because of all the driving you'll be doing—rolling along the coast, down Rodeo Drive, and through the mountains—and partly because Benzes, Hummers, and heritage Mustangs are there to mock you at every stoplight.

Beverly Hills Rent-A-Car
9220 S. Sepulveda Blvd., Los Angeles, 310-337-1400

The Draw: A yellow Lamborghini Diablo? There may be one more in the back. SoCal's best-known provider of luxury and exotic automobiles wouldn't dream of embarrassing you at the Spago valet.

The Scene: Bentleys, Ferraris, Hummers, Jags, Land Rovers, Porsches, Maseratis, and some classic Cadillac convertibles.

Hot Tip: It offers complimentary pickup and drop-off at all area airports, along with an extra VIP, meet-you-at-the-gate service if you prefer.

EagleRider
11860 S. La Cienega Blvd., Los Angeles, 310-320-3456

The Draw: Los Angeles may not be a terrifically accommodating city for motor-cycles, but all the traffic jams do provide a great opportunity for leaving those four-wheeled drivers sucking your exhaust fumes. And just think how exhilarated you'll feel when you make it back to the rental office alive.

The Scene: Electra Glides, Road Kings, Sportsters: Pick your own shiny Harley from this nice-sized fleet by the airport. Then head out to Angeles Crest Highway or Lake Castaic.

Hot Tip: If you want some company, EagleRider's guided tours cover the entire country, including an eight-day adventure from L.A. to the Grand Canyon and Utah.

Rent-A-Wreck
12333 W. Pico Blvd., West L.A., 310-826-7555

The Draw: If Steve McQueen came back as an L.A. tourist, he'd take this back-woods rental counter over Enterprise any day of the week. Dave Schwartz's orig-inal Rent-A-Wreck location, run by the owner himself, is full of the usual newer cars and vintage classics you haven't driven or seen in decades.

The Scene: What's your pleasure? A '66 Mustang convertible, a '68 Cadillac Coupe de Ville, a '70 Oldsmobile Cutlass? Choose from T-Birds, Skylarks, and a Ford Woody Station Wagon that'll make the trip to Santa Barbara.

Hot Tip: Don't let the slightly out-the-way location in West L.A. deter you. Rent-A-Wreck offers 24-hour pickup and drop-off service from LAX every day of the week.

Power Lunches

#58–60: Throughout history, very important people have been required to Do Lunch. L.A. has perfected this art. Who will (or won't) take a lunch with you is a direct statement of your position on the food chain. No less important is where the meal takes place—a bite at The Grill is very different from a sandwich at Canter's.

Barney Greengrass

9570 Wilshire Blvd., 5th Floor, Beverly Hills, 310-777-5877 • Hot & Cool

The Draw: See some famous faces over matzo brei and whitefish salad at this imported New York deli on the top floor of Barneys.

The Scene: Weight-deprived actresses almost eat here between shoplifting sprees, spaced out between agents and clients noshing comfort food. There are great views of Beverly Hills from the outdoor terrace and a dependable cast of recognizable regulars. *Mon-Wed 8:30am-6pm, Thu-Fri 9am-7pm, Sat 9am-7pm, Sun 9am-6pm.* $ ⎘⊟

Hot Tip: If you want to check out the scene solo, there's comfortable counter seating in front. If you're looking for the traditional Naugahyde deli with waitresses who call you "honey," Nate 'n' Al's is just up the street (310-274-0101).

The Grill on the Alley

9560 Dayton Way, Beverly Hills, 310-276-0615 • Hot & Cool

The Draw: For the quintessential Who's-Who lunch, look no further: It's steaks, chops, martinis, strawberry shortcake, and other corporate American comfort food, served in the presence of Hollywood's chieftains.

The Scene: There's no egalitarianism here. Open tables are held for very important players, from Geffen to Spielberg. Dinner (seven days a week) is also a scene in this dignified and clubby dining den. *Mon-Thu 11:30am-10:30pm, Fri-Sat 11:30am-11pm, Sun 5-9pm.* $$$ ⎘≡

Hot Tip: Booths are the coveted spots, but seats at the bar are fun, with a great view of all the players.

Spago

176 N. Cañon Dr., Beverly Hills, 310-385-0880 • Classic

The Draw: Everyone who's watched the Oscars knows Spago. It's the flagship of über-chef Wolfgang Puck's culinary empire.

The Scene: Power lunchers, industry players, stars, and a medley of 90210 types gather in this boldly designed dining room and out on the fountained patio. The menu is playfully indefinable, including sashimi, risotto, Wienerschnitzel, and strudel. *Mon-Fri 11:30am-2:15pm, Sat noon-2:15pm; Sun-Thu 5:30-10pm, Fri-Sat 5:30-11pm.* $$$ ≡

Hot Tip: Everyone wants a patio seat, but for action-packed views into the open kitchen, ask for the back tables inside.

Best Presidential Suites

#61–63: Five grand for a room. Per night. Okay, so presidential suites cost as much as a good heart surgeon, which you might need after you get the bill. Still, these rooms are booked more often than not in L.A.'s high-roller world. And feel free to take the towels. You deserve them.

Beverly Wilshire Four Seasons Hotel, Penthouse and Presidential Suites
9500 Wilshire Blvd., Beverly Hills, 310-275-5200 • Classic

The Draw: What other L.A. hotel has two presidential-type suites of such high caliber? At 4,000 square feet, the Presidential Suite is referred to by some— but not the hotel—as the *"Pretty Woman* suite" because it's where Julia Roberts' character supposedly stayed (though they didn't shoot here). The Penthouse Suite is 1,000 square feet bigger and six stories higher.

The Scene: The hardwood floors, Roman columns, and high ceilings give the two-bedroom Presidential Suite a palatial feel more in line with a penthouse apartment on Fifth Avenue. The three-bedroom Penthouse Suite (which costs $7,500, versus $5,500 for the Presidential) has a more modern decor and a 360-degree view with wraparound balcony. $$$$

Hot Tip: This is where some Oscar nominees shack up before the big night.

The Peninsula Beverly Hills, Peninsula Suite
9882 S. Santa Monica Blvd., Beverly Hills, 310-551-2888 • Classic

The Draw: The most spectacular living quarters here cost just $3,500 a night, in what is often called L.A.'s finest hotel.

The Scene: More than 2,000 square feet of lush living space overlooks the hotel's front courtyard. The Peninsula Suite includes a dining room for ten, and a living room with a fireplace and a baby grand. $$$$

Hot Tip: The grandest of 16 self-contained units on the property is the two-story Peninsula Villa.

Shutters on the Beach, Presidential Suite
1 Pico Blvd., Santa Monica, 310-458-0030 • Hot & Cool

The Draw: A mere $2,500 a night gets you one of three presidential suites at L.A.'s best beachfront hotel. Lots of famous guests stay here, and if you opt for the seventh-floor suite, they'll all be sleeping where they belong—beneath you.

The Scene: The 1,500-square-feet suite includes a full-sized living room and fireplace, kitchen, marble bathroom, and three balconies, all with front-row ocean views. $$$$

Hot Tip: Two suites look out on nothing but big blue. The third, north-corner suite (745) also has views of the Santa Monica pier and its lit-up Ferris wheel.

Romantic Dining

#64–66: What's your idea of a perfect spot for gazing lovingly into each other's eyes? By the ocean? In the hills? On a candlelit patio bursting with bougainvillaea? Roscoe's Chicken and Waffles? However you define romance, L.A. has the table set.

Il Cielo

9018 Burton Way, Beverly Hills, 310-276-9990 • Classic

The Draw: Sharing an evening at this intimate Italian hideaway is like a quick honeymoon in Positano, without leaving Beverly Hills. Beautifully prepared dishes and traditional wines from "the Boot" live up to one of L.A.'s most fanciful dining settings.

The Scene: The interior exudes romance, with a fireplace, frescoed ceilings, and private rooms. But for the real deal, reserve a table under the stars in the front courtyard or on the rear garden patio. *Mon-Sat 11:30am-3pm, 5:30-10pm. $$$* ▭

Hot Tip: As desserts go, is there a greater aphrodisiac than rose crème brûlée with candied rose petals on a bed of white chocolate and raspberry sauce?

Inn of the Seventh Ray

128 Old Topanga Canyon Rd., Topanga, 310-455-1311 • Hot & Cool

The Draw: The Topanga Canyon patio has hosted many a marriage proposal, not to mention a lot of weddings. Also, homemade bread and veggie selections highlight an amazing organic dining experience that isn't rushed.

The Scene: The couples-dominated lush garden patio, replete with a babbling brook and that "million miles from L.A." feel, makes this a really bad spot for a man to bring his girlfriend if he isn't proposing, because she'll take one look at the surroundings and assume that's the plan. *Mon-Fri 10:30am-3pm, Sat 10:30am-3pm, Sun 9:30am-3pm; Nightly 5:30-10pm. $$$$* ▭

Hot Tip: Reserve a table by the creek for the optimal romantic setting.

Yamashiro*

1999 N. Sycamore Ave., Hollywood, 323-466-5125 • Classic

The Draw: A 600-year-old pagoda (the oldest structure in California), a Japanese garden with a koi-filled pond, and a stellar view that makes Hollywood look a lot cleaner than it actually is make this a no-brainer for a romantic night out.

The Scene: Smartly dressed couples dine on Cal-Asian cuisine in the intimate, dimly lit dining room. The view coupled with the Zen vibe (Yamashiro is a replica of a Japanese temple) makes you feel like you're at a hilltop restaurant above Tokyo. *Nightly 5-9:45pm, bar until 2am. $$$$* ▭

Hot Tip: Not all tables are created equal—ask for one along the front windows.

Seafood

#67–69: Los Angeles has some of the best seafood restaurants in the country, though there are days when the ocean is so polluted that swimming is not advised. So don't be surprised if your salmon is Alaskan and the shrimp from Thailand. Even if your dinner has traveled farther than you, this is a town of high standards, and you can be sure it's fresh and delicious.

The Hungry Cat

1535 N. Vine St., Hollywood, 323-462-2155 • Hip

The Draw: Trained in classic French cooking, chef David Lentz went back to his Maryland roots when putting together a simple and approachable menu that stars tasty lobster rolls and crab cakes.

The Scene: Conversation bounces off the walls of this black-and-white modernist restaurant that looks like a slick movie version of an alternative-universe East Coast seafood shack. Trendy young filmgoers from the nearby Arclight Cinema pack in nightly. *Tue-Fri 11:30am-2pm, Mon-Sat 5:30pm-midnight, Sun 11am-3pm, 5-10pm. $$* B=

Hot Tip: The bar serves drinks made with fresh fruit juices—try the Bloody Mary.

Providence (G)

5955 Melrose Ave., Los Angeles, 323-460-4170 • Hot & Cool

The Draw: Providence owner Michael Cimarusti, formerly of Water Grill, is referred to by some as the best seafood chef in town.

The Scene: Porcelain barnacles cling to the chocolate-brown walls, and a certain *je ne sais quoi* makes it less stuffy and pretentious than Patina, the old tenant of this space. Suits of all kinds—from lawyers to studio heads—stretch their expense accounts here, while sophisticated foodies oogle the complex plates. This is a destination spot. *Fri noon-2:30pm, Mon-Fri 6-10pm, Sat 5:30-10pm, Sun 5:30-9pm. $$$$* =

Hot Tip: The main dining room is the best place to sit for good buzz, but if privacy is a priority, ask for the patio or the alcove. And try the oysters.

Water Grill (G)

544 S. Grand, Downtown, 213-891-0900 • Classic

The Draw: Many people dine here just to see how the menu has changed since David Lefevre took over from Michael Cimarusti. Lefevre employs slow-cooking techniques—with amazing, complex results that make you savor every bite.

The Scene: The formal, clubby feel gives away its status as a power-lunch spot that's a favorite with politicos. At night, the culture crowd of theater and concertgoers fills the dim, comfortable space. *Mon-Fri 11:30am-9pm, Sat 5-9:30pm, Sun 4:30-8:30pm. $$$$* B=

Hot Tip: Order the tuna tartare. Just do it.

Singles Scenes

#70–72: L.A. is a singles city. The young and restless fill the clubs and restaurants looking for companionship and connections. "What do you do?" is the new millennium update of "What's your sign?" And if your careers aren't compatible (meaning you can't help that gorgeous little thing land an audition), you might as well be an Aries tying to pick up a Cancer. It just won't work.

Circle Bar

2926 Main St., Santa Monica, 310-450-0508 • Hot & Cool

The Draw: Observe the Main Street meet market where Westside singles go to hit a home run.

The Scene: Faux Far East–inspired decor spices up a corny, dimly lit, oval-shaped interior conducive to getting up close and personal. Played-out party tunes blast as top-heavy bartenders serve stiffies to a roomful of sweaty 20- and 30-somethings thirsting for some noncommittal fun. *Sun-Wed 9pm-2am, Thu-Sat 8pm-2am.* ©≡

Hot Tip: Get a leg up on the competition at the late happy hour ($3 beers and $5 wells), which runs from 8:30-10:30pm Sunday-Tuesday.

Mood

6623 Hollywood Blvd., Hollywood, 323-464-6663 • Hip

The Draw: A sin-tillating scene casts a sensuous mood for Hollywood's elite and their entourages.

The Scene: An A-list aura and attitude defines this exotic club. Indonesian flavors fill the lush, layered space, while pouty-lipped bubblegum divas of both sexes flash more than flirtatious smiles. *Wed-Sun 10pm-2am.* ©≡

Hot Tip: If you're rolling with a "softball team" (anything over three guys), your best bet to get in would be to reserve a table, which is usually a two-bottle minimum at no less than $250 a pop.

Spider Club

1737 N. Vine St., Hollywood, 323-462-8900 • Hot & Cool

The Draw: Hollywood stars (or at least their look-alikes), aspiring models, and nightlife professionals fill this famous party playpen.

The Scene: This club-within-a-club spins a nightlife web that catches A-list celebrities and sexy singles with an ultraexclusive vibe and a Moroccan disco setting complete with stripper pole. *Hours vary.* ©≡

Hot Tip: The door policy is slightly more lenient midweek.

Spas

#73–75: Why are there so many spas in Los Angeles? Because people here are totally stressed out. Never mind that they're lounging at cafes drinking iced lattes on warm Tuesday afternoons in February. Stay here long enough and you'll need to get steamed, rinsed, wrapped, and twisted into a pretzel, too.

Bliss

W Hotel, 930 Hilgard Ave., Westwood, 323-930-0330 • Hip

The Draw: You can watch movies during your manicure, pig out at the locker-room snack buffet, and lounge around after your treatment is done.

The Scene: Clouds greet you at the entrance of the 7,000-square-foot space, which features shelf after shelf of Bliss's popular skin-care products. It took ten years for Bliss to make it to Los Angeles. Apparently, heaven could wait. *Daily 9am-9pm. $$$$*

Hot Tip: Weekends here can be a scene, and the small space can get loud, even in treatment rooms. For serenity, book a morning massage or come during the week.

Kinara Spa

656 N. Robertson Blvd., West Hollywood, 310-657-9188 • Hot & Cool

The Draw: The massages and manicures are predictably fantastic, but most people—numerous celebrities among them—come here for the custom facials.

The Scene: The rooms are warm and dimly lit, the bowls in the manicure-pedicure area are built into the ground, and the 100 percent cotton blankets you're swaddled in are imported from Japan. *Tue-Fri 9am-9pm, Sat 9am-7pm, Sun 10am-6pm. $$$$*

Hot Tip: Come for a half-day treatment, starting with the massage, then a facial, and finally the manicure-pedicure. End it all with lunch in the cafe garden, and a little champagne … for therapeutic purposes.

Ole Henriksen Face/Body

8622-A W. Sunset Blvd., West Hollywood, 310-854-7700 • Hot & Cool

The Draw: Run by a famous Beverly Hills skin care guru, this spa offers home-spun treatments like "Effleurage Massage with Mango and Cocoa Butter" and "Dry Brush Exfoliation and Swedish Massage with Anti-Cellulite Formulation" designed to whip your epidermis into shape.

The Scene: Glowing candles light this lovely facility in Sunset Plaza. Japanese shoji doors glide apart between treatment rooms. Multistep body treatments include herbal washes, mineral scrubs, tropical rain rinses, and cranial massage. *Sun-Mon 9am-5pm, Tue-Sat 8am-8pm. $$$$*

Hot Tip: Don't leave before doing penance with a viciously divine salt scrub.

Steakhouses with Atmosphere

#76–78: There's lots of flash in L.A., but when it comes to great steakhouses, it's all about the history. These spots have an entrenched sense of place—as if the city itself somehow grew up around their cracked leather booths and dark wood bars. Walk in the door and you'll instantly feel like the ghost of Cary Grant or Clark Gable might still be hanging around.

Dan Tana's

9071 Santa Monica Blvd., West Hollywood, 310-275-9444 • Classic

The Draw: This beloved Italian restaurant has been moonlighting as an A-list steak place for more than 40 years. But none of the Tom Jones–era regulars will laugh at you for ordering pasta instead of cow. Not to your face, at least.

The Scene: Red leather booths, checkered tablecloths, and suspended Chianti bottles are the backdrop for a crowd of goodfellas planted on bar stools, and a maître d' named Jimmy. The place is relaxed enough to have a TV set above the tiny bar and Jerry West's Lakers jersey on the wall—but make no mistake, this is Hollywood central. *Nightly 5pm-1am.* $$$$ B≡

Hot Tip: There's one steak on the menu, the New York strip. You just have to decide whether it'll be the 12- or 16-ounce.

Musso & Frank Grill*

6667 Hollywood Blvd., Hollywood, 323-467-7788 • Classic

The Draw: Hollywood's oldest restaurant doesn't look a day over 87. The moment you walk in, you'll see that you haven't come here just for the steak—which is still pretty good.

The Scene: Red leather, mahogany, chandeliers, and inebriated ghosts hover everywhere. If *The Shining* had been set in a Hollywood restaurant, this would've been the location. *Tue-Sat 11am-11pm.* $$ B≡

Hot Tip: Vegetarians can come for breakfast (flannel cakes) or lunch (Bloody Marys). If you're in Hollywood, this is also a great bar for martinis.

Pacific Dining Car

1310 W. Sixth St., Downtown, 213-483-6000 • Classic

The Draw: Almost as old as Musso's, this round-the-clock class act is best known for its USDA Prime Eastern corn-fed, dry-aged, mesquite-grilled beef and its Russian-novel–sized wine list.

The Scene: The railcar theme comes and goes once you're past the front bar entrance. After that, it's a hushed ambience of cozy booths and high-backed chairs that's popular with politicos and lawyers from Downtown. *24/7.* $$$$ ≡

Hot Tip: Great happy-hour spreads include ribs, wings, and shrimp. There's also a second location at 2700 Wilshire Blvd., Santa Monica, 310-453-4000.

Best

Studio Tours

#79–81: Hollywood studios have been inviting people in for a peek since the silent era, when Universal boss Carl Laemmle came up with the idea of selling bleacher seats on the back lot during shoots. While most studios opt to stay out of the public eye, a handful of tours are still offered by some of the best studios in the biz.

NBC Studios

3000 W. Alameda Ave., Burbank, 818-840-3537 • Hot & Cool

The Draw: You've stared at its product in the box for long enough. It's time to step behind the scenes at the Burbank headquarters to see how it's done.

The Scene: The 75-minute walking tour roams through wardrobe, makeup, and set construction departments. There are some nifty hands-on demos in the sound and FX rooms, plus possible visits to *The Tonight Show* and *Days of Our Lives* sets. *Tours depart regularly 9am-3pm weekdays, plus Saturdays during the summer (starting July 1).* $

Hot Tip: For free tickets to *The Tonight Show with Jay Leno*, be at the NBC ticket counter well before 8am, or request in advance by mail (NBC Tickets, 3000 W. Alameda Ave., Burbank, CA 91523).

Universal Studios Hollywood

100 Universal City Plaza, Universal City, 800-864-8377 • Hot & Cool

The Draw: Famous for its theme park, Universal Studios is also, of course, a blockbuster film factory. Hiding behind all those rides is the world's largest movie and television studio.

The Scene: The standard 45-minute Studio Tour is basically an over-rehearsed warmup for the park. The more personal VIP Experience Pass is pricey ($149), but provides two hours on the lot and far more behind-the-scenes access. *VIP tours depart daily, generally on the hour between 9am and noon.* $$$$

Hot Tip: VIP treatment includes four privileged hours in the park (meaning you can cut to the front of every line). Reserve at least a week in advance (818-622-5120).

Warner Brothers Studios

4000 Warner Blvd., Burbank, 818-972-8687 • Classic

The Draw: It's a refreshingly candid and unstaged tour in one of Hollywood's oldest, most famous movie and television studios.

The Scene: Small groups board a studio tram and are whisked all over the hundred-acre lot, visiting historic sets, prop warehouses, wardrobe departments, and sound stages of prime time shows when the cameras aren't running. *Tours depart weekdays on the half hour, 8:30am-4pm, varied hours in summer.* $$$$

Hot Tip: Warner's has a worthwhile Deluxe Tour (Wednesdays only) that is twice as long and includes lunch.

Sushi

#82–84: Delicate slabs of raw fish are about as prevalent in Los Angeles as 72-ounce steaks are in Amarillo, Texas. If you're just looking for a quick California roll and a few morsels of yellowtail, sushi bars are everywhere. On the other end of the spectrum, some of the world's top sushi chefs call L.A. home.

Matsuhisa (G)

129 N. La Cienega Blvd., Los Angeles, 310-659-9639 • Hot & Cool

The Draw: Innovative sushi master Nobu Matsuhisa runs what many foodies continue to call the best restaurant in the city.

The Scene: Surprisingly casual. There's very little to look at besides some posters on the wall and the odd celebrity in jeans and a T-shirt sitting across the room. *Mon-Fri 11:45am-2:15pm; Nightly 5:45-10:30pm. $$$* ☰

Hot Tip: Just say "omakase" (chef's choice) and let Nobu's talented disciples spare you the hassle of choosing from more than 100 possible dishes.

Sushi Katsu-ya

11680 Ventura Blvd., Studio City, 818-985-6976 • Hip

The Draw: Colorful, creative dishes have a certain wow factor that doesn't take away from the freshness and taste of the food.

The Scene: The interior looks like every other place along "sushi row"— Japanese scrolls, blond-wood bar—but it soon distinguishes itself with inventive dishes like seared scallop with foie gras and salmon caviar sashimi. It's so busy, even Oscar winners are sometimes forced to find a spot at the bar. *Mon-Thu 11:30am-2:30pm, 5:30-10pm, Fri-Sat 5:30-10:30pm, Sun 5:30-9:30pm. $$$* ☰

Hot Tip: If you're on the Westside, the new Philippe Starck–designed Katsu-ya in Brentwood (310-207-8744) will save you the drive out to the Valley.

Urasawa (G)

218 N. Rodeo Dr., Beverly Hills, 310-247-8939 • Hot & Cool

The Draw: You'll forget all about spicy tuna rolls at this sushi-purist oasis, where $250 gets you a 29-course dinner experience that's as sacred as eating gets.

The Scene: A maple bar that seats ten, a couple of tables, and a private room are all that make up this Beverly Hills sushi bar. Chef Hiroyuki Urasawa smiles knowingly while diners back for their fifth or sixth meal here gush about how they can't eat toro anywhere else now that they've had his. *Nightly 6-9pm. $$$$* ▭

Hot Tip: If you're forced to cancel less than 24 hours before your reservation, you will be charged a hefty penalty.

Best   Theme Bars

#85–87: Theme bars offer patrons a nightlife experience rather than just a scene. A good theme bar has a soul, straddling the fine line between kitschy and cool, while never crossing into cheese (Hooters). Theme bars are booming in Los Angeles thanks in part to the following trio of trend-setting hipster hangs.

Ivan Kane's Forty Deuce
5574 Melrose Ave., Los Angeles, 323-465-4242 • Hip

The Draw: This groundbreaking burlesque bar is a titillating combination of sexy showgirls, shining Hollywood stars, and Roaring '20s revelry.

The Scene: Ivan Kane's cutting-edge cabaret has been the subject of a Bravo reality mini-series, while drawing the likes of George Clooney, Hugh Hefner, and Naomi Watts. The plush parlor features cushy lounge seating and a T-shaped bar that doubles as a runway for the shimmying showgirls. *Wed-Sat 9pm-2am.* C =

Hot Tip: VIP service here isn't a bank-breaker and is worth the guaranteed entry. For $75 per person, you get a "lounge seat," and the cover is applied to your bar tab—but you have to hold with a credit card and arrive by 10pm.

L'Scorpion
6679 Hollywood Blvd., Hollywood, 323-464-3026 • Hip

The Draw: This sexy Spanish-inspired destination from the nightlife gurus behind Table 8 and Rokbar draws the young and trendy in droves.

The Scene: A sultry ambience permeates the narrow confines of this Hollywood tequila and tapas bar that has a legal occupancy of only 60 (and an average crowd of 125) and a tequila menu of more than 160 bottles. *Nightly 6pm-2am.* C =

Hot Tip: Educate yourself on Tequila Tasting Thursdays (7pm to 10pm) when hand-picked tapas dishes are paired with a variety of specialty tequilas (some regularly priced at $50), all for $45. And note: Dinner reservations let you skip the line.

Le Velvet Margarita Cantina*
1612 Cahuenga Blvd., Hollywood, 323-469-2000 • Hip

The Draw: Tijuana chic meets Gothic creep at this Cahuenga Corridor ultra lounge. The husband and wife owners ("Big Daddy" Carlos and Ava Berman) are longtime L.A. scenesters who keep things inviting, yet underground, making it a favorite with iconic *Swingers* like like Vince Vaughn and Jon Favreau.

The Scene: The pulp- and pop-culture–laced decor channels Tarantino: velvet walls, leopard skin, cult movie classics, and black-lit pictures of Sinatra, Elvis, and Che. Strolling mariachis, fruity margaritas, and an award-winning Nuevo Latino menu add authenticity. *Sun-Thu 11:30am-2am, Fri-Sat 11:30am-3am.* =

Hot Tip: The back patio is a great place to smoke and meet new people.

Trendy Tables

#88–90: Trendy in L.A. comes and goes faster than a Paris Hilton single. When you're talking about the latest restaurants, it's usually all about design and flash—who's behind it and who's out front with the paparazzi. Every once in a while, there's even decent food involved.

Bridge Restaurant and Lounge*

755 N. La Cienega Blvd., West Hollywood, 310-659-3535 • Hot & Cool

The Draw: This is the new venture from the backers of Koi (across the street), and it's quickly becoming even more sceney than its sibling.

The Scene: The long, sleek, two-story dining room is done in rich tones of chocolate and gold with wood accents. Inside these stylish rooms, L.A.'s trendiest crowd dines on passable Italian food and lingers in the sunken bar. *Restaurant: Mon-Sat 6-11pm; Lounge: Mon-Sat 8pm-2am. $$$$* ▤

Hot Tip: The lounge here serves food until 2am—a rarity in this neighborhood. For dining, ask for a booth in the main room.

Cut

The Regent Beverly Wilshire, 9500 Wilshire Blvd., Beverly Hills, 310-276-8500 • Hot & Cool

The Draw: Wolfgang Puck's latest undertaking—a swank steakhouse—is Los Angeles' hottest reservation.

The Scene: Crowds are dying to get into this chic, white-on-white dining space not just for a taste of excellently prepared cuts of meat, but more importantly, because everyone from foodies to Hollywood elite wants a table here. *Mon-Thu 5:30-10pm, Fri-Sat 5:30-11pm. $$$* ▤

Hot Tip: The wait for reservations can be up to two months—but the Beverly Wilshire concierges do have some tables held aside for their clients.

Social Hollywood*

6525 W. Sunset Blvd., Hollywood, 323-462-5222 • Hip

The Draw: This classic building, once the Hollywood Athletic Club, hosted the first Academy Awards in 1949. These days, hip style-setter Jeffrey Chodorow has once again revived the spot's allure.

The Scene: The lounge is dim, with red leather seats and jittery movies playing on the wall. The dining room is pure *Casablanca*. The clientele is young, beautiful, and dying to be noticed—celebs from Orlando Bloom to John Stamos and Jessica Biel have been spotted here. Upstairs is a private club for Hollywood elite. *Sun-Wed 6-11pm, Thu-Sat 6pm-1am; bar until 2am. $$$* ▤

Hot Tip: On Wednesdays, a club night is hosted on the exclusive second floor. Call 310-262-6728 or email viptableservice@aol.com to try to get on the list.

Best | Views of L.A.

#91–93: On a smoggy day, gazing down over Los Angeles from the Hollywood Hills might make you want to write a sympathy card to your lungs. Locals describe the yellow-brown filter as smoky, hazy, or even optimistically as a "marine layer." But somewhere underneath that pollution are a big blue ocean, chapparal-covered mountains, and a world-class city waiting to be discovered.

Briles Wing & Helicopter

16303 Waterman Dr., Van Nuys, 877-863-5952 • Hot & Cool

The Draw: Make like a local traffic reporter and launch yourself above L.A. in a helicopter for the best bird's-eye view of the city.

The Scene: The standard tour takes just 30 minutes to cover the Hollywood Hills, the Getty Center, Universal Studios, Beverly Hills, and Downtown. $$$$

Hot Tip: Add some airtime along the coast on the City of Angels Flight. Another option includes limousine pickup service from your hotel (for groups of ten or more) and a special Destination Dinner Flight to either Santa Monica Airport's Typhoon or LAX's Encounters restaurant.

Catalina Island

20 miles southwest of Los Angeles

The Draw: Gazing at Los Angeles from this getaway 20 miles offshore erases all the city's buildings and highways from view, leaving behind the hills, mountains, and sweeping coast. Here's what L.A. looked like when the dinosaurs ruled.

The Scene: A charming island retreat that's as removed from the hustle of the city as it appears, Catalina draws everyone from families to romance-seeking couples. Several trails from the port town of Avalon lead up to the best vistas of the Southern California coast.

Hot Tip: Reservations, reservations, reservations. Catalina is a small island town, and hotels get booked lightning fast for events like JazzTrax (October) or the triathlon (November). See *Leavings*, p.190.

Mulholland Drive

Between U.S. 101 and I-405

The Draw: Gaze down over the Los Angeles flats on one side and the San Fernando Valley on the other from this famous road that wends its way through the Hollywood Hills.

The Scene: Winding past mansions and celebrity estates, Mulholland Drive straddles the Hollywood Hills and Santa Monica Mountains for more than 20 miles. There are several turnoffs and lookout points between U.S. 101 and Coldwater Canyon.

Hot Tip: Come at night for the best city lights show, but drivers should try to give the road at least cursory attention.

Wine List

#94–96: California is wine country, and until the northern part of the state splits from the southern part (and don't think it hasn't been discussed), a trip to Los Angeles is as much about enjoying the state's grape offerings as anything else. You don't need to be a *Sideways* snob to enjoy the wine lists at these friendly spots.

A.O.C.

8022 W. Third St., Los Angeles, 323-653-6359 • Hot & Cool

The Draw: This hot spot on the Third St. corridor has been luring scenesters and connoisseurs alike since opening its stylish doors.

The Scene: The bar buzzes with afterwork cocktail seekers, snacking on small plates and sampling the large by-the-glass wine list. The lively dining room is a hustle and bustle of 30-and-up-somethings searching out good food and good fun in the sophisticated, wood-paneled room. *Mon-Fri 6-11pm, Sat 5:30-11pm, Sun 5:30-10pm.* $$ B=

Hot Tip: Don't leave without trying one of the cheese plates for which it's famous, and for greater privacy, ask for an upstairs seat.

Melisse (G)

1104 Wilshire Blvd., Santa Monica, 310-395-0881 • Hot & Cool

The Draw: Fine dining at its finest is set in a formal yet comfortable environment, featuring a wine list predictably heavy in French selections.

The Scene: Comfy banquettes, soft lighting, and monogrammed plates are the backdrop for an eager crowd dressed in everything from T-shirts to suits. The wine list changes often, including many bottles from smaller vineyards in France. Not that high-end standbys like Château Petrus and Château Latour aren't well represented. They are. *Tue-Thu 6-9:30pm, Fri 6-10pm, Sat 5:45-10pm.* $$$ =

Hot Tip: Special wine dinners often highlight lesser-known vintages. Check the website (melisse.com) for upcoming dates.

Valentino (G)

3115 Pico Blvd., Santa Monica, 310-829-4313 • Classic

The Draw: Some of the best Italian food in the country is served in some of the plushest surroundings in the city, creating a special-occasion eating experience.

The Scene: Set back from a generic strip of Pico Boulevard near the 405 freeway, Valentino has several dining rooms filled with complex floral arrangements, mosaic mirrors, faux frescoes, and of course, well-dressed, knowledgeable diners. The wine list includes more than 2,500 selections from all over the world. Total number of bottles? It used to have around 150,000 but recently scaled back to a mere 60,000 or so. *Mon-Fri 5:30-10:30pm, Sat 5-11pm.* $$$$ =

Hot Tip: For the most privacy, ask for a table in one of the alcoves just off the main dining room.

Best

Workouts

#97–99: With a high per capita of body-conscious people, Los Angeles is filled to the brim with places to sweat, strain, and grimace that have nothing to do with driving in traffic. This brings up the problem of choice. Do you want to work out your body or check out everybody else's? At the following gyms, both are possible.

Crunch Fitness

8000 W. Sunset Blvd., West Hollywood, 323-654-4550 • Hip

The Draw: An emphasis on classes like strip aerobics and washboard abs makes this the best place to get a cardio workout under adult supervision.

The Scene: A sex-fueled environment either adds to or detracts from one's attempts to get in shape, but web-surfing on the stationary bikes and the rhythm-challenging jump-rope class should keep your mind on other things besides the hot bodies around you. *Mon-Fri 5am-midnight, Sat-Sun 7am-10pm.* $

Hot Tip: For a boost, treat yourself to an energy shake at the juice bar halfway through your regimen.

Gold's Gym

360 Hampton Dr., Venice, 310-392-6004 • Classic

The Draw: This is the mecca of bodybuilding, the place where many of those guys in the ego-and-Crisco bodybuilder contests like "Mr. World" and "Mr. Universe" have actually trained.

The Scene: You lift weights here and do little else. It's serious business, and though you'll probably feel intimidated when you first come in, it will soon become clear that the approachable staff and pumped-up patrons see you as a welcome presence in their world. *Mon-Fri 4am-midnight, Sat-Sun 5am-11pm.* $$

Hot Tip: Getting a personal trainer for your first visit is the best way to learn how to use the gym.

The Sports Club / LA

1835 Sepulveda Blvd., Los Angeles, 310-473-1447 • Hot & Cool

The Draw: Valet parking and celebs who haven't yet ascended to the "home gym" phase of their careers pack this über-trendy spot.

The Scene: Beautiful, silicone-enhanced people climb, run, and walk in state-of-the-art workout rooms, compete on several courts of the racquetball, squash and paddle-tennis variety, and swim laps in a junior Olympic–size pool, before repairing to Splash spa for an emergency massage or facial. *Mon-Fri 5am-11pm, Sat-Sun 7am-8pm.* $$

Hot Tip: Day passes are not for general sale, but guests of the Peninsula, Hotel Bel-Air, and the Regent Beverly Wilshire get special privileges.

EXPERIENCE LOS ANGELES

Los Angeles is huge and diverse. Getting from one side of town to the other can be an all-day event. But you don't have time to waste, so strut into the L.A. of your choice with one of three themed itineraries: *Hot & Cool* (p.50), *Hip* (p.90), and *Classic* (p.124). Each is designed as a special invitation to a unique style of enjoying this glamorous city. The experiences will put you in the right place at the right time—with the best restaurants, nightlife, and attractions. Whether you're looking to indulge in a decadent meal created by a celebrity chef, or party with A-listers at one of the hottest clubs, you'll find what you need to know right here.

Hot & Cool Los Angeles

Hot & Cool starts in L.A. This city shapes au courant culture like no other. Turn on your TV—that's not Milwaukee you're looking at. It's a celebrity-obsessed world out there, from Lohan to Clooney, and the trends and treats that make A-list life so glamorous are all born on this stretch of Southern California coast. From dimly lit dive bars to stylish, buzzing restaurants, this version of L.A. is about hitting the places where paparazzi hang out waiting for star sightings, and searching out the stops that aren't even on their radar yet. Grab your entourage and get ready to see what keeps this silicone-studded playground at the epicenter of fun.

Note: Venues in bold are described in detail in the listings that follow the itinerary. Venues followed by an * asterisk are those we recommend as both a restaurant and a destination bar.

Hot & Cool Los Angeles:
The Perfect Plan (3 Nights and Days)

Perfect Plan Highlights

Thursday

Lunch	The Grill on the Alley, Barney Greengrass
Afternoon	Getty Center, cemetery, shopping
Cocktails	Cameo Bar, Ma'Kai*, Casa del Mar
Dinner	Wilshire*, Melisse, JiRaffe
Nighttime	Renee's, Circle Bar, Rokbar
Late-Night	Mor, Busby's*, Privilege

Friday

Morning	Universal Studios, Disney Concert Hall
Lunch	Patina, Clafoutis
Afternoon	Spa, Msm. TV and Radio
Cocktails	Saddle Ranch*, Falcon*
Dinner	Koi, Providence, Ago
Nighttime	LAX, Holly's
Late-Night	Basque, Cinespace*

Saturday

Morning	Bike ride, hike, horseback riding
Lunch	Jer-ne, Geoffrey's
Afternoon	Beach
Cocktails	Four Seasons Bar, Geisha House*
Dinner	Lucques, A.O.C., Ortolan
Nighttime	Skybar, Citizen Smith
Late-Night	Cabana Club, Lobby Lounge at the Standard, 24/7

Morning After

Brunch	Breadbar

Hotel: **Raffles L'Ermitage**

Thursday

12:30pm Lunch Jump right into the sleek midday scene in Beverly Hills by booking a table at **The Grill on the Alley**. Consider yourself a true player if you manage to get a booth. For something more casual, but no less likely to net you a star sighting, head to the top floor of Barneys, where you'll find **Barney Greengrass**. Grab a table on the rooftop patio.

2pm The **Getty Center** is a must-see museum not only for the art, but also for the panoramic view from the ocean all the way to the San Bernardino Mountains. It's a good idea to call ahead and reserve a parking spot, and don't think it's all paintings and marble—the gardens here are lovely.

4:30pm Swing around through Westwood and visit the famous dead at the **Pierce Bros. Westwood Village Memorial Park**, where you'll find Marilyn Monroe's grave. Or join the living filling the shops and cafes at the **Third Street Promenade** for a quick shopping fix.

6pm In Santa Monica, grab a seat in the Viceroy Hotel's **Cameo Bar**, or slip into a chaise amidst the palm trees in the outside lounge area. Not tropical enough for you?

Then make your way to teak-rich **Ma'Kai*** a few blocks over, where the waterfalls are flowing and the singles-heavy clientele gets less discerning as the night goes on. For a refined cocktail, grab one of the comfortable armchairs in the elegant lobby of **Casa del Mar** and pretend you're taking a meeting.

8pm Dinner Make the short drive to **Wilshire***, where the valet line of Mercedes and BMWs is so long it backs up traffic. You'll want a seat out on the patio. If romance is what you're seeking, check out the refined offerings at **Melisse**, a Westside favorite. Or try sublime Cal-French at **JiRaffe**.

10pm At **Renee's Courtyard Café**, an outside-inside bar on Wilshire, plant yourself in the central courtyard. Tables there are harder to come by as the night goes on because it's great real estate for people-watching. If Main Street beckons, try **Circle Bar**, a former biker hangout with Far East pretensions that considers itself king of the area's singles scene. The smallish dance floor gets packed, which sort of proves its point. If you're looking for a savvier club scene, head east to Hollywood and **Rokbar**—this sleek space from rockers Tommy Lee and Dave Navarro is a stellar place to start the night.

Midnight Mor Bar on Main Street is a great locale to keep the momentum going. The sexy Moroccan space is small, with just enough room for dancing.

As the evening goes on, **Busby's*** on Santa Monica Boulevard morphs from a cozy sports bar into a lively spot for singles. But if you're in Hollywood, head up Sunset to **Privilege**, where you'll find trendy young things packing a stylish space.

Friday

9am Start a luxurious day with some room service.

10am For a taste of behind-the-scenes moviemaking, make a trek to the Valley and check out a VIP tour at **Universal Studios**. You could spend a whole day here, but a few hours will do the trick for all but the most hard-core thrill ride fans. Or head downtown: The **Walt Disney Concert Hall** is a soaring feat of architecture, and worth the drive. Take the self-guided audio tour, then wander down the block to the Cathedral of Our Lady of Angels, a modern wonder with delicate alabaster panels for windows and tombs in the basement.

1pm Lunch If you're Downtown, **Patina** is the spot for lunch. Score a booth inside, or on a nice day, enjoy the outdoor patio. If you're in the Valley, cut across Laurel Canyon and land on the Sunset Strip at **Clafoutis**, where you can dine like a star at the sidewalk tables.

2:30pm Time to relax. The minute you walk into **Ole Henricksen** at

Sunset Plaza, you'll catch a whiff of some of the divine fragrances you'll be pampered with when you have one of this spa's famous facials. If your whole body is in need, check out **Kinara Spa** on trendy Robertson, where you'll also find über-trendy shops like Lisa Kline and Kitson. You could also spend a few hours at the **Museum of Television and Radio**, where patrons tuck away in private cubicles to view the huge collection of TV shows, from *Wonder Woman* to *Saturday Night Live*.

6pm For pre-dinner drinks, you can either go Western or undercover. At **Saddle Ranch***, a mechanical bull holds court, daring you to make a fool of yourself. Go ahead—they'll start you out slow. **Falcon*** is a hard place to find. You have to know to climb concrete stairs to a side door. No password needed, just head in, order a martini, and decide whether you want to take your drink outside or stay in the lounge.

8pm Dinner A sushi feast replete with sure-fire celeb sightings is yours at **Koi** on La Cienega's restaurant row. You can request a seat out on the stone patio, though the stars are known to eat inside as well. Looking for a meal to brag about? Try **Providence**, Michael Cimarusti's restaurant a few miles east on Melrose. Set in the former Patina spot, it's one of the most sought-after eating experiences in the city. Of course, there's also **Ago**, De Niro's hot spot, and **Bridge**, where the food plays backup to the very Hollywood scene.

10:30pm Next up: **LAX**, an airport-lounge-inspired retro bar and high-profile celeb hangout. For another young Hollywood hot spot with less flash but equal star allure, head to **Holly's**. Convince the doorman you're one of owner Rick Calamaro's long-lost and obscenely rich friends (better hope Rick's out of town), and head into the candle-lit, sexy club.

Midnight Dance the night away at tapas bar and nightclub **Basque** near Hollywood and Vine. Elsewhere in the neighborhood, **Cinespace*** is where hipsters choose to spend the entire evening, starting early with cocktails, then doing dinner and a movie (they show indie flicks or documentaries while you eat), all before the music starts up.

Saturday

9am Bike or hike? That's the question this morning. If the choice is two wheels, head south to **Martha's 22nd Street Cafe** in Hermosa Beach and immerse yourself in the SoCal lifestyle of volleyball, surfing, and flip-flops over breakfast. Then walk south on the beach path called The Strand to the area around Hermosa Pier, where you can rent a bicycle at one of several shops. You could ride all the way up to Malibu if you're feeling up to it, but remember that you'll have to ride all the way back, too. If you'd rather hike, then the mountains up the coast are calling. Drive north to **Point Mugu State Park** and explore the trails, or head out on horseback through Topanga Canyon in the Santa Monica Mountains with **Los Angeles Horsebackriding**. You get stunning views of Zuma Beach and Catalina Island when it's clear.

1pm Lunch Drive back up Vista del Mar to Marina del Rey, where the Asian-fusion restaurant **Jer-ne**, overlooking the marina, serves a popular brunch. Or, relax at **Geoffrey's** in Malibu, where you never know what misbehaving star will be at the bar.

2:30pm If you're down south, lay out a towel on the beach near the pier and get some sun. If you're up the Malibu way, stop into the **Malibu Country Mart** for refreshments, then spend a few hours soaking up the scene on Zuma Beach.

6:30pm Back in town, join the scene at the **Four Seasons lobby bar** in Beverly Hills, which is filled with celebs, dignitaries, and assorted other VIPS. This is L.A. at its most high-falutin. A sexier vibe can be had at **Geisha House***, Ashton Kutcher's sushi restaurant, which is good for a couple of starter drinks and a small plate or two. And if Santa Monica is close, try **Chaya Venice***, just down the street from the "binocular building" designed by Frank Gehry.

8pm Dinner Saturday night is a hot scene at **Lucques**, especially considering Suzanne Goin recently won the Best Chef in California Award from the James Beard Foundation. You can also still enjoy Goin's bold flavors at her restaurant and wine bar, **A.O.C.** For dessert, get a cheese plate. An equally delicious option is the stylish room at **Ortolan**.

10pm It's time to check out the infamous **Skybar** at the Mondrian Hotel. You can also head back into Hollywood for the action at **Citizen Smith**, a trendy restaurant/bar with a lively crowd.

Midnight **The Cabana Club** is a favorite of beautiful young things. But the **Lobby Lounge** at **The Standard** is the perfect place to cap off a swanky evening in mellow style. If you're jonesing for food, the sandwich- and appetizer–heavy menu at the Standard Hotel's high-end coffeeshop **24/7** should do the trick.

The Morning After

Breadbar isn't for the carb-conscious, but everyone else is in this small and bustling spot having brunch.

Hot & Cool Los Angeles:
The Key Neighborhoods

Beverly Hills is the world capital of celebrity, glamour, and, of course, money. As such, it runs the gamut from upscale restaurants to upscale drinking holes, with lots of middle-aged, wealthy patrons in each.

Hollywood It's the anti–Beverly Hills, with equal amounts of starpower. This stretch of clubs and restaurants is one of the hottest destinations in L.A., but remains a marginal, up-and-coming area.

Santa Monica is both trendy and moneyed. This unofficial capital of L.A.'s Westside has some of the best dining in the city and a shopping street—Montana Avenue—that's chic, but refreshingly understated compared to some of the city's more famous browsing strips. And, of course, there's the beach.

South Bay includes Manhattan, Hermosa, and Redondo beaches and has for decades been a scruffy surfer hangout. Times are changing along with real estate prices, and the sand-in-your-ears scene has become much more sophisticated in recent years.

West Hollywood, a gay-friendly area also called WeHo or Boystown, is filled with modern spas, trendy restaurants, a plethora of martini-type bars, and a heightened sense of fashion.

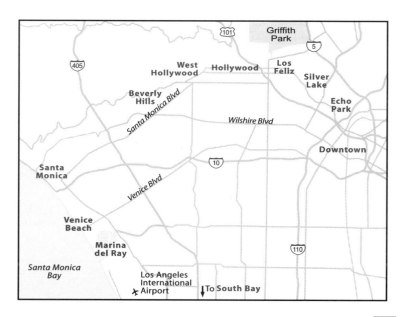

Hot & Cool Los Angeles:
The Shopping Blocks

Beverly Boulevard

With an emphasis on home design, this is the street to go for mid-20th-century creations, though it also hosts some one-of-a-kind stores where form and function come together.

Modernica This trailblazing Beverly Boulevard furniture store specializes in high-quality replicas of minimalist furniture. 7366 Beverly Blvd. (Martel Ave.), 323-933-0383, modernica.net

Stella McCartney The fluid creations of the former Chloe designer are a must-browse for any woman with style on her mind. 8823 Beverly Blvd. (Robertson Blvd.), 310-273-7051, stellamccartney.com

Williams-Sonoma Home Browse high-end furniture and accessories at the company's flagship home furnishings store. 8772 Beverly Blvd. (Robertson Blvd.), 310-289-2420, wshome.com

Melrose Heights

The doorbells used by many of the upscale clothes stores along this strip running from La Cienega to Fairfax are ostensibly for security purposes, but funny how they also help keep the celebrities in and the riff-raff out. Who's the riff-raff? You could be if you don't have the sophisticated look down pat. But isn't that why you wanted to visit these stores in the first place?

Decades Head upstairs for vintage evening wear from the '50s, '60s, and '70s, or stay downstairs (Decades Two) for modern wear. 8214 Melrose Ave. (Harper Ave.), 323-655-1960

Fred Segal This vine-covered building, sans doorbell, holds a warren of shops selling everything from cosmetics to children's fashions. 8100 Melrose Ave. (Crescent Hts.), 323-655-3734, fredsegalbeauty.com

Maxfield Expensive fashion, gifts, furniture, and gadgets help you further refine your discriminating taste. 8825 Melrose Ave. (Robertson Blvd.), 310-274-8800

Miu Miu The austere interior allows men and women plenty of room to browse Miuccia Prada's ready-to-wear creations. 8025 Melrose Ave. (N. Laurel Ave.), 323-651-0072, miumiu.com

Soolip Paperie & Press Get a designer card and some imported wrapping paper to cover that gift for the person who has everything. 8646 Melrose Ave. (Norwich Dr.), 310-360-0545, soolip.com

Montana Avenue

This understated street, which serves up the best concentration of stylish shops on the far Westside, is Santa Monica's more mature, quainter answer to Robertson Boulevard.

The Blues Jean Bar Men and women can try myriad blue jean styles by sidling up to the bar and whispering their sizes. 1409 Montana Ave. (14th St.), 310-656-7898, thebluesjeanbar.com

Jill Roberts Clothing, home goods, shoes, and jewelry with a perfect mix of elegance and hipness. 920 Montana Ave. (Ninth St.), 310-260-1966

Planet Blue Larger than its Malibu location, this store gives shoppers room to roam among rows of casual but definitely not dowdy designer duds. 800 14th St. (Montana Ave.), 310-394-0135

Shabby Chic With fabrics and other furniture restoratives, this is the shop that launched the popular television show. 1013 Montana Ave. (Tenth St.), 310-394-1975, shabbychic.com

Robertson Boulevard

The hottest shopping street in Los Angeles is rife with trendy clothes for young actresses who flock here en masse to be photographed by paparazzi. Lacking the sniffy atmosphere found in Melrose Heights and along Rodeo Drive, these stores have employees who actually care about helping you, sort of, even if you're not the next Hilary Duff.

Curve Edgy designer-wear highlights this women's shop hidden from onlookers by frosted glass. 154 N. Robertson Blvd. (Beverly Blvd.), 310-360-8008, shopcurve.com

Diavolina This sassy, sexy footwear has nothing to do with practicality. 156 S. Robertson Blvd. (W. Third St.), 310-550-1341

Kiehl's Lab-coat-wearing salespeople give this animal-friendly skin-care shop that much more credibility. 100 N. Robertson Blvd. (Beverly Blvd.), 310-860-0028, kiehls.com

Kitson Perhaps the most talked about store in the city specializes in cutesy clothes for perfect bodies. 115 S. Robertson Blvd. (Third St.), 310-859-2652, shopkitson.com

Lisa Kline Girly fashions including Barbie T-shirts and Joe's Jeans for the hip and trendy at heart. Kline's men's store is across the street. 136 S. Robertson Blvd. (Alden Dr.), 310-246-0907, lisakline.com

Hot & Cool Los Angeles:
The Hotels

Beach House at Hermosa • Hermosa Beach • Modern (96 rms)
Off the beaten path by some standards, this deluxe property in the South Bay is a well-kept four-star secret. Savvy couples and corporate execs who like to jog along the ocean before meetings get a real deal down here compared to the ransom rates they could be paying up at Santa Monica's swanky beach hotels. Just steps from one of the city's loveliest and liveliest beaches, more than 100 identical studio suites are tastefully assembled with large king beds, down comforters, and generous work spaces with high-speed internet access in loft-style bedrooms. There's a mini-kitchen with a microwave, small stove, and fridge. Spacious bathrooms have deep soaking tubs and come stocked with Aveda products. Sunken living rooms are dressed with plush couches, wood-burning fireplaces, stereo systems, and walk-onto balconies with ocean views. A complimentary continental breakfast is included, and room service is provided by two nearby restaurants. The hotel's holistic spa service offers private yoga sessions on the beach and in-room massage treatments The 500-square-foot studios have a balcony and a sunken tub. $$$ 1300 The Strand (14th St.), 310-374-3001 / 888-895-4559, beach-house.com

Casa del Mar • Santa Monica • Timeless (131 rms)
A new heyday has dawned at this posh seaside landmark, which was the toast of Santa Monica's private beach club scene back in the '20s. Stunningly restored in Renaissance revival style and reopened in 1999, Casa del Mar joins its neighboring sister property, Shutters (see p.61), as the most celebrated L.A. digs on the coast. The immense lobby lounge is the first showstopper, with its lavish wood- and ironwork, huge stone hearth, plush velvet sofas, club chairs, and a gorgeous bar overlooking the Pacific. To your left, the elegant Oceanfront dining room serves innovative New American cuisine accompanied by the same postcard views. All of this tasteful opulence continues throughout 131 guest rooms and suites, dressed in fruitwood furnishings, handpainted armoires, Matisse-inspired art, and gauzy white curtains with thick wood Venetian blinds. Stereos, DVDs, VCRs, and high-speed internet access are all standard, as are large Italian marble bathrooms with glass-enclosed showers and computer-controlled whirlpool tubs. For sweeping views, reserve an oceanfront room with king-size bed on the 7th floor. A full fitness area boasts state-of-the-art Cybex cardio equipment and individual workout stations with headphones and TVs. A range of spa treatments can be enjoyed in private cabanas on the lovely fifth-floor pool deck above Santa Monica Bay. $$$$ 1910 Ocean Way (Pico Blvd.), 310-581-5533 / 800-898-6999, hotelcasadelmar.com

Chateau Marmont • West Hollywood • Timeless (63 rms)
Since 1927, L.A.'s homage to some castle in Amboise, France, has been hiding above a curve at the top of the Sunset Strip—well, "hiding" the way that stars "hide" from the public. (Lots of Garbo- and De Niro–caliber guests have engaged in that very activity here.) With its lovely garden cafe, a funky attic exercise room, and a secluded, brick-decked pool court, this elegant yet quirky

spot offers as much peace, privacy, and European-style charm as one could expect from a celebrity-studded chateau on the most frenzied stretch of Sunset Boulevard. If small doesn't charm you, avoid the standard rooms and opt for one of the suites with balconies and Shangri-La views of the Hollywood Hills. Or splurge on a Spanish-style garden cottage or a famous poolside bungalow. Renting bungalow 3 lets you stand in the very kitchenette where in 1940 Robert Mitchum fried bacon (much better than bungalow 2, where John Belushi checked in and permanently checked out). Each of the Chateau's 63 rooms are uniquely decorated, ranging from Gothic and Arts and Crafts to Fabulous '50s. Standard rooms on the first floor have the most privacy. $$$ 8221 W. Sunset Blvd. (Marmont Ln.), 323-656-1010, chateaumarmont.com

Four Seasons Hotel • Beverly Hills • Timeless (285 rms)

As 90210 as any hotel in Beverly Hills, the five-diamond Four Seasons exists in its own quiet residential pocket, providing easy access to, but also relief from, Rodeo Drive and the nearby Beverly Center. The lobby's outstanding floral displays and 24-hour concierge service are pure Four Seasons. Furnished in tasteful pastels, the well-appointed guest rooms and suites provide extra-stuffed Sealy mattresses, Heavenly linens, marble bathrooms, and French doors opening out to balconies that, in the lavish upper suites, wrap around for full panoramic views. Certain Premier accommodations offer a garden view, a 430-square-foot room, and a wraparound balcony. Guests converge on the fourth floor terrace with its always-80-degree lap pool, Jacuzzi, fully-equipped fitness center, and poolside grill specializing in light spa cuisine. A 4,000-square-foot spa is a recent addition, stocked with eight treatment rooms and a range of sybaritic options, from the signature Punta Mita Massage and Margarita Salt Scrub to one of the most raved-about 75-minute facials in town. Gardens restaurant serves award-winning Cal-Med cuisine in a tranquil indoor/outdoor setting. Windows lounge is known for its martinis and its schmoozing industry regulars. $$$$ 300 S. Doheny Dr. (Burton Way), 310-273-2222 / 800-332-3442, fourseasons.com

Luxe Hotel Rodeo Drive • Beverly Hills • Modern (86 rms)

Just how Rodeo Drive is this boutique hotel smack in the middle of the Golden Triangle? How does a pair of Valentino boutiques—his and hers—right inside the building grab you? If you're looking for an oversized room and lots of great on-site facilities, truth be told, this compact little gem from the Luxe gang doesn't fit the bill. But for the novelty of living right above one of the world's most famous fashion districts in a classy, somewhat European-style setting, it can't be beat. Eighty-six charming guest rooms and suites feature Frette linens, DSL, CD players, a small desk, and well-appointed bathrooms with signature robes. Deluxe rooms have either balconies or Rodeo Drive views. Rooms 209, 309, and 409 are the only three of the bigger rooms that face Rodeo Drive. $$$ 360 N. Rodeo Dr. (Brighton Way), 310-273-0300 / 866-589-3411, luxehotels.com

Malibu Beach Inn • Malibu • Contemporary (47 rms)

Malibu's stretch of premium coast offers very little in the way of accommodations, which is just the way those private Colony folks like it. The next best thing to crashing at Johnny Carson's place is a few nights at the Malibu Beach Inn, which accurately enough calls itself the neighborhood's only luxury beachfront hotel. With its assortment of "Beachcomber" and "Surfrider" rooms and suites done up in soft pinks and greens, the relaxed vibe here is more about a quick weekend escape with front-row ocean views than five-star luxury. Mexican-tiled bathrooms, casual wicker furnishings, and private balconies are standard, and most suites have gas fireplaces and Soft Tub Jacuzzis right above the surf. Best non-suite rooms are on the first floor and have 550 square feet with Jacuzzi and California king bed. For a small extra charge, the "romantic-getaway" package includes champagne, Godiva chocolates, rose petal turn-down service, and breakfast in bed. Complimentary continental breakfasts are otherwise served out on the patio; roomservice is 24 hours; and stairs lead right down to the beach. If you can't live in Malibu, this charming fixture right on PCH provides a sweet taste. $$$ 22878 Pacific Coast Hwy. (Sweetwater Canyon Dr.), 310-456-6444 / 800-462-5428, malibubeachinn.com

Raffles L'Ermitage Beverly Hills • Beverly Hills • Modern (121 rms)

Just before residential Burton Way curves into Little Santa Monica Boulevard and downtown Beverly Hills, there it is—a five-star, five-diamond 90210 boutique hotel that you can drive right past every day and somehow never notice. That's just how the entertainment and recording industry fat cats who hole up in this gorgeous eight-story sanctuary would like it to stay: kind of hidden, yet just around the corner from everything. Tasteful contemporary Euro-Asian decor meets state-of-the-art technology in the 121 double-size guest rooms, which include large separate living and work spaces, plus a vanity area stocked with Aveda products and your choice of terry or plain cotton robes. French doors open onto private balconies with mountain or city views. Rooms come with 40-inch TVs, CD/DVD players with Bose speakers, DSL, five phone lines, a cell phone for use during your stay, and a panel of bedside controls that has everything but a steering wheel. Executive rooms on floors 7 and 8 are 650 to 700 square feet, and have the largest balconies and best city views. Outstanding facilities include a full-service spa, a state-of-the-art fitness center, a rooftop pool with private cabanas, and a French-Indochine restaurant, Jaan. $$$$ 9291 Burton Way (Foothill Rd.), 310-278-3344 / 800-800-2113, raffleshotels.com

Shade • Manhattan Beach • Trendy (38 rms)

This boutique hotel is further proof that Manhattan Beach, possibly California's most picture-perfect beach town (sorry, Malibu), is getting the proverbial sand out of its ears and becoming more urbane. The 38 rooms—all with balconies, but no ocean views—are simplistic and modern, with rich, glossy woods, ambient lighting you control, and Mascioni linens and feather duvets on the Tempur-Pedic mattresses. Bathrooms are cordoned off with Shoji screens (except in the five suites) and have spa tubs with chromatherapy lighting. Rooms on the second floor are quieter and have fireplaces. Room 212 is the only one from which you can see the ocean. For splurging's sake, the northwest-corner Penthouse Suite has king- and queen-sized beds and looks out over the adjacent and brand-spanking-new shopping pavilion. A rooftop bar is open weekend nights during the summer. Like the lounge, Zinc, room service shuts down at 11pm, but if you really need some grub, walk a block or so to the nearby Kettle restaurant, a South Bay institution that's open 24 hours. If you're not much for walking, it can deliver. $$$ 1221 N. Valley Dr. (Manhattan Beach Blvd.), 310-546-4995 / 866-987-4233, shadehotel.com

Shutters on the Beach • Santa Monica • Timeless (198 rms)

Best Presidential Suites If you haven't seen a celebrity yet and you want to, have a seat in Shutters' fireplace lobby lounge and wait. Honored time and again as L.A.'s finest luxury hotel right on the sand, Shutters hasn't much competition in this category save for Casa del Mar (see p.58) next door, which boasts the same cosmic room rates without the balconies (something about tampering with a historic landmark). But Shutters has balconies, three per room sometimes, and they're all close enough to the surf so you can hear the waves, smell the salt, and spot bobbing sea lions (or are those empty oil drums?) with the handy binoculars provided in some of the upper suites. Shutters has a pair of destination restaurants, One Pico (formal, upstairs) and Pedals (casual, downstairs), serving top contemporary American cuisine with front-row ocean views. In your room, you can close the pretty clapboard shutter doors, crank the AC, and pretend you're wintering in the Hamptons. Then you can open them to reveal that you are (in case we failed to mention this) right on the sand in Santa Monica. Guest rooms are outfitted with warm wood furnishings, upholstered beds, oversized Jacuzzis in spacious marble bathrooms, and soft aqua color schemes. If you want a fireplace and those three balconies, check into a Presidential Suite (just $2,500 a night). Deluxe oceanfront rooms on the seventh floor have vaulted ceilings and a great view of the pier. All guests can enjoy the small but pretty pool deck and a fully-equipped fitness room where spa treatments may be arranged. $$$$ 1 Pico Blvd. (Ocean Way), 310-458-0030 / 800-334-9000, shuttersonthebeach.com

Hot & Cool Los Angeles:
The Restaurants

A.O.C. • Los Angeles • Mediterranean

Best Wine List Occasionally, Third Street's restless roster of "hot new restaurants" produces one with enough style and substance to make it through one year and draw an even hungrier crowd the next. Enter A.O.C., the latest A-list hangout on this mini restaurant row, which draws in flocks of stylish 30-something patrons for drinks at the chic wine bar and dinner in the stark but inviting room. Delicate small-plate creations on the revolving menu—a French take on tapas—are meant to be savored and shared. The menu starts with a robust list of cheese and charcuterie selections, followed by fish, meat, and wood-burning-oven dishes that might include seared albacore with shell beans and bottarga, lamb skewers with carrot purée and cumin yogurt, or steamed fingerlings with crème fraîche. More than 50 wines are available by the bottle, carafe, glass, or even half-glass. The best scene is at the bar and in the sleek main dining room; for a more intimate setting, request a table upstairs on the back patio (where the no-smoking rule still applies). *Mon-Fri 6-11pm, Sat 5:30-11pm, Sun 5:30-10pm.* $$ B= 8022 W. Third St. (S. Laurel Ave.), 323-653-6359, aocwinebar.com

Ago • West Hollywood • Italian

Best Celebrity-Owned Restaurants This trendy trattoria in West Hollywood has enjoyed a constant buzz ever since word somehow got out (on day one, seven years ago) that Robert De Niro and a handful of other movie types had a piece of the place. Thankfully, Ago isn't resting on these laurels alone. Power-lunchers (and -dinnerers) don't mind paying a little extra to savor perfectly done pastas, risottos, grilled fish, and chef Agostino Sciandri's signature bistecca alla fiorentina (a 22-ounce Angus T-bone steak prepared in the wood-burning oven). If you pick the right evening, you'll be dining with the in-crowd and usually some guest stars. On weekend nights (which seems to include Wednesdays and Thursdays here), don't think of walking into this discreet-from-the-outside, happening-on-the-inside, split-level dining room without a reservation. Alfresco fans can ask or beg for a table on the leafy patio. *Mon-Fri noon-2:30pm; Mon-Sat 6-11:30pm, Sun 6-10:30pm.* $$ B= 8478 Melrose Ave. (Crescent Heights Blvd.), 323-655-6333, agorestaurant.com

Angelini Osteria • Los Angeles • Italian

Gino Angelini has cooked for everyone from Luciano Pavarotti to François Mitterand to Pope John Paul II, but at Angelini Osteria you wouldn't know it—the atmosphere in his home-style restaurant is unpretentious, right down to the friendly waiters, lively buzz (okay, it's loud), and bar seats for Angelini fans who don't have time to call a friend when they get the sudden craving for his spaghetti alla carbonara or famous lasagna verde, a recipe honoring his grandmother. On any night, you'll find young fashionistas dining elbow to elbow with suits and even a kid or two. Lovers of Italian wine should be suitably overwhelmed by this local gem's extensive menu covering every major region in Italy. Daily specials begin to disappear as the night goes on, so get there early or you'll miss out. *Tue-Fri noon-2:30pm, Tue-Sun 5:30-10:30pm.* $$$ B≡ 7313 Beverly Blvd. (Poinsettia Pl.), 323-297-0070, angeliniosteria.com

Asia de Cuba • West Hollywood • Fusion
The scene at this Asian-Latin eatery is everything you'd expect from a dining room in the trendy Mondrian—it's all well-coiffed, well-dressed, and ready for fun. For starters (besides the eye candy, tasty mojitos, and great views), try the calamari salad or the signature oxtail spring rolls. Favorite entrees (like hacked lime-and-garlic chicken and Hunan-wok crispy whole fish stuffed with crab escabeche) arrive in let's-share portions, as do some very decadent desserts. Food is served either in the chic narrow dining room or out on the hotel's famous patio area. Contrary to what you might hope, dining here does not guarantee you entry into the Mondrian's ultrachic poolside bar, Skybar. *Daily 7-11am, 11:30am-3:30pm, Mon-Thu 5:30-11:30pm, Fri-Sat 5:30pm-1am, Sun 5:30-10:30pm.* $$$ B≡ 8440 W. Sunset Blvd. (La Cienega Blvd.), 323-848-6000, mondrianhotel.com

Avenue • Manhattan Beach • New American
Fine dining finally arrives in Manhattan Beach with chef Christian Shaffer's progressive-American restaurant a few blocks from the sand, although the swanky interior, with upholstered banquettes and linen-covered tables, tends to scare off the flip-flop–wearing crowd. The menu changes monthly and might include duck confit with okra or roasted sturgeon with asparagus purée. Shaffer also likes to throw in the occasional whimsical creation, like escargot pot pie, just for fun. This is the beach, after all, so enjoy the relaxed vibe and allow for the possibility of inter-table conversation while you're putting the extensive wine list through its paces. *Sat-Sun 10:30am-2:30pm, Wed-Thu, Sun 5:30-10pm, Fri-Sat 5:30-11pm.* $$ B≡ 1141 Manhattan Ave. (Manhattan Beach Blvd.), 310-802-1973, avenuemb.com

Barney Greengrass • Beverly Hills • Deli
Best Power Lunches This fancy-ish deli on the top floor of Barneys in downtown Beverly Hills is your best shot at noshing on chicken matzo ball soup, pickled herring, or, for that matter, $165 Beluga caviar beside someone sort-of-famous. At lunch, the sleek wood tables and expansive rooftop patio are crammed with entertainment industry folks doing business, of sorts. The biggest hit here is the smoked fish—sturgeon, Nova Scotia salmon, sable, whitefish, house-cured gravlax—all flown in from the Big Apple and served à la carte or beside a mess of eggs any style. Top deli sandwiches include the smoked fish club (Nova Scotia salmon, sturgeon, cream cheese, sprouts, and avocado) and the straight-out-of-New-York pastrami sandwich piled high on a rustic roll with slaw on the side. Top non-deli desserts include German chocolate cake and apple strudel. *Mon-Wed 8:30am-6pm, Thu-Sat 9am-7pm, Sun 9am-6pm.* $ B≡ 9570 Wilshire Blvd., 5th Floor (Rodeo Dr.), 310-777-5877, barneys.com

BlackSteel* • Hollywood • French/Japanese
Almost everything Pamela Anderson touches turns to gold—*Baywatch*, plastic surgery, celebrity sex tapes—which bodes well for her very industrial, very severe, very black new restaurant. BlackSteel offers Asian-inspired dishes like Kobe beef filet mignon, as well as vegetarian dishes handed down from Pamela's ancestors. (Health food in a Goth setting? Only in Hollywood.) It's an open space, with an open kitchen, and huge opaque-glass doors that slide open in the summer months. That welcoming look doesn't deter young fashionable types from filling the tables, along with passing tourists who wander in. *Tue-Sat 6pm-2am.* $$$ B≡ 6683 Hollywood Blvd. (Las Palmas Ave.), 323-469-3456, blacksteel.tv

Brandywine • Woodland Hills • Continental

The best restaurant in the Valley (yes, that's a compliment) is a smallish place with just a handful of tables and private booths. You won't find a phalanx of celebrities here, just a devoted crowd of West Valley diners who swear by the steaks and the John Dory that melts in your mouth. Service is attentive without being smothering, and it's also personable, yet another reason this dining room feels more like your living room. Some preparation is done tableside, and when you combine that with nightly guitar music and an owner who calls you by your first name, this place begins to feel like home. *Tue-Fri 11:30am-2:30pm, Mon-Sat 5:30-10:30pm.* $$ ≡ 22757 Ventura Blvd. (Fallbrook Ave.), 818-225-9114

Breadbar • Los Angeles • American

You can almost smell it as you're shopping on trendy Robertson Boulevard: the sweet whiff of baking bread. Follow your nose east about a block down Third Street and you're at Eric Kayser's bakery-cum-cafe, a descendant of his Paris restaurant, where a fashionable set orders eggplant-gorgonzola omelets, cucumber soup, and, of course, an assortment of croissants. Yes, carb-cautious Angelenos are finally warming up to bread. *Daily 7am-7pm.* $ ≡ 8718 W. Third St. (Arnaz Dr.), 310-205-0124, breadbar.net

Bridge Restaurant and Lounge* • West Hollywood • Italian

Best Trendy Tables With a conspicuously large valet-parking crew, dining spaces of warm wood, and patterned walls that are practically dipped in gold and New York sensibility, this Italian hot spot on La Cienega's restaurant row is the more high-profile sister restaurant of Koi (see *Hot & Cool Restaurants,* p.71) across the street. It gets the same hip, celebrity-driven crowds, but there's a red-carpet feel outside Bridge, as if a special party—Jay-Z's birthday perhaps?—is in the offing. But he's just here to eat like everybody else, so go right on in to savor everything from risotto with seafood and bistecca alla fiorentina to late-night pizzas and pressed sandwiches that are served until 2am in the voluminous lounge area. In any other city, Bridge might adversely affect Koi's business, but on happening La Cienega Boulevard, one senses there's plenty of room for both. *Restaurant: Mon-Sat 6-11pm; Lounge: Mon-Sat 8pm-2am.* $$$$ ≡ 755 N. La Cienega Blvd. (Waring Ave.), 310-659-3535, bridgela.com

Busby's* • Santa Monica • American

The four-star menu at this upscale sports club offers standard grease grub, but is known for its filet mignon and salmon dinner entrees. See *Hot & Cool Nightlife,* p.77, for details. *Daily 10am-midnight, bar until 2am.* $$ ≡ 3110 Santa Monica Blvd. (Berkeley St.), 310-828-4567, busbysonline.com

La Cachette • Century City • French (G)

You could call the cuisine at this hidden Century City restaurant French-Lite, but chef and owner Jean Francois Meteigner prefers the term *cuisine naturelle*. Mostly gone is the heavy cream and butter of traditional French cooking, but enough punch remains in classic dishes like frog's legs and foie gras. The name La Cachette means "the hideaway," a moniker that first-time visitors will find appropriate since it's so hard to find the alley entrance off busy Little Santa Monica Boulevard. With peaches, golds, and navy blues, the decor of the dining room is definitely geared toward an older crowd, many from the surrounding well-heeled area, but when you're dining on French food, that's not a bad thing—although some may find it bordering on stuffy. *Mon-Fri noon-2:30pm, Mon-Thu 6-9:30pm, Fri-Sat 6-10pm, Sun 6-9pm.* $$$ ▤ 10506 Little Santa Monica Blvd. (Thayer Ave.), 310-470-4992, lacachetterestaurant.com

Café Pinot • Downtown • Continental

Part of the distinguished Pinot restaurant group run by über-chef Joachim Splichal, this small brasserie is known for its lighter interpretations of Cal-French cuisine—a relative term that still includes duck leg confit and a bowl of French onion soup dripping in cheese if you require it. Both the leafy patio, the best place to sit in good weather, and the canopied sky room overlook the Central Library's lovely Maguire Gardens. Both provide an oasis beneath all the bank towers for business lunches or pre-theater dining for a mature, sophisticated crowd during the week. On weekends, the scene is more eclectic, but this is a place for casual fine dining, so the patrons are always upscale. If you come during the day, wander into the attractive gift shop in the library for a quick shopping fix. *Mon-Fri 11:30am-2:30pm, Sun 4:30-9pm, Mon-Tue 5-9pm, Wed-Thu 5-9:30pm, Fri-Sat 5-10pm.* $ ▤ 700 W. Fifth St. (S. Flower St.), 213-239-6500, patinagroup.com/cafePinot

Capo • Santa Monica • Italian (G)

Homemade pastas, heirloom tomato salads, and fire-grilled chops don't come cheap at this exclusive spot, which hides its 16 candlelit tables behind a thick velvet curtain in a little gabled building with no sign. The message is clear. Nobody's going to be just walking in off the street (especially since weekend reservations can require a week's notice). This modern Italian mecca bursting with Cal creativity is the latest endeavor of chef and owner Bruce Marder, whose culinary range (from the late West Coast Cafe to Rebecca's to Broadway Deli) has made an indelible mark over the last few decades. His most haute effort yet is housed in the sort of rustic-yet-refined wood-beamed room you'd sooner expect to find in Vail than a block from the beach. The regular clientele is as affluent and the service as flawless as the menu demands. Highlights include the burrata and heirloom tomato appetizers, a perfectly grilled Dover sole, and steaks cooked right over the dining room fireplace. A 900-bottle wine list assures finding just the right vintage with your verdure. *Tue-Sat 6-10:30pm.* $$$$ ▤ 1810 Ocean Ave. (Pico Blvd.), 310-394-5550, caporestaurant.com

Chaya Venice* • Venice • Fusion

Japanese art on the ceilings, French posters on the walls, floating rice-paper sea sculptures, white linen tablecloths, an open kitchen, and *Venice* magazine by the door—not to mention a low-key celebrity or two. It's just what you'd expect from a trendy Pan-Asian restaurant that's just a tad too boho to be in Santa Monica but draws droves of artsy types (with full wallets) one block over to Venice. The sushi is excellent if you can tear yourself from the main menu, which includes lobster enchiladas topped with cilantro cream sauce, sesame-crusted bluefin tuna with wasabi mashed potatoes, and sea scallops wrapped in New York steak. If you like bananas, the warm banana tart with banana ice cream and a frozen chocolate-covered banana wants you to save room for dessert. A sushi "happy hour" 5-7pm every day pulls a very lively afterwork crowd to the bar. *Mon-Fri 11:30am-2pm, Mon-Thu 6-10:30pm, Fri-Sat 6-11pm, Sun 6-10pm.* $$ Ⓑⓔ 110 Navy St. (Main St.), 310-396-1179, theychaya.com

Chinois on Main • Santa Monica • Fusion

Once you've got Spago under your belt, this action-packed production, brought to you by Wolfgang Puck and his designer wife Barbara Lazaroff, is your next stop. After more than two decades, this compact dining room is still drawing in the stars—and other scene-conscious Westsiders—with its neon lights, modern art, bursts of bright flowers, and an open kitchen that doesn't help in keeping the noise down. The menu, a melange of bold Cal-French-Asian creations (with an eight-dollar plate of brown fried rice thrown in just to make a point) is pure Puck. Dishes change, as do the chefs, but some classic items have gained a religious following, namely the Shanghai lobster with spicy ginger curry sauce and crispy spinach, the sizzling catfish stuffed with ginger and ponzu sauce, and the grilled Mongolian lamb chops with cilantro vinaigrette and wok-fried vegetables. *Wed-Fri 11:30am-2pm, Mon-Sat 6-10:30pm, Sun 5:30-10pm.* $$$ ≣ 2709 Main St. (Hill St.), 310-392-9025, wolfgangpuck.com

Cicada • Downtown • Italian

Any more gold leaf on the ceiling of this eye-popping Deco dining room and it would have to be moved from the historic Oviatt Building to Fort Knox. One of Downtown L.A.'s classic formal dining destinations, Cicada is a favorite venue for weddings, corporate dinners, and any other events requiring chenille sofas and a 600-label wine list that's difficult to lift. Its colosseum-close location also draws upscale game and concert-watchers. Antipasti at this elegant Nouvelle Northern Italian spot include seared foie gras with caramelized mango, microgreens in vanilla coulis, and tarragon-scented crab cake on a bed of white coleslaw in a Dijon mustard remoulade. This might be followed by duck ravioli with shiitake mushrooms, sweet peas, and shallots, or tournedos of sesame salmon with skinned red potatoes, baby carrots, and Swiss chard in a pinot noir sauce. *Mon-Fri 5:30-9pm.* $$$ ≣ 617 S. Olive St. (Sixth St.), 213-488-9488, cicadarestaurant.com

Cinespace* • Hollywood • American

Best Date Spots Wine and dine on California cuisine in a supper club setting while watching a classic film. See *Hot & Cool Nightlife*, p.78, for details. *Thu-Sat 6-10pm, bar until 2am.* $$ ≣ 6356 Hollywood Blvd., 2nd Floor (Ivar St.), 323-817-3456, cinespace.info

Citizen Smith* • Hollywood • American

Best Date Spots Southern-inspired gourmet comfort food hits the late-night lounge scene. See *Hot & Cool Nightlife*, p.78, for details. *Mon-Fri 11am-1:30am, Sat-Sun 6pm-1:30am.* $$ ≣ 1602 N. Cahuenga Blvd. (Selma Ave.), 323-461-5001, citizensmith.com

Clafoutis • West Hollywood • French

What could be better than lounging in shades at a sidewalk table on the swankier end of Sunset with a plate of eggs or a salade Niçoise, seated beside a bunch of Europeans yapping on their cells? This popular, recently reopened Cal-French bistro at the Sunset Plaza offers it all. The tireless menu runs all the way from a Paris ham and Swiss cheese omelet with a fresh croissant to a grilled filet mignon with garlic spinach and herbed potatoes topped with a brandy peppercorn sauce. Marvelous people-watching is also served all day. *Mon-Thu 11am-11pm, Fri-Sun 8am-11:30pm.* $ ≣ 8630 W. Sunset Blvd. (Sunset Plaza Dr.), 310-659-5233, le-clafoutis.com

Crustacean • Beverly Hills • Seafood

Sure, there's an epidemic of hot fusion restaurants in L.A. But only one has a long, koi-filled aquarium walkway leading into its main dining room and a famously secret kitchen where prized family recipes from the old country (French Colonial Vietnam) are heavily guarded. Euro-Asian Crustacean is a phenomenon even by Beverly Hills standards. Try the signature roasted Dungeness crab in garlic sauce and you'll understand why the recipe is padlocked. Major celebrities flock to the side entrance and eat amongst themselves upstairs. Let them. The garlic noodles, lobster in tamarind sauce, and that amazing crab are just as ambrosial down below, where the crowd is mixed between power-lunchers and ladies who lunch in the day, and romantic couples and sophisticated foodies at night. *Mon-Fri 11:30am-2:30pm, Mon-Sat 5:30-10:30pm.* $$$ ≡ 9646 Little Santa Monica Blvd. (N. Bedford Dr.), 310-205-8990, anfamily.com

Cut • Beverly Hills • Steakhouse

Best Trendy Tables Another month, another Wolfgang Puck restaurant. Or so it seems. This Richard Meier-designed steakhouse is more than just a white modernist interior with white-oak floors and skylights that take advantage of the world-famous Southern California light. Cut also serves a mean steak. The creamed spinach and the French fries in sauce may be a bit comfort food-y—a well-worn theme in Los Angeles—which is striking coming from a man who is known for starting culinary trends, not following them. Nevertheless, the Puck magic continues. Cut draws an A-list crowd (the location near Rodeo Drive assures that), the steaks are indeed good (particularly the tender bone-in ribeye), and the room has an interesting aesthetic—and we're not talking about the face-lifts of the Beverly Hills socialites who dine here. *Mon-Thu 5:30-10pm, Fri-Sat 5:30-11pm.* $$$ ≡ Regent Beverly Wilshire, 9500 Wilshire Blvd. (Beverly Dr.), 310-276-8500, wolfgangpuck.com

Dakota • Hollywood • Steakhouse

Every table is hot at this columned steakhouse punctuated with dark leather, chocolate suede, and ambient lighting, all of which work with the old Hollywood vibe of its host, the renovated Roosevelt Hotel, site of the first Academy Awards. The specialty is steaks, and lots of them: filets, rib eyes, Kobe beef, New York strip. If you want a porterhouse, you have to order it for two, but be sure to add a tower of the thick, battered-but-not-greasy onion rings, possibly the best in the city (the truffle fries are also tasty). It's a see-and-be-seen atmosphere heavy on the young Hollywood clientele at the Roosevelt, where people are known to grab seats in the lobby bar just to check out the action. *Daily 6-11am, Mon-Fri 6-10:30pm, Sat-Sun 6-11pm.* $$$ B≡ The Roosevelt Hotel, 7000 Hollywood Blvd. (Orange Dr.), 323-769-8888, dakota-restaurant.com

Derek's Bistro • Pasadena • California French

This strip-mall restaurant with a hedge for privacy may attract a slightly older, more formal clientele, but even the hippest foodie will find the service a refreshing change from the sniffy attitudes of too many L.A. waitstaff. The lauded menu is Cal-French and might include seared foie gras with kumquat marmalade or Belgian endive with honey-ginger syrup followed by wild salmon with beluga lentils or a dry-aged New York strip. A jacket is definitely required—another attractive departure from the usual local protocol. *Tue-Sat 5:30pm-closing.* $$ ≡ 181 E. Glenarm St. (S. Marengo Ave.), 626-799-5252, dereks.com

Dolce Enoteca e Ristorante* • West Hollywood • Italian

Not even constant press or a flaming backlit bar can fully guarantee a trendy restaurant's future. But this chic young Italian eatery co-owned by Hollywood stallion Ashton Kutcher is the place to dine among stars like Ashton, his wife Demi Moore, and their cohorts. Heavy on the leather and marble, the main dining room is lined with spacious booths built for VIPs and a candlelit patio that feels more like a room with no ceiling. The classic Italian menu may be secondary to the scene, but it holds up admirably. Diners on a budget or a diet can opt for smaller bites by requesting the separate Enoteca tasting menu. Thursdays through Saturdays, DJs arrive after the plates are cleared, so stay a while and join the star soirée. *Sun-Thu 6-10:30pm, Fri-Sat 6-11pm, bar until 2am.* $$$ B≣ 8284 Melrose Ave. (Sweetzer Ave.), 323-852-7174, dolceenoteca.com

Falcon* • Hollywood • American

Vegans and carnivores enjoy upscale comfort food while sipping specialty martinis. See *Hot & Cool Nightlife*, p.79, for details. *Mon-Sat 7-11pm, bar until 2am.* $$ ⊟ 7213 Sunset Blvd. (N. Alta Vista Blvd.), 323-850-5350, falconslair.com

Geisha House* • Hollywood • Japanese

Best Celebrity-Owned Restaurants Partly owned by Mr. Demi Moore, aka Ashton Kutcher, Geisha House announces its sexy self with a pair of lips—the restaurant's logo—on the front doors. Red, red, and more red is the backdrop to a hip, younger crowd of vamped-up women and painfully trendy men who drink Geisha Kisses and try to look cool while imagining what it is the geishas walking around actually do. A four-tiered fireplace that dominates the main dining space is the only obstacle keeping you from scoping the entire room as you mark your prey from a perch on the balcony. Oh yes, and it serves food, too. The Japanese menu is dominated by inventive sushi dishes and a short list of steaks and seafood, culminating in the eight-ounce Kobe beefsteak. But you didn't come here for the food, did you? *Nightly 6-11pm, bar until 2am.* $$$ B≣ 6633 Hollywood Blvd. (Cherokee Ave.), 323-460-6300, geishahousehollywood.com

Geoffrey's • Malibu • American

More than a decade after that power-lunch scene from *The Player* was shot here, Geoffrey's is still the place to eat outdoors in Malibu—whether you're a tourist or a local. You're just as likely to see Pierce Brosnan dining on the patio as a family from Iowa. You'll pay a little more for only decent seafood, chicken, or chops on this north stretch of coast, but a big part of that investment is the location—an unbeatable perch right above the ocean. Lunches, brunches, and cocktails at sunset are very popular. The most romantic time to be here, though, is at night when the midday schmoozers are gone, the waves are crashing, and the heaters are glowing. Request a table by the outer rail for the best views. *Mon-Fri 11am-10pm, Sat-Sun 10am-10pm.* $$$ ≣ 27400 Pacific Coast Hwy. (Meadows Ct.), 310-457-1519, geoffreysmalibu.com

Grace • Los Angeles • American

A warm and inviting place bathed in earth tones and furnished with comfy banquettes (the tables of choice), Grace leads Beverly Boulevard's latest dining renaissance with a creative New American menu from renowned local chef Neal Fraser. The menu at this hit newcomer changes regularly, but keep an eye out for the Dungeness crab salad appetizer, halibut wrapped in Swiss chard, grilled

Hawaiian ono, braised New Zealand lamb shank, and tenderloin of wild boar. *Tue-Thu 6-10:30pm, Fri-Sat 6-11pm, Sun 6-10pm.* $$ ≡ 7360 Beverly Blvd. (N. Fuller Ave.), 323-934-4400, gracerestaurant.com

The Grill on the Alley • Beverly Hills • Steakhouse

Best Power Lunches There's a time and a place to drink martinis, eat chicken pot pie, and order strawberry shortcake—all while seated next to a table full of showbiz gods and monsters. That time is around midday. That place is at this power-lunch capital of Beverly Hills. If you just got bumped from the next open table, it's probably because David Geffen or his equivalent just walked through the door. You will continue to be bumped until those deemed more worthy have eaten. Dinner (seven days a week) is also a scene in this dignified and clubby den, but it's a bit easier to get a table. Reservations are always recommended. *Mon-Thu 11:30am-10:30pm, Fri-Sat 11:30am-11pm, Sun 5-9pm.* $$$ B≡ 9560 Dayton Way (Wilshire Blvd.), 310-276-0615, thegrill.com

HamaSaku • West Los Angeles • Sushi

Why are so many top-notch L.A. sushi bars located in strip malls? Who knows? But it does make for an interesting transition to step out of the mini-mall's bourgeois environs and into HamaSaku, with Japanese scrolls and a slatted ceiling that could have been inspired by a Zen-garden rake job. Despite the modest location just off the 405 (or maybe because of it), this is celebrity-driven sushi at its most shamelessly indulgent. The decor includes signed movie posters and head shots, and the creatively prepared custom rolls are named after clients like Harrison Ford, Christina Aguilera, and Jennifer Aniston. It does have traditional omakase offerings, but don't worry about fascist chefs: You can order a California or spicy tuna roll without fear of being yelled at. *Mon-Fri 10:30am-2:30pm, Mon-Sat 5:30-10:30pm.* $$ ≡ 11043 Santa Monica Blvd. (Sepulveda Blvd.), 310-479-7636, hamasakula.com

Inn of the Seventh Ray • Topanga • American/Vegetarian

Best Romantic Dining Over the last century, this one-of-a-kind spot tucked into the hills of Topanga Canyon has done time as a church, a garage, a gas station, and a junkyard before blooming into one of the city's most stunning natural dining spots. In keeping with the earthy neighborhood and clientele, there's an unmistakable New Agey vibe going. Organic entrees are listed "in order of esoteric vibration," and an assortment of goddessy statues adorns a spectacular terrace surrounded by trees, flowering vines, and a babbling brook. Wholesome lunch selections include the Buddha Salad (naturally raised chicken, Chinese snow peas, roasted red bell peppers, julienne vegetables, sesame seeds, and water chestnuts in ginger dressing) and the I-can't-believe-it's-seitan Seventh Ray Burger. For dinner, there's vegan "duck," smoked tofu, rack of naturally raised lamb, and two five-course tasting menus (one of them vegetarian). *Mon-Fri 11:30am-3pm, Sat 10:30am-3pm, Sun 9:30am-3pm; Nightly 5:30-10pm.* $$$$ ≡ 128 Old Topanga Canyon Rd. (Topanga Canyon Blvd.), 310-455-1311, innoftheseventhray.com

Ivy at the Shore • Santa Monica • American

If you don't need to eat your chopped salad or crab cakes with celebrities and paparazzi, this laid-back spinoff of the original Ivy in Beverly Hills (see p.136) features the same impeccable service and reliable but pricey New American menu. For the best oceanfront dining, request a table on the terrace. *Mon-Thu 11:30am-10:30pm, Fri-Sat 11:30am-11pm, Sun 10:30am-10pm.* $$$ Ⓑ≡ 1535 Ocean Ave. (Broadway St.), 310-393-3113

Jer-ne • Marina del Rey • Fusion

This forward-thinking New World reinvention has gotten local buzz for its five- and eight-course tasting menus, as well as the variety of cuisine—everything from Hawaiian swordfish to Kobe beef carpaccio to Maine lobster and brie cheese fondue. New chef Dakota Weiss has gone heavier on French technique, but regulars, mainly beach-loving South Bay locals, are always happy to see a longtime favorite on the menu, the wasabi shrimp served on a hot river rock. For the aesthete in you, the two-level restaurant has French windows, hardwood floors, a classic wood-and-glass bar, and an outdoor patio overlooking the marina. *Daily 6:30am-10pm (late-night dining at the bar until 2am).* $$$$ ≡ 4375 Admiralty Way (Promenade Way), 310-574-4333, ritzcarlton.com

JiRaffe • Santa Monica • California French

JiRaffe has managed to survive the rousing reviews of its first few years in the late-'90s without getting too full of itself. The Cal-French menu is fairly consistent, and with dishes like baked chicken and pork chops with applesauce and chutney, local fans of Raphael Lunetta ("the surfing chef") can eat here two or three times a week and not feel gluttonous. The crowd gets younger and livelier on Monday nights, when Lunetta serves a less expensive three-course menu on butcher-paper–covered tables, with bistro lamps, and wines served by the carafe—but whichever night you come, you'll find a room full of well-dressed Westsiders sipping wine, flirting, and vying to be seen. *Mon 6-9pm, Tue-Sat 6-10pm, Sun 5:30-9pm.* $$ ≡ 502 Santa Monica Blvd. (Fifth St.), 310-917-6671, jirafferestaurant.com

Josie • Santa Monica • American (G)

On the corner of a nondescript block on Pico Boulevard, across from a car wash and a few doors down from Rite-Aid, this softly lit space seems out of sync, but in an entirely pleasant way. The open kitchen is staffed by three women, one of whom, restaurant namesake Josie Le Balch, creates a menu that includes dishes like sautéed frog legs and Millbrook Farm venison for a savvy crowd of 30-and-up locals. Her cuisine is infused with fresh ingredients from the infamous Santa Monica farmer's market, where every Westside chef worth his or her organic produce goes to pick up fixings for the week. *Mon-Thu 6-10pm, Fri-Sat 6-11pm, Sun 5:30-9pm.* $$ ≡ 2424 Pico Blvd. (25th St.), 310-581-9888, josierestaurant.com

Katana • West Hollywood • Japanese

Best Patio Dining A high concept in all regards, this instant hit rises above the Sunset Strip while remaining firmly rooted in it. Walk up the stone steps to the Piazza del Sol building, and into this brilliantly done Japanese eatery. Late night, you'll find a crowd of industry types and in-the-know yuppies plowing through tasty skewers of robatayaki (traditional open-flame cooking) and realizing just how much tastier a spear of filet mignon wrapped in fois gras and asparagus is than a slab of raw fish—which is also widely consumed here, too. For a show with dinner, sit at the robata bar, where a crew of busy chefs finds time to yell greetings and farewells to guests. Drinks and sushi selections are $5 during weekday happy hours (5:30-7pm). *Sun-Mon 6-11pm, Tue-Wed 6-11:30pm, Thu-Sat 6pm-12:30am.* $$ ▣ 8439 W. Sunset Blvd. (La Cienega Blvd.), 323-650-8585, katanarobata.com

Koi • Los Angeles • Japanese

Sushi snobs might not be as taken with this stylin' Japanese joint as the trend-conscious bunch who flock here to sip sake martinis on the firelit patio, but don't knock it 'til you try it. Catering perfectly to its young Hollywood audience and feng shui'd just so, Koi is a seriously hip place to linger over sea urchin, shiitake tempura, and an assortment of Cal-inflected signature entrees that further tempt the taste buds. Hot dishes include black cod bronzed with miso, jumbo softshell crab with ponzu sauce, and Alaskan king crab legs with garlic butter. Make weekend reservations fashionably late (not before 9pm), at least a few days in advance. *Mon-Wed 6-11pm, Thu 6-11:30pm, Fri-Sat 6pm-midnight, Sun 6-10pm.* $ Ⓑ▣ 730 N. La Cienega Blvd. (Melrose Ave.), 310-659-9449, koirestaurant.com

The Little Door • Los Angeles • Mediterranean

The door may be little, but it's what's behind it (and the buff attendant blocking the way) that counts. Reservations are a must at this white-hot French-Mediterranean charmer that doesn't deign to hang a sign out front. If you're on the list, the door opens onto a fabulous canopied patio where young, beautiful people smoke and laugh and drink and propose to each other between mouthfuls of mussels. Hustling French waiters are as charming as can be, right up to the presentation of the sobering bill. Beyond the patio is a tighter crunch of indoor tables strewn with rose petals. Unless you like eavesdropping, request a patio berth up front. *Sun-Wed 6-10pm, Thu-Sat 6-11pm.* $$$ ▣ 8164 W. Third St. (La Jolla Ave.), 323-951-1210, thelittledoor.com

The Lobster • Santa Monica • Seafood

Shuttered for years, this former shack on Santa Monica Pier now reels in both A-list crowds and schools of tourists with its seafood, some of the finest on the coast. Great oceanfront views are capitalized on in an all-glass building that thankfully isn't just about scoring a window or patio table for cocktails and calamari at sunset. The real show-stealers are the Maine lobsters, sold by the pound and either steamed, herb roasted, or—a house specialty—pan roasted with Jim Beam bourbon sauce. Top toque Allyson Thurber (formerly of L.A.'s Water Grill and Philadelphia's Striped Bass) is behind a menu of superb fish dishes, like pepper-crusted rare yellowfin with shrimp, asparagus, and a hearts of palm salad. Save room for the chocolate bread pudding with Tahitian vanilla ice cream. Reservations are advised. *Sun-Thu 11:30am-10pm, Fri-Sat 11:30am-11pm.* $$ ▣ 1602 Ocean Ave. (Colorado Ave.), 310-458-9294, thelobster.com

Lucques • West Hollywood • California French (G)

Gaining even greater buzz with their latest hit restaurant, A.O.C., celebrated local chef Suzanne Goin and business partner Carolyne Styne warmed up for nearly five years at this unique Cal-French hot spot in West Hollywood, which continues to draw a stylish crowd—and tons of celebs—craving something more inspired after a movie than another ahi burger. It starts with the setting itself—an old brick and wood-beam room with a fireplace and adjoining patio that was once the carriage house for the Harold Lloyd estate. The innovative seasonal menu might begin with a salad of apples, Asian pears, radicchio, and mint in a buttermilk dressing or a medley of reed avocado, beets, and Dungeness crab with chili, lime, and crème fraîche. Ambitious entrees sometimes sound better on paper but most often hit the mark. They include a grilled pancetta-wrapped trout with sorrel, fennel, verjus, and crushed grapes, and a very successful plate of braised beef short ribs with sautéed greens, pearl onions, and horseradish cream. One of the neighborhood's best late-dining spots on the weekend, Lucques keeps its bar menu going until midnight on Fridays and Saturdays. *Tue-Sat noon-2:30pm, Mon-Tue 6-10pm, Wed-Sat 6-11pm, Sun 5-10pm.* $$$ B≡ 8474 Melrose Ave. (La Cienega Blvd.), 323-655-6277, lucques.com

Ma'Kai* • Santa Monica • Tapas

Indoor waterfalls and a Polynesian decor accent an exotic island tapas menu. See *Hot & Cool Nightlife*, p.81, for details. *Sun-Thu 11:30am-1am.* $ B≡ 101 Broadway Ave. (Ocean Ave.), 310-434-1511, makailounge.com

Maison Akira • Pasadena • Fusion (G)

A veteran of Maxim's in Paris and the Los Angeles restaurants L'Orangerie and dearly departed Citrus, Akira Hirose offers a Franco-Japanese menu that might include miso-marinated Chilean sea bass (a dish Hirose once served to the Emperor of Japan) and grilled duck foie gras. The dining room, which has several nooks, is dramatically appointed with crystal chandeliers and red drapes. It's a fairly roomy, quiet space—a rarity in insecure, loud L.A.—but this is Pasadena, so it all makes sense. The crowd is mostly locals from the gracious, elegant neighborhoods that epitomize Pasadena. Maison Akira is the sort of restaurant that makes the drive East worth it, even if you might have no other plans there. *Tue-Fri 11:30am-2pm, Tue-Thu 6-9pm, Fri 6-9:30pm, Sat 5:30-9:30pm, Sun 11am-2pm, 5-8pm.* $$ ⊔ 713 E. Green St. (Oak Knoll Ave.), 626-796-9501, maisonakira.com

Martha's 22nd Street Grill • Hermosa Beach • American

On sunny weekend mornings, the wait for a patio seat at Martha's can be 45 minutes, which is plenty of time for a walk or a bike ride on the Strand just a block away. When you get back, you have to decide if it's going to be the stuffed French toast with seasonal berries and fruit, one of seven different types of eggs Benedict, or perhaps Martha's best seller, the white-corn scrambled eggs with Havarti cheese. When the sun is shining, and the South Bay's toned, skimpily dressed residents abound, this patio feels like the center of the world. *Daily 7am-3pm.* $ ≡ 25 22nd St. (Hermosa Ave.), 310-376-7786

Matsuhisa • Los Angeles • Sushi (G)

Best Sushi Only a few top chefs in Los Angeles have been granted celebrity status, and only one of them is a sushi master. At the founding location of his empire of destination Japanese restaurants (which now stretches from Aspen to Milan), Nobu Matsuhisa runs what many foodies continue to call the best restaurant in the city—although the patrons are pure California casual. There's lobster ceviche with lime stone lettuce, halibut cheeks with pepper sauce, and about a hundred more special plates to choose from. Just say "omakase" (chef's choice) to let Nobu's staff spare you the hassle of figuring it all out. *Mon-Fri 11:45am-2:15pm; Nightly 5:45-10:30pm.* $$$ ≡ 129 N. La Cienega Blvd. (Wilshire Blvd.), 310-659-9639, nobumatsuhisa.com

Melisse • Santa Monica • French (G)

Best Wine List At Melisse, your tasting menu selections may arrive on fine china and your wine pairings in crystal glasses, but you never have to worry about which fork to use—your server will provide the proper utensils as you need them. Chef Josiah Citrin opened Melisse in the midst of a late-'90s fine-dining wave, and hard-core diners and a good many food critics swear it is now the best restaurant in the city, a reputation you'll find reflected in the prices. But you won't argue with the French-influenced New American cuisine and picture-perfect service that lends itself to a surprisingly relaxing evening in spite of all the heavy-duty finery that lures wealthy Westsiders. *Tue-Thu 6-9:30pm, Fri 6-10pm, Sat 5:45-10pm.* $$$ ▤ 1104 Wilshire Blvd. (11th St.), 310-395-0881, melisse.com

Nobu Malibu • Malibu • Japanese (G)

Japanese fusion master Nobu Matsuhisa is best known for his Beverly Hills flagship restaurant, Matsuhisa, short-listed among the world's top dining destinations. Hiding out alongside a New Age bookstore and a yogurt shop in the Malibu Country Mart is Matsuhisa's lower-key little sister, Nobu Malibu, perfectly positioned to serve the casual but wealthy patrons who call Malibu home. Superb sushi, delectable sizzling plates, delicate bento box desserts, and many Matsuhisa-born innovations can be found here at bargain prices—comparatively speaking. On warmer nights, reserve a table on the enclosed garden patio. *Sun-Thu 5:45-10pm, Fri-Sat 5:45-11pm.* $$$ ▣▤ 3835 Cross Creek Rd. (Pacific Coast Hwy.), 310-317-9140, nobumatsuhisa.com

Norman's • West Hollywood • American

In 2004, chef Norman Van Aken opened a branch of his Coral Gables institution on Sunset Boulevard in West Hollywood. The New World menu now includes some lighter fare (a nod to Southern California's health-food pretensions), but the big ticket is the Friday night pig roast, as festive a dining experience as the city has to offer, particularly in a restaurant with such an open feel thanks in part to a glassed-in kitchen. Large parties should try the chef's table inside the kitchen. *Tue-Thu 6-10pm, Fri-Sat 6-10:30pm.* $$ ▣▤ 8570 Sunset Blvd. (Alta Loma Rd.), 310-657-2400, normans.com

One Pico • Santa Monica • American

Three walls of windows encase this elegant beachfront restaurant at Shutters, which on any given night hosts many more chic, stylish locals than it does hotel guests. The dining room's unbeatable seaside setting more than makes up for whatever excitement may be lacking in the broad "New American" menu, meant to keep everyone perfectly happy if not totally enthralled. Favorites include Brentwood corn and tortilla soup with lobster, seared scallops with arugula and mascarpone risotto, pan roasted Alaskan halibut with tomato, fennel, and basil, and a New York steak with big, chunky cowboy fries. *Mon-Sat 11:30am-2:30pm, 6:30-10pm, Sun 11am-2:30pm.* $$ ▤ Shutters on the Beach, 1 Pico Blvd. (Ocean Ave.), 310-587-1717, shuttersonthebeach.com

Ortolan • Los Angeles • French (G)

Best Celebrity-Owned Restaurants Ortolan is named after diminutive Eurasian songbirds that were force-fed oats and millet, then ... well, let's just say it's a delicacy that's off limits now. Co-owned by actress Jeri Ryan, this contemporary French restaurant is a bit delicate as well, with cream-colored booths, mismatched chairs, velvet drapes, copious chandeliers, and a communal table in what looks like a wine cave crossbred with King Arthur's dining room. Chef Christophe Emé's playful sense of humor may have been one of the reasons he was recently dubbed "Best New Chef" by *Food & Wine* magazine—an otherwise simple amuse-bouche of fresh soup might show up in a test tube that you empty with a straw. The scene is a happening mix of Hollywood celebs and hard-to-please foodies, but to be a part of it all, you'll need to make reservations at least two weeks in advance. *Tue-Sat 6-10pm.* $$$ B⬚⬚ 8338 W. Third St. (King's Rd.), 323-653-3300, ortolanrestaurant.com

Patina • Downtown • California French (G)

Celebrated chef Joachim Splichal launched a restaurant and catering empire starting with this 18-year-old dining destination, the only Relais Gourmand kitchen in the city. The playful yet stunning Cal-French and prix fixe menus and impeccable waitstaff are now in a new location inside the Walt Disney Concert Hall. It's a sleek minimalist space with a leafy patio in front—but the most sought-after tables are the booths in the back of the main room. At lunch, politicos and lawyers from the nearby courthouses and City Hall flood in for a quick gourmet fix. At night, crowds come just before and after concerts, leaving normal dining hours less crowded. A private behind-the-scenes chef's table can accommodate up to 10 guests for a special seven-course meal with wine pairings. *Tue-Fri 11:30am-1:30pm (Sun on performance days); Nightly 5-9:30pm (5-11pm on performance nights).* $$$ Walt Disney Concert Hall, 141 S. Grand Ave. (First St.), 213-972-3331, patinagroup.com/patina

Pedals • Santa Monica • American

Casual meals at Shutters are taken downstairs at this wood-beamed cafe, where the best tables front the big glass windows overlooking the crashing waves, or are out on the 50-seat patio, just a lattice fence away from the Santa Monica beach promenade. At breakfast and lunch, you'll dine with entertainment industry types taking meetings, and Westside casual socialites gossiping with friends. Dinner is a fancier affair, with dim lights and a lively afterwork bar scene. *Daily 6:30am-9pm.* $ B⬚ Shutters on the Beach, 1 Pico Blvd. (Ocean Ave.), 310-587-1707, shuttersonthebeach.com

Providence • Los Angeles • Seafood (G)

Best Seafood Many considered Water Grill in Downtown to be the best seafood restaurant in Los Angeles before its chef, Michael Cimarusti, struck out on his own and opened Providence in the former site of Patina. Cimarusti's menu comes with suggested wine pairings—a sauvignon blanc with the Santa Barbara spot prawns, a chardonnay with the scallops in aged vinegar—and though he does include non-seafood dishes, it seems beside the point to order Muscovy duck or the prime rib eye mignon, no matter how good you're sure they are. However, maybe on the eighth visit ... Providence is very much a dining destination—the room is filled with hardcore foodies and business people serious about impressing, or at least maxing out their expense accounts. There's a small alcove room if you're looking for privacy, but for a lively scene in the heart of the action, sit in the main room. *Fri noon-2:30pm; Mon-Fri 6-10pm, Sat 5:30-10pm, Sun 5:30-9pm.* $$$$ ⬚ 5955 Melrose Ave. (Cole Ave.), 323-460-4170, providencela.com

Saddle Ranch Chop House* • Los Angeles • American
Texas-size platters of high-grease grub are surprisingly delicious. See *Hot & Cool Nightlife*, p.82, for details. *Daily 8am-2am.* $ ▣ 8371 W. Sunset Blvd. (La Cienega Blvd.), 323-656-2007, srrestaurants.com

Sona • West Hollywood • French (G)
One look at the minimalist decor and the six-ton wine-decanting stone centerpiece and you know it's all about the food here—which lives up to the meditative atmosphere. An à la carte menu and an assortment of prix fixe meals from classically trained executive chef and pastry chef duo David and Michelle Myers change almost nightly at this gourmet hot spot. A recent *Food & Wine* Best New Chef, David is known for creations like pickled papaya soup, confit of salmon with braised oxtail, and creamy macaroni with crispy sweetbreads. Michelle's wildly creative chocolate beignet is the famous dessert here—ambrosial and vaguely Tim Burton–ish. The crowd here is as beautiful as the plates—and maybe even as good-looking as the waitstaff, who are clearly waiting (tables) until their big break comes. On weekends, a late-night, small-plate kappo menu takes over after 11pm, when chefs from other top restaurants tend to swing by for bite-sized tastes. *Tue-Thu 6-10pm, Fri 6-11pm, Sat 5:30-11pm.* $$$ ᴮ▣ 401 N. La Cienega Blvd. (Melrose Ave.), 310-659-7708, sonarestaurant.com

Table 8 • Los Angeles • American
Everyone from foodies to young trendoids appreciates something about this California seasonal restaurant located beneath a tattoo parlor. It must be the air of relaxed sophistication which goes well with a lychee martini. Or maybe it's the smallness of the room, which makes it feel cozy, not cramped. Ordering the porterhouse for two (in advance) means you'll miss out on the Kurobata pork chop or the New Zealand lamb, but this restaurant is like a movie with a complex plot: Subsequent viewings will reveal even richer layers of meaning. *Mon-Thu 6-10pm, Fri-Sat 6-11pm (lounge open until 11pm on weekdays and 1am on weekends).* $$$ ᴮ▣ 7661 Melrose Ave. (Stanley Ave.), 323-782-8258, table8la.com

Tower Bar • West Hollywood • American
A two-piece band—baby grand and bass—provides the soundtrack at the Sunset Tower Hotel's Tower Bar, where white-jacketed waiters, deferential almost to the point of being invisible, serve sumptuous dishes like beef carpaccio and Kurobuta pork chops to an eclectic crowd of diners. It's an extremely civilized atmosphere done up in wood paneling and portraits of old-time celebrities, and if you try hard enough, you can almost picture Humphrey Bogart holding court at the long bar, or Bette Davis ordering another drink ("WAAAY-tuh, maah-TEEEE-nee") from the shadows of a cozy nook. *Tue-Sat 6-11:30pm.* $$$ ᴮ▣ 8358 W. Sunset Blvd. (Sweetzer Ave.), 323-848-6677, sunsettowerhotel.com/tower-bar.html

Urasawa • Beverly Hills • Sushi (G)
Best Sushi Dinner here is beyond the "special occasion" rating. "Once-in-a-lifetime" might be more like it. Urasawa consists of a ten-seat bar, a couple of tables, and a private room. Unless you've gone scouting for the best Tokyo has to offer, the sushi here is fresher than anything you've had. For $250 you get a 29-course meal that includes beef, scallop and duck foie-gras shabu shabu, and egg custard with sea urchin, Japanese chive gelée, caviar, and gold flake. Did we mention that chef and

owner Hiroyuki Urasawa is one of the few people in the U.S. licensed to serve blow-fish? Eating here and then eating at your neighborhood sushi bar is probably akin to sitting in coach after a flight on Air Force One. *Nightly 6-8:30pm (reservations only).* $$$$ ⊑ 218 N. Rodeo Dr. (Wilshire Blvd.), 310-247-8939

White Lotus* • Hollywood • Asian Fusion

Times really are changing in Hollywood. The makers of the Sunset Room and Pig 'n Whistle have feng-shui'd a former dance dungeon (Crush Bar) into one of the hottest "it" dining and clubbing scenes on either side of La Brea Ave. The restaurant includes a full sushi bar and a canopy-tented patio serving fancy Euro-Asian grub that covers all the bases—dim sum, deep-fried red snapper, duck leg confit, a New York steak. Once the meal is over, a separate club area draws the same well-heeled eye candy, and you're invited because dinner gets you into the club. People eat fashionably late here, so take the last booking (usually 10pm—sometimes 10:30pm on Saturdays), unless you like eating alone and wondering what all the fuss is about. *Fri-Sat 6-10pm; Club: 9pm-2am.* $$ ≡ 1743 Cahuenga Blvd. (Hollywood Blvd.), 323-463-0060, whitelotushollywood.com

Wilshire Restaurant* • Santa Monica • Californian

You may have to wait for your table in the crowded front bar at popular Wilshire Restaurant, purveyor of New American cuisine. But that's okay, because there's a lot to look at, whether it's the chocolate-and-orange color scheme, geometric wood ceilings and mood-heightening votive lighting, or your fellow diners—an attractive lot—who have to walk through the bar to get anywhere else in the restaurant. Request a seat in the patio area, the most sought-after space, where the lucky few pretend to understand the 15-page wine list, order the must-have beet salad, and finish with the wild boar tenderloin or the braised boneless beef short ribs, which Wilshire regulars tend to opt for more than a cardiologist might prefer. *Mon-Fri noon-2pm, happy hour 4:30-6:30pm; Mon-Sat 6-10pm, bar until 12:30am.* $$$$ ≡ 2454 Wilshire Blvd. (26th St.), 310-586-1707, wilshirerestaurant.com

Zucca • Downtown • Italian

Joachim Splichal's charming Tuscan villa–style dining room, patio, and sculpture garden is short listed among the city's top Italian restaurants—and not just for its amazing looks. Pre-theater or Laker crowds (the restaurant's just two blocks from the Staples Center) are drawn to homemade pastas, fresh fish, and fine cheeses from the old country, paired with an equally tantalizing Italian wine list. *Mon-Fri 11:30am-2:30pm, Sun-Thu 5-9pm, Fri-Sat 5-10pm.* $$ 801 S. Figueroa St. (W. Eighth St.), 213-614-7800, patinagroup.com/zucca

Hot & Cool Los Angeles:
The Nightlife

Basque • Hollywood • Nightclub
Best Nightclubs Bask in voyeuristic vices at this Spanish-flavored cabaret that takes over where legendary club Deep left off. The remodeled black and red bordello interior is an artful blend of erotic Euro-chic that still packs more sexual energy than a bottle of Viagra. Nearly naked dancers strike promiscuous poses behind the Red Light District, a set of one-way mirrors behind the bar. Inspired exhibitionists can shake their assets on the revamped dance floor, which opens up to the surrounding bottle-service VIP booths. The California cuisine now features a tapas menu and the weak drinks are still pricey. The new look and old vibe is bringing back the likes of the Hilton and Simpson sisters, but is still a favorite with club commuters from the 714 to the 818. *Mon, Thu-Sat 10pm-2am.* C≡ 1707 N. Vine St. (Hollywood Blvd.), 323-464-1654, basquehollywood.com

BlackSteel* • Hollywood • Restaurant/Lounge
Asian-inspired dishes like Kobe beef are served in a Goth setting. See *Hot & Cool Restaurants,* p.63, for details. *Tue-Sat 6pm-2am.* CB≡ 6683 Hollywood Blvd. (Las Palmas Ave.), 323-469-3456, blacksteel.tv

Bridge Restaurant and Lounge* • West Hollywood • Restaurant/Lounge
Hollywood heavy clientele enjoy so-so Italian and a hot scene. See *Hot & Cool Restaurants,* p.64, for details. *Mon-Sat 8pm-2am; Restaurant: 6-11pm.* ≡ 755 N. La Cienega Blvd. (Waring Ave.), 310-659-3535, bridgela.com

Busby's* • Santa Monica • Sports Bar
Sports junkies with hot-wing stains, Budweiser bellies, and Sportscenter-track minds might argue that this spot is too upscale—but it knows its Westside clientele. The comfy, multiroom interior has an Old English boys' club feel complete with a fleet of flat-screens at every turn and pool tables, board games, foosball, video games, and darts. The menu offers standard grease grub, but is known for its filet mignon and salmon dinner entrees. The flirtatious staff look like they strutted straight out of an Aaron Spelling casting call. The surprisingly even ratio of tanned and toned Westside singles come out for Lakers games and football season, but seem more interested in a different kind of scoring, especially after 10pm when it turns into a flashback frat party. *Daily 10am-1:45am, 9am Sat during football season.* C≡ 3110 Santa Monica Blvd. (Berkeley St.), 310-828-4567, busbysonline.com

Cabana Club • Hollywood • Nightclub
Best Nightclubs The sun never sets at this beach club oasis located in the heart of Hollywood. The nightlife impresarios behind White Lotus and the Pig 'n Whistle have transformed the former Sunset Room into a versatile indoor/outdoor venue that also includes the adjacent Sterling Steakhouse. The brown and gold decor, swaying palm trees, tented bungalows, cascading waterfalls, and walkway bridges over an L-shaped pool create a manufactured Mediterranean look that's more Las Vegas hotel pool than St. Tropez resort. Expect lots of Cristal popping, blinking bling, and too-tight designer duds from the crowd of

urban-flavored professionals and industry types. The late-arriving crowd tends to show up after 11pm, so get there early to avoid the lengthy line. The dress code is fashionable, meaning no throwback jerseys or shorts. *Thu-Sat 10pm-2am.* C= 1439 N. Ivar Ave. (Hollywood Blvd.), 323-463-0005, cabanaclubhollywood.com

Cameo Bar • Santa Monica • Hotel Bar

Best Hotel Bars The stylish lobby lounge in the new and very chic Viceroy Hotel saves a drive out to West Hollywood for hipsters and industry types who'd rather be schmoozing, posing, and sipping cosmopolitans near the ocean. Outfitted with bold custom furnishings, glass cocktail tables, Colonial green walls, and a shag-rug library area with angled bookshelves, the main draw is still the outside deck with its twin plunge pools and private cabanas starting at $500 a day. This is also a great outdoor drinking spot on a warm day. *Tue-Sat 11am-1am, Sun-Mon 11am-midnight.* — Viceroy Hotel, 1819 Ocean Ave. (Pico Blvd.), 310-260-7500, viceroysantamonica.com

Chaya Venice* • Venice • Lounge

A Pan-Asian menu draws artsy types, especially for the sushi happy hour when the bar fills with afterwork drinkers. See *Hot & Cool Restaurants,* p.65, for details. *Mon-Thu 6-10:30pm, Fri-Sat 6pm-midnight, Sun 6-10pm.* B= 110 Navy St. (Main St.), 310-396-1179, thechaya.com

Cinespace* • Hollywood • Nightclub/Restaurant

Best Date Spots Film, food, and nightlife converge at this innovative supper club conveniently overlooking the Hollywood Walk of Fame. The versatile, multiroom interior of this minimalist space is capable of hosting a student film festival, music video wrap party, and dance club in the same night—which it often does. Canoodling couples and film fanatics come out for the dinner and a movie show-case (Thu-Sat 8pm) where they can wine and dine on fine California cuisine while watching everything from *The Wizard of Oz* to *Pulp Fiction.* If you're more club kid than cineaste, then the midweek modern rock crowd is much cooler than the invading weekend warriors. *Nightly 6pm-2am.* C= 6356 Hollywood Blvd., 2nd Floor (Ivar St.), 323-817-3456, cinespace.info

Circle Bar • Santa Monica • Bar/Nightclub

Best Singles Scenes This cheesy guilty pleasure is a one-stop meet market for ready-to-mingle singles. Main Street's main nightlife attraction is ironically a former long-time biker bar turned yuppie lounge. The red and black interior has a faux-Oriental flavor with the stereotypical Bruce Lee poster and feng shui candles. Packs of wolves in collared shirts lap up booze at the centralized bar, hunting for wild game or wounded gazelles. Nightly DJs spin frat rock favorites over a sweaty, too-close-for-comfort dance floor. The tight oval-shaped room fills up quickly, so come early and grab a booth or a barstool. If not, be prepared to wait in a DMV-like line out-side, especially on the weekends. *Sun-Wed 9pm-2am, Thu-Sat 8pm-2am.* C= 2926 Main St. (Kinney St.), 310-450-0508, thecirclebar.com

Citizen Smith* • Hollywood • Bar/Restaurant

Best Date Spots The latest hyphen to hit La-La-Land is the restaurant-lounge. Designer Thomas Schoos (Koi, Wilshire) brings Hollywood sex appeal to the down and dirty Cahuenga Corridor with this upscale urban bistro. The long, nar-row, black and tan, high-ceilinged interior is an interesting mix of gaucho chic (cowhide "wallpaper," worn wood) meets Gothic glamour (rococo chandeliers, wrought iron fixtures). Licorice-thin model-actress-waitress types are wined and dined in cushy leather booths, while roaming packs of writer-director-actor-producers scope the scene looking for fresh meat—not on the menu. Kitschy classic rock blares throughout the main dining area, which leads to a packed bar and brick-lined outdoor patio. The Southern-leaning gourmet comfort food menu is served till the early morning, making it a prime late-night dining destination. *Mon-Fri 11am-1:30am, Sat-Sun 6pm-1:30am.* ⊟ 1602 N. Cahuenga Blvd. (Selma Ave.), 323-461-5001, citizensmith.com

Dolce Enoteca e Ristorante* • West Hollywood • Lounge
Classic Italian cuisine takes a backseat to the star-studded scene at this young, trendy spot. See *Hot & Cool Restaurants, p.68,* for details. *Nightly 6pm-2am.* B⊟ 8284 Melrose Ave. (Sweetzer Ave.), 323-852-7174, dolceenoteca.com

Falcon* • Hollywood • Bar/Restaurant
Glamour and gourmet come together at this swanky restaurant/bar on the eastern edge of the Sunset Strip. Sky-high concrete walls enclose the unsigned, stylishly minimalist two-level venue that divides into a lair-like, open-air patio and a posh, low-lit upper dining area. The American menu offers an array of upscale comfort food favorites for carnivores and vegans alike, as well as an extensive list of specialty martinis. The festive, if highbrow, atmosphere draws martini-sipping, gossip-dropping *Sex and the City* types and the deep-pocketed Mr. Bigs they love to hate. Ironically, actor-musician and part-owner John Corbett (Carrie Bradshaw's other true love) is known to go "unplugged" on Monday nights. *Mon-Sat 7pm-2am.* ⊟ 7213 Sunset Blvd. (N. Alta Vista Blvd.), 323-850-5350, falconslair.com

Geisha House* • Hollywood • Lounge
Young hipsters drink stylish cocktails while eyeing the very chic young things who call this spot a second home. See *Hot & Cool Restaurants, p.68,* for details. *Nightly 6pm-2am.* B⊟ 6633 Hollywood Blvd. (Cherokee Ave.), 323-460-6300, geishahousehollywood.com

Guy's • West Hollywood • Nightclub
Hot guys and dolls flock to this WeHo party playpen for its private intimacy. Although it's now open to the common clubber, it was originally a member's-only spot that drew the likes of Madonna, Prince, and Bruce Willis. The living room–like interior consists of cushy gray couches, a marble bar, and onyx trimmings. The fenced-in outdoor patio in back features another bar and looks and feels like an upscale backyard keg party. The club's close-knit quarters make it the perfect place to host a party. It still is often reserved for private engagements (Rod's daughter Kimberly Stewart's birthday bash, Denzel Washington's movie wrap party). DJs including Jake Hoffman (son of Dustin) and Danny Masterson utilize the booming new sound system to get the party started. The space fills up quickly, so get there early and be prepared to wait in line, especially for the bathroom—which is only two stalls. *Tue-Sun 9pm-2am.* C⊟ 8713 Beverly Blvd. (La Cienega), 310-729-4031

Holly's • Hollywood • Ultra Lounge
Best Celebrity Hangouts If you aren't a part of owner Rick Calamaro's community (Hollywood heavyweights, hotties, hangers-on) then the odds of you getting in are slimmer than the waists of the parade of cadaverous cuties you'll see strutting past

you. Less is more at this exclusive party playpen that caters to all things celebrity. The intimate candlelit interior (formerly Paladar) is decked out in deep dark woods, while the decor is nothing more than an island bar, a digital DJ stand, and a few bottle-service booths separated by billowing silver curtains. Lace lingerie–clad waitresses and black and white burlesque portraits provide eye-candy as the young and restless *Entourage*-esque crowd talk shop(ping), schmooze, and booze. *Thu-Sat 10pm-2am.* CB≡ 1651 Wilcox Ave. (Hollywood Blvd.), 323-461-1400

LAX • Hollywood • Nightclub

Best Celebrity Hangouts When Hollywood jet-setters like Jessica Alba and Wilmer Valderrama are at home, you can bet you'll find them at mash-up master DJ AM and copilot Loyal Pennings' retro-futuristic "mile high" club. The spot's sleek aero-chic decor, spread out over multiple rooms, takes its red and silver hue cues from a '60s airport terminal. Hangar-shaped lounge areas, tinted airplane windows, a hydraulic-raised side door, and specialty drinks like the "Red Eye" add to the kitschy look and feel, while a colorful jellyfish tank is the club's only link to its Las Palmas past. The crowd is more first-class than coach, making the entrance lines as long as those at the real LAX—so be patient or have the killer B's: boldness, beauty, bills, and babes. *Wed-Sun 10pm-2am.* C≡ 1714 N. Las Palmas Ave. (Hollywood Blvd.), 323-464-0171, laxhollywood.com

Lobby Bar at the Four Seasons • Beverly Hills • Bar/Lounge

There's good reason why celebrities take their cocktails in this swank bastion of old-school elegance. From the moment you take a seat in the dim, comfortable, and very quiet bar, you're surrounded by a feel of exclusivity. Well-spaced tables leave lots of room for private conversations. But don't worry, there's plenty of light to see who's sitting nearby. *Mon-Sat 11pm-1:30am, Sun 5pm-12:30am.* ⬚ Four Seasons Hotel, 300 S. Doheny Dr. (Gregory Way), 310-273-2222, fourseasons.com

Lobby Lounge at the Standard Hollywood • West Hollywood • Ultra Lounge

Best Daytime Drinking Spots If the Skybar is for the haughty, then its Sunset Strip neighbor—the Lobby Lounge at the Standard—is for the hip. This equally surreal and calculatingly cool vision of Hollywood features floor-to-ceiling white shag carpeting, bubble-shaped swing chairs, and a half-naked nymph in an aquarium behind the front desk. DJs spin ambient grooves throughout the adjoining, dimly lit Cactus Room, and the blue Astroturf-lined pool deck is a sip-and-dip community pool of sorts, offering ping-pong, chaise longues, a delectable lunch menu, and a breath-taking view of the L.A. skyline. The exclusive Purple Lounge in back is reserved for private parties hosted for the likes of Mark Wahlberg and Hugh Hefner. *Daily 9:30am-2am.* ⬚ Standard Hotel, 8300 W. Sunset Blvd. (Sweetzer Ave.), 323-650-9090, standardhotel.com

Ma'Kai* • Santa Monica • Nightclub/Restaurant

This oceanside singles retreat is a welcome addition to the Westside scene. A Polynesian paradise that's become a neighborhood favorite among the local tanned and toned, the lush, tropical-themed dinner lounge has teak fixtures, bamboo furnishings, indoor waterfalls, and an exotic island tapas menu. Two outdoor patios offer happy hour professionals a stunning sunset ocean view— which they can enjoy from a warm fire pit or more intimate porch swing. Relaxation gives way to nighttime revelry as MILF-hunters, perky divorcees, and game-faced desperados troll the center bar in search of partners to bring out to the makeshift dance floor. The Hawaiian-style brunch is a perfect Sunday get-away with a seafood luau platter that serves four to five people. *Sat-Sun 11am-3pm, Sun-Thu 5pm-midnight, Fri-Sat 5pm-1am.* Ⓒ≣ 101 Broadway Ave. (Ocean Ave.), 310-434-1511, makailounge.com

Mor Bar • Santa Monica • Nightclub

Right in the heart of Main Street's coffee shops and pubs, you'll find the sleek and chic Mor bringing a cool, Hollywood nightlife vibe to the Westside. The Moroccan-themed space is all dark woods and velvety accents, with a killer round of rotating DJ's that heat up the very small dance floor with everything from salsa to worldbeats. It's an intimate spot, but one that consistently draws crowds— albeit young crowds on Tuesday's two-dollar night. Weekends see a savvier set, when Jimmy Choos replace thongs. *Nightly 5pm-2am.* Ⓒ≣ 2941 Main St. (Kinney St.), 310-396-6678, themorbar.com

Nacional • Hollywood • Nightclub

Evoking visions of a romanticized, 1950s Havana, this revolutionary lounge played a central role in Hollywood Boulevard's recent rebirth. The black and tan color scheme, dim lighting, and sexy, army fatigued–bartenders provide a sultry flair, while the framed images of real-life Cuba add a touch of authenticity. The working-class, multicultural crowd unites on the tiny, booty-to-booty dance floor as neophyte DJs deliver standard hip-hop, rock, and soul. If you want to lay low, hit the upstairs patio where you can start up a conversation or light up a ciga-rette. The strict door policy might feel a bit Communist, so if your patience runs out, there's plenty of other options just around the corner. *Tue-Sat 10pm-2am.* Ⓒ≣ 1645 Wilcox Ave. (Hollywood Blvd.), 323-962-7712, nacional.cc

Privilege • West Hollywood • Nightclub

Best Nightclubs Nightlife mogul Sam Nazarian's nightclubs have gone through more makeovers than Madonna. "Renovate it again" Sam keeps his creations stylish and fresh—essential elements in the trendy Hollywood nightlife scene which goes through hot spots like Paris Hilton does dates. Privilege (formerly Shelter) pampers partygoers with a luxurious and sensual look that's as glamorous as its A-list clien-tele. The soundstage-like setup is constantly in flux, but the general floor plan remains the same: curtained VIP bottle-service booths, three accessible bars, a packed dance floor, and a black-veiled smoking patio pit. DJs spin hip-hop, rock, and '80s for high-heeled fashionistas, power players, and industry fakers. The only pain bigger than the congested valet service is getting past the CIA-like doorman. So be prepared to pay in both time and money. *Tue, Wed, Fri-Sat 10pm-2am.* Ⓒ≣ 8117 Sunset Blvd. (Crescent Heights Blvd.), 323-654-0030, sbeent.com

Renee's Courtyard Cafe • Santa Monica • Bar

Known for its Old World charm, stiff drinks, and cheesy singles scene, this long-time Santa Monica spot is a favorite with laid back locals looking to hook up or hang out. The converted Victorian house is more homely than hip with five intimate rooms and three tiny bars. At the center is an open-air courtyard dotted with Christmas lights, shady trees, and rustic patio furniture. Renee herself often serves as host, zig-zagging from room to room greeting familiar faces. The late-arriving, 30-something, Banana Republican crowd packs in Thursdays through Saturdays, while the more mellow live jazz on Sundays makes it the perfect place to wind down. *Nightly 5:30pm-2am.* ⊟ 522 Wilshire Blvd. (Fifth St.), 310-451-9341

Rokbar • Hollywood • Nightclub

Rock 'n' roll bad boys Tommy Lee and Dave Navarro bring '80s excess to Hollywood with their "anti-club." The trashy cocktail lounge ironically adjacent to LAX uses the same bawdy blueprint as its sister club in Miami. A life-size picture of a half-naked girl flipping you the bird greets you at the entrance, setting up the sinfully sexy, yet no-drama nightlife scene inside. More centerfold shots of hotties dot the minimalist black-on-black interior, including walls lined with some of Lee and Navarro's favorite song lyrics. The worthwhile menu puts a new spin on comfort food classics like grilled cheese with short ribs and fried chicken. Retro rock videos and concert footage play on TVs, while The Sex Pistols, Guns N' Roses, and AFI blast from the speakers. Celebrity and rock royalty like Pamela Anderson, Courtney Love, and Slash are regulars, but the video vixenish staff are the ones whom you can't keep your bloodshot eyes off. *Nightly 6pm-2am.* ≣ 1710 N. Las Palmas Ave. (Hollywood Blvd.), 323-461-5600, rokbaronline.com

Rooftop Bar at the Standard Downtown* • Downtown • Hotel Bar

Best Hotel Bars Leave it to hotel guru Andre Balazs to transform an abandoned industrial building in Downtown L.A.'s grim financial district into one of the city's trendiest hot spots. The rooftop bar is the hotel's main attraction, drawing a wide range of jet-setting tourists, decompressing 9-to-5 suits, and curious club commuters. The candy apple red and virgin white decor, space-pod waterbed cabanas, Twister board dance floor, and naughty nurse waitress uniforms are straight out of a sci-fi fairy tale. The mature scene is hit-or-miss, with the martini-sipping afterwork crowd giving way to random revelers at night. The weekend pool parties during the summer season are pure bikini bliss—as you can sit poolside, sip mimosas, get a back massage, and take in the stunning view of the L.A. skyline or the hot bod next to you. *Daily noon-2am.* Ⓒ⎕ The Standard Downtown, 550 S. Flower St. (Fifth St.), 213-892-8080, standardhotel.com

Saddle Ranch Chop House* • Los Angeles • Bar/Restaurant

Best Daytime Drinking Spots *Animal House* meets chop house at this Wild West–themed bar on the Sunset Strip. This guilty pleasure of "Bluto" Blutarsky proportions looks like a Knott's Berry Farm attraction complete with cowboy and saloon girl mannequins and horse and buggy models. If the bouncing coed sloppily riding a mechanical bull doesn't tell you that this is an "adult" theme park, then the annoyingly attentive staff pushing giant-sized cocktails on you will. The everyone-from-everywhere crowd consists of suburban cowboys, white-trash chic cuties, red-faced tourists, and reality TV show refugees who both work and play here—and even occasionally film here. The Texas-sized platters of greasy grub are surprisingly delicious, while the fleet of indoor/outdoor TVs make it a prime spot to catch a game. A guitar-fiddle duo roam the wraparound outdoor patio deck, while lip-locking lovers can roast s'mores over open fire pits. *Daily 8am-2am.* ≣ 8371 W. Sunset Blvd. (La Cienega Blvd.), 323-656-2007, srrestaurants.com

Skybar • West Hollywood • Hotel Bar

Best Hotel Bars Find everything you love to hate about Hollywood at this pretentious playground of the rich and famous. The Mondrian Hotel's open-air oasis conveys the image of a surreal life of leisure filled with leggy supermodels, panoramic views, sarong-clad servers, and poolside cocktails. Superficiality comes at a price—namely egos as big as bra sizes, $20 drinks, and a draconian door policy. In reality, the cabana-style lounge is nothing more than a posh poolside deck featuring a raised ivy-covered hut surrounded by cushy mattresses and chaise longues. Although the once white-hot scene has cooled down some, the well-heeled and well-connected still consider it a Sunset Strip institution, and the view of the L.A. skyline is unmatched. *Daily 11am-2am.* ⊟ The Mondrian Hotel, 8440 Sunset Blvd. (La Cienega Blvd.), 323-848-6025, mondrianhotel.com

Spider Club • Hollywood • Nightclub

Best Singles Scenes Intimacy and exclusivity go together like sex tapes and the Internet in "Hollow-wood." Thus, it's no surprise that the usual *US Weekly* suspects (Britney, Paris, and Lindsay) come here to crack the Cristal and swing from the in-house dancing pole. Designer Donovan Leitch Jr.'s Moroccan-themed lounge is conveniently hidden above super club Avalon and behind a requisite velvet rope. Guest-list credentials or a bevy of babes ensure entrance into the plush playpen, which is decked out in Persian rugs, soft pillows, and cushy booths. Eclectic DJs funk things up in front of a tiny dance floor, while the sweeping outdoor patio features a retractable ceiling. The weekend after-hour club nights are less restricted, but are purely for revved-up beat junkies who just "wanna dance." *Hours vary.* ⓒ≣ 1737 N. Vine St. (Hollywood Blvd.), 323-462-8900

White Lotus* • Hollywood • Restaurant/Nightclub

Dine on a tented patio before hitting the hot club scene next door. See *Hot & Cool Restaurants*, p.76, for details. *Fri-Sat 9pm-2am; Restaurant: 6-10pm.* ⓒ≣ 1743 Cahuenga Blvd. (Hollywood Blvd.), 323-463-0060

Wilshire Restaurant* • Santa Monica • Restaurant/Bar

Wilshire's front bar draws a crowd under its geometric wood ceilings and mood-heightening votive lighting afterwork and before and after dinner. See *Hot & Cool Restaurants,* p.76, for details. *Mon-Sat 6-10pm, bar until 12:30am.* ⓒⒷ≣ 2454 Wilshire Blvd. (26th St.), 310-586-1707, wilshirerestaurant.com

Hot & Cool Los Angeles:
The Attractions

Beverly Hot Springs • Los Angeles • Spa

An errant oilman once struck hot mineral water at this unlikely sybaritic site, which now houses L.A.'s only natural thermal baths. Steamy soaks, scrubs, and shiatsus are rejuvenating experiences at this traditional Korean-style spa adorned with rock waterfalls and a soothing soundtrack of chimes, hissing steam, and easy-listening Brahms. Treatment rooms are only semiprivate, but after a few minutes that won't matter. Call ahead for frequent promo specials. *Daily 9:30am-9pm.* $$$$ 308 N. Oxford Ave. (Beverly Blvd.), 323-734-7000, beverlyhotsprings.com

Briles Wing & Helicopter • Van Nuys • Tour

Best Views of L.A. The name may have changed from Heli USA to the less cool-sounding Briles Wing & Helicopter, but whatever you choose to call it, this helicopter touring company still offers Hollywood/Skyscraper flight packs. Soar over famous movie locations, Bel-Air mansions, The Getty Center, Universal Studios, Beverly Hills, the Hollywood sign, and Downtown's batch of high-rises. Hand over $125 more, and the City of Angeles Flight will take you on a romantic sunset flight along the beach. *Hours vary.* $$$$ 16303 Waterman Dr. (Roscoe Blvd.), 877-863-5952, toflyla.com

The Getty Center • Los Angeles • Museum

Only a portion of the vast J. Paul Getty collection fits into its dream home and Foundation headquarters. Rumor has it that there was no budget set for this modern architectural wonder, designed by Richard Meier and perched like an urban San Simeon in the Santa Monica Mountains. Construction took just under 15 years and the final cost was ... well, it's only money. A short tram ride from the parking structure leads to five pavilions full of paintings, decorative arts, photographs, manuscripts, drawings, and other masterpieces that require at least a few visits, especially if you take time to enjoy the gardens and views. Admission is free, but it's seven dollars to park your car. Parking is first-come, first-served and busiest at midday. A free shuttle operates from the overflow lot two miles south of the museum on the northwest corner of Sepulveda Boulevard and Constitution Avenue. *Tue-Thu, Sun 10am-6pm, Fri-Sat 10am-9pm.* 1200 Getty Center Dr. (Sepulveda Blvd.), 310-440-7300, getty.edu

Hollywood & Highland • Hollywood • Shopping

Hollywood is back! At least this $700 million, 1.3-million-square-foot, five-story entertainment complex, modeled after D.W. Griffith's *Intolerance* set, with its 60-plus shops and restaurants, 640-room hotel, and gala Kodak Theatre (home to the Academy Awards), would have you think so. Spoilsports may call it a glorified mall—the majority of stores here are the same ones you'll find back home, from Aveda to Sephora. But as far as Hollywood's latest renaissance goes, this may be as good as it gets. *Mon-Sat 10am-10pm, Sun 10am-7pm (theaters, clubs and some restaurants have extended hours).* 6801 Hollywood Blvd. (Highland Ave.), 323-467-6412, hollywoodandhighland.com

Kiehl's • Los Angeles • Shop
Imagine the indignity of having to order body-care products by mail. Luckily for L.A. acne-phobes, New York shop Kiehl's opened a store on Robertson's tony stretch of celebrity boutiques, forever changing the way Los Angeles residents moisturize. The counter people aren't actual chemists, but they do wear lab coats, which tends to make their skin-care advice all the more believable. *Mon-Thu, Sat 10am-7pm, Fri 10am-8pm, Sun 11am-6pm.* 100 N. Robertson Blvd. (Beverly Blvd.), 310-860-0028, kiehls.com

Kinara Spa • West Hollywood • Spa
Best Spas Even if it's only 10am, pretend you've done enough to deserve a thirsty skin quencher facial, a deep detox hydrotherapy bath, a Bora Bora body scrub, or a hydrating shea butter wrap. Everything's good for your mind and body at Kinara Spa, even the interiors inspired by Bali and Eastern India, and the cafe, which serves an organic, skin-friendly menu put together by Christine Splichal, wife of chef Joachim of Patina fame. It's a celebrity scene here, so if you see Halle Berry or Anjelica Huston parading around in a bathrobe, remain calm. When your treatment is over, try the cafe's three-course anti-aging menu before seizing what's left of the day. *Tue-Fri 9am-9pm, Sat 9am-7pm, Sun 10am-6pm.* $$$$ 656 N. Robertson Blvd. (Melrose Ave.), 310-657-9188, kinaraspa.com

Kitson • Beverly Hills • Shop
Celebs like Lindsay Lohan and Jessica Simpson come here for the store's colorful assortment of denim, purses, necklaces, sweater beanies, designer sneakers and myriad other "of the moment" accessories. Often labeled (in tabloids at least) L.A.'s hottest celebrity shop, Kitson plays the celebrity-watcher game with T-shirts that read "Team Nick" and "Team Jessica" (or whichever famous couple is breaking up at the time). Note of caution: It helps if you're a size two. *Mon-Fri 10am-7pm, Sat 9am-7pm, Sun 11am-6pm.* 115 S. Robertson Blvd. (Third St.), 310-859-2652, shopkitson.com

Kodak Theatre • Hollywood • Site
The Oscars have had many homes over the years, but its grandest venue yet promises to be permanent. If you're not nominated for anything this year, you can still get inside for a variety of other shows ranging from Barry Manilow, Prince, and Harry Connick Jr. concerts to *Sesame Street Live* and American Ballet Theatre performances of *The Nutcracker*. The best way to snoop around is on a guided tour, which includes a visit to the exclusive George Eastman VIP room (where those post-show Oscar parties are held) and an introduction to an Oscar statuette, presented to the Eastman Kodak Company in 1991. *Tours run daily every half-hour 10:30am-2:30pm (June–Aug 10:30am-4pm).* $ 6801 Hollywood Blvd. (Highland Ave.), 323-308-6300, kodaktheatre.com

Los Angeles Horseback Riding • Topanga Canyon • Tour
The back yard of this friendly ranch high up in the Santa Monica Mountains is a vast chaparral-covered wilderness with miles of trails and dramatic views of the coast. Saddle up for a 90-minute ride with an experienced guide who'll let you canter if you can handle a horse. Groups rarely exceed six people, and intimate two-person rides can be arranged with advance notice. Romantic sunset rides in the hills with a gourmet dinner are also offered. *Hours vary.* $$$$ 2623 Old Topanga Canyon Rd. (Pinehurst Rd.), 818-591-2032, lahorsebackriding.com

Malibu Country Mart • Malibu • Shopping

This complex of shops, dining, and services is the tony enclave of Malibu's answer to a strip mall, though they'd be very distressed to hear it called that. From Starbucks to a branch of trendy Lisa Kline, and even a pet shop to the stars, you'll find a bit of everything here—including celebrity sightings. It's a great place to stop for refreshments on the way to the beach. *Hours vary by store.* 3835 Cross Creek Rd. (Civic Center Way), malibucountrymart.com

Marina del Rey Sportfishing • Marina del Rey • Sport

This 30-year-old company has built a sturdy reputation for finding the fish. Experienced and novice anglers alike can choose from a variety of open-party half- or three-quarter–day trips. Licensed vessels comb Santa Monica Bay for all seasonal game fish including yellowtail, bass, barracuda, halibut, and bonita. Rods and tackle can be rented, bait is included, lunch is served on the longer excursions, and even fish cleaning and packaging is offered. During gray whale migration season (January–March), whale watching trips are also offered every morning during the week and twice daily on weekends. *Half-day fishing trips leave at 7:30am and 12:30pm, returning approximately five hours later. Three-quarter-day trips depart at 7am or 8am, returning at around 3pm.* $$$ Dock 52, Fiji Way (Admiralty Way), 310-822-3625, mdrsf.com

Marina Sailing • Marina del Rey • Sport

One of six Marina Sailing locations scattered along the SoCal coast between Ventura and San Diego, this one lets you pull out of the world's largest pleasure-craft marina on vessels ranging from a 20-foot Santana to a 42-foot catamaran. *Quarter-day, half-day, and full-day rentals are offered with or without skippers. Weekend sailing lessons can also be arranged.* $$$$ 13441 Mindanao Way (Admiralty Way), 800-262-7245, marinasailing.com

Museum of Television & Radio • Beverly Hills • Cultural Museum

Like that of its sister facility in New York, the name's a tad misleading. You won't be finding any examples of old transistors or '50s-era Zenith user's manuals at this stark Richard Meier–designed building in the heart of Beverly Hills. In fact, except for a few art exhibits, the joint appears pretty empty until you get your paws on a library database of more than 100,000 radio and television programs spanning 80-odd years. After enough time with a headset on a private console, you'll forget where you are and what year it is—which is what good TV has always been about. Stuff from the collection is also screened in the facility's two main theaters. *Wed-Sun noon-5pm.* 465 N. Beverly Dr. (Little Santa Monica Blvd.), 310-786-1000, mtr.org

NBC Studios • Burbank • Site/Tour

Best Studio Tours NBC is, as it proudly claims to be, "the only network that opens its doors to you!" How wide that door opens is beside the point. You do get some behind-the-scenes perspective when you take the studio's walking tour. Just over an hour long, it pokes inside the wardrobe, makeup, set construction, and other departments, which nicely deflates the myth that working in Hollywood is the least bit exciting. Your chipper guide will also lead you through a soundstage and an FX room or two and very likely the set of the *Tonight Show.* For free tickets to *The Tonight Show with Jay Leno* (which usually tapes at 3pm), be at the NBC ticket counter well before 8am or request in advance by mail (NBC Tickets,

3000 W. Alameda Ave., Burbank, CA 91523). *Tours depart regularly 9am-3pm weekdays, plus weekends during the summer.* $ 3000 W. Alameda Ave. (W. Olive Ave.), 818-840-3537, nbc.com

Ole Henriksen Face/Body • West Hollywood • Spa

Best Spas Whip your epidermis into shape at this full-service spa run by one of the great authorities on skin care (he's served as a Ms. Universe judge and he's been on *Oprah*). The soothing environs of this 4,000-square-foot Japanese-style spa include several Zen-like treatment rooms with glowing candles and shoji doors. If there's a signature treatment on the aptly named menu of "tranquility packages," it's the Six-Step Body Treatment—a rapturous 90 minutes that includes the famous sea mineral scrub. Don't leave Ole's without one. *Sun-Mon 9am-5pm, Tue-Sat 8am-8pm.* $$$$ 8622-A W. Sunset Blvd. (Sunset Plaza Dr.), 310-854-7700, olehenriksen.com

Paradise Bound Yacht Charters • Marina del Rey • Tour

The "Silver Eagle," a 42-foot Catalina sailing yacht with three private double cabins and gourmet meal service, operates out of the Ritz-Carlton for luxury sunset cruises, marriage proposals, birthdays, and all other occasions—all in the able hands of Captain Alex. *Hours vary.* $$$$ Ritz-Carlton Hotel, 4375 Admiralty Way (Bali Way), 310-578-7963, aaparadiseboundyacht.com

The Pierce Bros. Westwood Village Memorial Park • Westwood • Site

Best Graveyards of the Stars This tiny cemetery close to UCLA didn't have cachet until Marilyn Monroe was buried here. She has subsequently been joined by the likes of Natalie Wood, Billy Wilder, Rodney Dangerfield, and Janis Joplin. Unlike many other cemeteries, this one's small enough to make finding the gravestone of your favorite celebrity a breeze. *Daily 8am-sundown.* 1218 Glendon Ave. (Wilshire Blvd.), 310-474-1579

Point Mugu State Park • Malibu • Hike

Best Hikes More than 70 miles of hiking trails at this 15,000-acre retreat in the Santa Monica Mountains include five miles of varied Malibu coastline and a lofty backdrop of river canyons, sycamore-dotted valleys, and one of the last remaining examples of indigenous California grassland. The La Jolla Valley Loop Trail is a moderately strenuous but crowd-free ten-mile ramble that starts at the Ray Miller trailhead and passes seasonal waterfalls, oak groves, and bursts of sage, lavender, and wildflowers in the spring. Near the junction of these two trails, the La Jolla Valley Camp provides piped water, restrooms, and oak-shaded picnic tables. Bag a few more miles and find higher vista points on this day hike by cutting west from the Valley Loop Trail to the Mugu Peak Trail. 9000 Pacific Coast Hwy. (Sycamore Canyon Rd.), Point Mugu State Park, 818-880-0350, parks.ca.gov

Rancho Park Golf Course • Los Angeles • Golf

One of the city's nicest public golf courses is just down the street from Beverly Hills. The bad news is that you're not the only one in on this little secret. Traffic is heavy at this hilly 6,681-yard, par 71, with an additional 9-hole par 3. Good facilities include a two-tiered driving range, an executive course, plus an onsite restaurant and bar. To reserve a time, you'll have to first obtain a City Parks golf card (213-473-7055). *Daily until sundown.* $$ 10460 W. Pico Blvd. (Patricia Ave.), 310-838-7373, lagolfclubs.com/clubs

South Bay Bicycle Trail • Various • Sport

Spanning 22 miles from Pacific Palisades to the South Bay with a few detours along the way, this paved bicycle path lets you check off as many beaches, boardwalks, and piers as your leg muscles will allow. Have coffee in Santa Monica and brunch in Marina del Rey. Or do breakfast in Venice, late lunch in Manhattan Beach, and happy hour in Hermosa. Just be back before the rental counter closes. Congestion is heaviest between Santa Monica and Venice, where you share the path with walkers, joggers, bladers, skaters, wheelchair riders, three-wheel recumbent bikers, and people on various other contraptions. Keep going and it lightens to almost nothing on long open stretches at Dockweiler State Beach and El Segundo Beach before traffic picks up again at Manhattan Beach. Bikes can be rented from the many, many places along the path. From Will Rogers State Beach to Torrance County Beach, coastalconservancy.ca.gov

The Sports Club / LA • Los Angeles • Gym

Best Workouts The gym of choice for serious gawkers and exercisers alike offers massage services and valet parking, among other cushy amenitites. But you also get plenty of opportunities to actually work out, from racquetball courts to an Olympic-size swimming pool to a huge main workout room dotted with televisions that help take your mind off the fact that the person on the Versa Climber next to you is doing twice your calorie-burn rate. Check your blood pressure and cardiovascular endurance at the FitLab, then enjoy your protein-laden smoothie at the Sidewalk Cafe. Day passes aren't available, unless you're a guest of the Peninsula, Hotel Bel-Air, or Regent Beverly Wilshire. *Mon-Fri 5am-11pm, Sat-Sun 7am-8pm.* $$ 1835 Sepulveda Blvd. (Olympic Blvd.), 310-473-1447, thesportsclubla.com

Third Street Promenade • Santa Monica • Shopping

Developed in the late '80s, downtown Santa Monica's lively three-block pedestrian zone of restaurants, shops, cafes, theaters, kiosks, and nonstop street performances is one of the great models of civic revitalization. Friday and Saturday nights can be a zoo here, when extended store hours often run past midnight. Popular stops include the Broadway Deli, Arcana Books, Z Gallerie, Anthropologie, and a new Krispy Kreme donut stand. Between Broadway and Wilshire Blvd., 310-393-8355, downtownsm.com

Universal Studios Hollywood • Universal City • Site/Tour

Best Studio Tours Somewhere on this huge lot, the world's biggest blockbusters are being produced. Of course, the spotlight at Universal Studios is reserved for movies that return home as theme park attractions—including old favorites like *Back to the Future* and *Jurassic Park* and a roster of newcomers including *The Mummy Returns: Chamber of Doom* and *Shrek 4-D*. The standard offering is the 45-minute Studio Tour, which whisks past sets and soundstages with enough fun surprises to keep the experience feeling very ride-like. To better appreciate what's going on back there, a VIP tour provides two hours of far less rehearsed access, plus six hours in the theme park with front-of-the-line privileges. At nearly three times the price of general admission it's an investment, but it's likely the best one you can make in the Valley on a crowded summer day. Reserve at least a week in advance (818-622-5120). *Summer park hours Mon-Fri 9am-8pm, Sat-Sun 9am-9pm. VIP tours depart daily 9am and noon, usually on the hour.* $$$$ 100 Universal City Plaza (Universal Studios Blvd.), 800-864-8377, themeparks.universalstudios.com

Walt Disney Concert Hall • Downtown • Concert Venue/Site

In 1988, renowned L.A. architect Frank Gehry turned in his winning design for what would become one of the world's most ambitious (and trouble-ridden) modern architectural projects. After a decade of feuding egos, budget fiascos, and construction stalemates followed by another three full years just to build the thing, the monumental new home of the L.A. Philharmonic and Master Chorale opened in October 2003 to nearly unanimous praise. And at a price tag of $274 million—phew! A swirl of facts and figures surround this eye-popper on Bunker Hill, described by Gehry as "a living room for the city," though one that required 30,000 pages of diagrams, a million square feet of wood, 12,500 unique shapes of structural steel, painstaking acoustical considerations and reconsiderations, and so on. Just how accessible this 2,265-seat "living room" will be to most of the city is another matter, but even outsiders will find it hard not admire this venue's arcing, looping, and soaring steel shell. Visitors can explore the hall's gardens and multilayered interior (though not the actual auditorium, where rehearsals are usually in progress) on a guided group tour arranged through the Music Center (213-972-4399). Concert tickets can be reserved by contacting the Los Angeles Philharmonic Box Office (323-850-2000). *Box office Tue-Sun noon-6pm.* $ 111 S. Grand Ave. (Second St.), 213-972-7211, musiccenter.org/wdch

Williams-Sonoma Home • Beverly Hills • Shop

In terms of style and prices, the flagship store of this new Williams-Sonoma venture floats somewhere between Restoration Hardware and its high-end neighbors, though admittedly a bit closer to the top end. What's here? A European-inspired line of furniture, expensive bed linens that made Oprah's best list, and prices that fall below those of the Ralph Lauren home store in Beverly Hills. *Mon-Sat 10am-7pm, Sun 11am-6pm.* 8772 Beverly Blvd. (Robertson Blvd.), 310-289-2420, wshome.com

Hip Los Angeles

There's a line across L.A., an unspoken boundary as solid as any wall—La Cienega Boulevard. It's the unofficial marker between east and west, and that's a big distinction. If the Westside is all about L.A. stereotypes—bleached, Botoxed blondes of both sexes cruising to yoga in designer cars—then the Eastside is stubbornly about the hip opposite. These neighborhoods crave alternatives—if by different you mean full-sleeve tattoos, rocker attitudes, and a dislike of "Westside Wendys" in all forms. But it takes commitment to be an L.A. hipster: the disdain, the clothes, the late-late nights! Not to mention all the time you have to devote to finding the latest hot spot and insinuating yourself into it. Lucky you—for three fun-filled nights and days you can pretend you're the real deal, and then you can go home. Put on your shades, grab your triple espresso, and hit the streets—this is the L.A. you don't see in magazines.

*Note: Venues in bold are described in detail in the listings that follow the itinerary. Venues followed by an * asterisk are those we recommend as both a restaurant and a destination bar.*

Hip Los Angeles:
The Perfect Plan (3 Nights and Days)

Perfect Plan Highlights

Thursday

Pre-dinner	Tropicana Bar, Jones
Dinner	Memphis*, BLD, Soot Bull Jeep
Nighttime	Acme Comedy, Mood, Dresden Room
Late-Night	Magnolia*, Sanamluang

Friday

Breakfast	Alcove Cafe, Fred 62
Morning	Shopping, Griffith Park, Dtox Day Spa
Lunch	R-23, 410 Boyd, Ciudad*
Afternoon	MOCA, Geffen
Cocktails	Golden Gopher, Ciudad*
Dinner	Michelangelo's, Dusty's, Cobras & Matadors
Nighttime	Good Luck Bar, Bigfoot Lodge, Spaceland
Late-Night	Ye Rustic Inn, The Well

Saturday

Breakfast	Toast, Joe's
Morning	Abbot Kinney, Bergamot Station, Venice Beach
Lunch	Ford's, Newsroom Cafe, King's Road Cafe
Afternoon	Runyon Canyon, Peterson Automotive Museum
Cocktails	Social*, L'Scorpion, L.A. Neon Tour
Dinner	Social*, Palms Thai, Jar
Nighttime	Velvet*, Lucky Strike
Late-Night	Forty Deuce, Arclight, 25 Degrees

Morning After

Breakfast	House of Blues*

Thursday

7pm Inside the Roosevelt Hotel, seat yourself at **The Tropicana Bar** for a smooth beginning to a weekend of fun. You'll find yourself in the company of the city's hippest scenesters getting ready for a night out. Another option is the nearby **Jones Hollywood**, close to the Warner Bros. Hollywood lot, where assistants to power players come to blow off steam.

8:30 Dinner Memphis* is known for its blood-red decor and real Southern cooking, set in the last residence left on this strip of Hollywood Boulevard. **BLD** (Breakfast, Lunch, Dinner) on Beverly draws a more posh type of hipster with comfort food in a sleek red and black space. But for a unique, delicious, and adventurous meal, head to **Soot Bull Jeep** in Koreatown, where you probably won't be able to decipher a single item on the menu, but will likely end up with Korean BBQ—tasty meats grilled right at your table.

10pm The show at **Acme Comedy Theatre** will have you rolling, no matter what the theme—famous faces like Wayne Brady have played here. A different sort of kitsch awaits you at **Mood**, with

HIP

its Bali-themed interior and bevy of young stars that have seen their fair share of MTV airtime. Reserve bottle service beforehand; otherwise moving beyond the velvet rope is not guaranteed. You can also venture farther east to **The Dresden Room** in Los Feliz where the swinger lifestyle lives on, and the rope is much easier to pass.

Midnight Slide into a booth at restaurant/bar **Magnolia*** and lose about ten years among the youthful clientele. You should probably be carding the bartenders, not the other way around. If you're in Los Feliz, head to **4100 Bar** where the night is still warming up.

1am The crowd at **Sanamluang Café** is a little older, but not by a whole lot. It's all about the Thai noodles and iced tea here, until well into the morning hours.

Friday

9:30am It's back to Los Feliz and Silver Lake for an outdoor breakfast: The brick patio of **The Alcove Cafe** gets packed with locals, from those wielding strollers to those just back from the clubs. At **Fred 62**, you can sit inside or out to enjoy upscale diner food with a lively if hung-over crowd.

10am If you need to work off breakfast, head to Griffith Park. Park your car at the end of Commonwealth Avenue and follow the trail into the park and up the hill to your right for a rewarding view of the Observatory, Downtown, and out to the ocean (on a clear day). It's about a two-mile loop if you take the return dirt trail just past the lookout point—just ask any hiker.

Of course, you could also just explore the gentrified backbone of Los Feliz along Vermont Avenue between Hollywood Boulevard and Franklin Avenue, which is loaded with stylish boutiques, as is the nearby Sunset Junction area. Then head to **Dtox Day Spa** for a massage and steam.

But golfers take note: Hidden in Griffith Park are the **Wilson and Harding Golf Courses,** some of the best public courses in the city, set among the lush hills.

12:30pm Lunch is being served Downtown, which means a drive about 15 minutes down Sunset. Stop in Echo Park for a quick walk around **Echo Park Lake**, where the lotus draw crowds when they bloom in late summer.

1:30pm Lunch R-23 is tricky to find, but well worth the trouble for great sushi. **410 Boyd** serves swell New American fare, but for a bustling patio scene, check out **Ciudad's*** tasty Cuban food.

3pm Now feast your eyes on L.A.'s bountiful art scene. The **Museum of Contemporary Art** (MOCA) is one of the country's finest collections of modern American and European works. Admission to

MOCA also includes entrance to its cool off-site property, **The Geffen Contemporary**, just five minutes away in Little Tokyo. The smaller and lesser-known **Museum of Neon Art** (MONA) is another worthy stop in the area. Since you're downtown, you must wander by The Walt Disney Concert Hall, a swooping silver feat of construction, and its down-the-block neighbor, Our Lady of Angels Cathedral, where each of the giant bronze doors weighs 25,000 pounds.

6:30pm The Golden Gopher is an old-school spot that's been given a new lease on life. If you didn't lunch at **Ciudad***, check out its afterwork drinks scene.

8:30pm Dinner Head back to Silver Lake and into **Michelangelo's**, a tiny, family-run Italian spot with the best spaghetti and meatballs around—as the crowd proves. There are also the charming, wood-detailed booths at **Dusty's Bistro**, where upscale American fare is served to hungry style-setters. The shared tapas plates at sleek **Cobras & Matadors** are another stellar option—let the waiter help you choose the perfect Spanish wine.

10:30pm The Good Luck Bar is a colorful spot with a friendly crowd. For a real neighborhood hangout, check out **Bigfoot Lodge**, behind a wood door on a nondescript block. If live music is what you're after, it's **Spaceland**,

just a few doors down from Michelangelo's.

Midnight Set in a shabby strip mall, **Ye Rustic Inn** doesn't look like much—which is exactly how patrons like it. Inside, it's loud, crowded, and fun. Back in Hollywood, you could also check out **The Well** for late-night action with a lively crowd.

Saturday

10am Head west, get to **Toast** early, and nab a sidewalk table with views of the industry crowd. The Magnolia Bakery treats are tasty, but you could also opt for the inventive pancakes or French toast. Even farther west is **Joe's**, where Santa Monica locals like to start the day on the patio or in the buzzing room.

11am Do some browsing in **Abbot Kinney's** edgy but upscale shops, where you might get the impulse to purchase a pair of jeans or a piece of 1960s French furniture. Don't miss the nearby **Bergamot Station**, where you can discover some of L.A.'s top artists. You could also visit the famous **Venice Beach** boardwalk, where you can shop for hip clothes, get your fortune read, buy some incense, and lie out on the surprisingly beautiful beach—the drug dealers don't come out until later.

1:30pm Lunch Ford's Filling Station in Culver City isn't hot just for its simple-but-great fare—this spot is owned by Harrison Ford's son. But for heavy-duty Hollywood scenes, check out the **Newsroom Cafe** or **King's Road Cafe**—two popular spots for the young and undiscovered.

3pm Want to see celebrities and the dogs that walk them? Drive up to **Runyon Canyon Park** for a little jogging, or a long uphill hike. To explore the last hundred years of automotive history, head to the **Peterson Automotive Museum**. Down the block you'll find the La Brea Tar Pits, a bit of early L.A. history.

6pm Back in Hollywood, the dark lounge at **Social Hollywood*** is a great place to sip a martini and plot the rest of the evening. It's also not too early for a little tequila at **L'Scorpion**, with its homey exposed brick and red stained glass. You can also head downtown and catch the 7pm **L.A. Neon Tour**, where a double-decker bus will show you the bright lights of the big city after a cocktail or two.

8pm Dinner If the chic Moroccan vibe of **Social*** has you enthralled, stick around for dinner. For a nothing-fancy-about-it spot, try **Palms Thai**, where locals come for the food and the singing Thai Elvis. That's all we're saying—you have to experience it for yourself. At **Jar**, you'll find comfort food, comfortable seating, and a very stylish crowd.

10pm Another vibey hot spot is **Le Velvet Margarita Cantina***. It's a skewed version of a dark Tijuana bar, with velvet walls and healthy Mexican food. You could also head through the subway-like façade of **The Bowery*** near the fabled corner of Sunset and Vine. Seat yourself at the bar and order a Belgian beer. Think bowling is too Midwest? Think again—**Lucky Strike Lanes** is filled with L.A.'s scenesters.

Midnight **Ivan Kane's Forty Deuce** is a burlesque bar with lots of well-turned-out people and a tough velvet rope. A few blocks up Sunset, a former dive has been transformed into **The Bar**, a sleek hangout for trendsetters—it doesn't have a velvet rope. Of course, **Arclight Theaters** also still has the projectors running.

2am The build-your-own-burger joint **25 Degrees** in the Roosevelt Hotel is open until 3am.

The Morning After
The **House of Blues*** has a most happening weekly ritual, the Sunday Gospel Brunch.

Hip Los Angeles:
The Key Neighborhoods

Downtown is where this city began. These days, it's home to courts, politicians, business visitors, and a lot of homeless people. However, recent years have seen an upswing in cool restaurants, clubs, and arts venues filling up the old buildings.

Echo Park For the past several years, this predominantly Latino area has been known as the next up-and-coming spot for artists and young couples to inhabit, and it has the boutiques, art galleries, and struggling creative types to prove it.

Hollywood is experiencing a revival. A once down-and-dirty area, it's still pretty bleak, with a large homeless population. But in between sex shops and tourist traps, you'll find tons of A-list clubs, restaurants, and even a new loft or two.

Los Feliz is the home of the city's zoo and Griffith Park. In the hills, you'll find old money in mansions, but lower down, it's a hip mix of mommies-who-rock, Eastside fashionistas, and artistic types.

Silver Lake sits just east of Los Feliz, and hosts an eclectic population of immigrants, yuppies who have taken over the hillside homes, artists, rockers, and those who like to hang out with them.

Venice Beach draws artists to the Boardwalk and Abbot Kinney Boulevard thanks to an inspiringly edgy vibe, touches of which are evident in the area's styles and cuisine. It used to be a dangerous place ... then rents skyrocketed. Yuppies have been moving here in droves, but they have yet to tame Venice's storied grit.

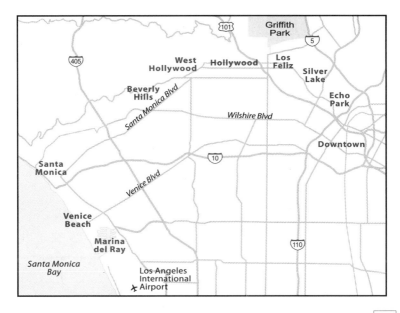

Hip Los Angeles:
The Shopping Blocks

Abbot Kinney Boulevard

Despite the influx of money, Venice Beach's revitalized Abbot Kinney has so far managed to avoid soul-deadening gentrification.

French 50s-60s Minimalist home furnishings from post-war French designers. 1427 Abbot Kinney Blvd. (Navarre Ct.), 310-392-9905, french50s60s.com

Heist Edgy basics, lots of denim, and handmade jewelry give this store a browsing-through-someone-else's-closet feel. 1104 Abbot Kinney Blvd. (Westminster Ave.), 310-450-6531, shopheist.com

Kevin Simon Custom clothing that just seems vintage, for men and women. 1358 Abbot Kinney Blvd. (California Ave.), 310-392-4630, kevinsimonclothing.com

The Perfect Piece Machine-age pieces like dentist's chairs reworked as home furnishings. 1216 Abbot Kinney Blvd. (Aragon Ct.), 310-581-1002, perfectpiece.com

Glendale Boulevard and Sunset Junction

On and around two of Silver Lake's main thoroughfares are myriad stores catering to a blend of the hip and sophisticated.

The Cheese Store of Silver Lake Gourmet foods and fine cheeses from around the world. 3926 W. Sunset Blvd. (Hyperion Ave.), 323-644-7511, cheesestoresl.com

Patty Faye Fashion-forward styles with a hippie-chick slant. 2910 Rowena Ave. (Herkimer St.), 323-667-1954

Rockaway Records Predictably hip (but not predictable) selection of vinyl, collectibles, and used CDs and DVDs. 2395 Glendale Blvd. (Brier Ave.), 323-664-3232, rockaway.com

Silver Lake Wine Specializing in small-production wines from all over the world. 2395 Glendale Blvd. (Brier Ave.), 323-662-9024, silverlakewine.com

La Brea Avenue

The place to go for home furnishings and antiques, from Wilshire up to Sunset, La Brea also has its share of vintage clothiers.

American Rag Used jeans, contemporary fashions, and a home store and French cafe next door. 150 S. La Brea Ave. (W. Second St.), 323-935-3154

Futurama Retro home furnishings read like 1950s ideas of what the future was supposed to look like. 446 N. La Brea Ave. (Oakwood Ave.), 323-937-4522, futuramafurniture.net

Jet Rag Low prices make this vintage shop the choice for theme-party fashions. 825 N. La Brea Ave. (Waring Ave.), 323-939-0528

Lower Melrose Avenue

If Melrose Heights is the clean-cut older brother, Lower Melrose is the black sheep who's sporting the tattoos, piercings, and dark fashions.

Sportie L.A. Your one-stop shop for vintage athletic footwear. 7753 Melrose Ave. (Genesee Ave.), 323-651-1553, sportiela.com

Wasteland Do some digging for barely worn secondhand designer clothes. 7428 Melrose Ave. (Martel Ave.), 323-653-3028, thewasteland.com

Sunset Boulevard (at Mohawk) and Echo Park Avenue

Picking up where Silver Lake and Los Feliz leave off, Echo Park is so hip it hurts. Sunset and Mohawk has vintage and home furnishings stores. And a one-block strip along Echo Park Avenue features avant-garde fashions.

Luxe de Ville Hard-to-find antique clothing and vintage jewelry. 2157 Sunset Blvd. (Mohawk St.), 213-353-0135, luxedeville.com

Show Pony Avant-garde fashions by just-out-of-art-school designers fill this cutting-edge store. 1543 Echo Park Ave. (Delta St.), 213-482-7676

Sirens & Sailors One-of-a-kind pieces by independent designers in a little purple house. 1104 Mohawk St. (Sunset Blvd.), 213-483-5423, sirensandsailors.com

Vermont Avenue

In Los Feliz, the east side of Vermont around Hollywood Boulevard has some of the hippest shopping and sidewalk café-going around.

Camille Hudson A DJ booth lends a certain cool factor to this shoe shop. 4685 Hollywood Blvd. (Vermont Ave.), 323-953-0377, camillehudson.com

Skylight Books Independent bookstore specializing in film, L.A. history, and pop culture. 1818 N. Vermont Ave. (Melbourne Ave.), 323-660-1175, skylighbooks.com

Soap Plant and WACKO Sex toys, Alfred E. Neuman salt and pepper shakers, and more. 4633 Hollywood Blvd. (Rodney Dr.), 323-663-0122, soapplant.com

West Third Street

Unique is a word often overused, but for this street of specialty stores that cater to your every whim, it's hardly an overstatement.

Plastica Hip, sometimes outlandish housewares made of, yep, plastic. 8405 W. Third St. (Orlando Ave.), 323-655-1051, plasticashop.com

Polkadots & Moonbeams Modern trendy, colorful fashions are made by both national and local designers. 8381 W. Third St. (Kings Rd.), 323-655-3880, polkadotsandmoonbeams.com

Satine Accessories, bags, clothing, and jewelry for the It Girl. 8117 W. Third St. (Crescent Heights Blvd.), 323-655-2142, satineboutique.com

Hip Los Angeles:
The Hotels

Avalon Hotel • Beverly Hills • Trendy (84 rms)

A full-on makeover earned this once ailing '50s apartment complex the 2000 Westside Historic Preservation prize. It also saved the place from resting too heavily on its laurels as former home to Marilyn Monroe and a handful of *I Love Lucy* episodes. The savvy media types who check in here now don't much care about all that stuff, but they do appreciate the modern-retro kidney-shaped pool, the cabanas, and the hip indoor/outdoor dining area called "Blue on Blue," serving lobster-and-pumpkin ravioli and a drink called "A Walk in Space." There's a state-of-the-art fitness center and a nifty house-call spa service that does shiatsus, facials, manicures and pedicures, seaweed marine wraps, and so on, in the comfort of your own room. Style and practicality coexist in the guest rooms, which flaunt Noguchi tables, Eames chairs, and bubble lamps, and don't skimp on the basics: Frette linens, internet access, fax machines, and Philosophy toiletries. Second-floor Premium king rooms (all are 450 square feet) have sought-after pool views. Tucked away in a residential pocket of lower Beverly Hills, this chic boutique hotel will be cool for at least another 50 years. $$ 9400 W. Olympic Blvd. (Cannon Dr.), 310-277-5221 / 800-535-4715, avalonbeverlyhills.com

Hollywood Roosevelt Hotel • Hollywood • Timeless (300 rms)

Best Hotel Pools The first Academy Awards were held in the Blossom Room here in 1929, and it took a merciful 15 minutes for the host, Douglas Fairbanks, to do the honors. An ambitious $15 million reno of this Spanish Colonial–style hotel firms up its reputation as Hollywood's best blast from the past. (Plans of boosting itself to a four-star establishment will see room rates bumped accordingly.) Some guests swear that suite 1200 is haunted by Marilyn Monroe, and rumor also has it that Montgomery Clift is still learning his lines on the ninth floor. The rooms include two dozen suites and 68 cabana rooms overlooking the pool. For a quiet night's sleep and a stellar view of the Hollywood sign, request a King Superior room high up in the front of this 12-story building. There's also a complete fitness center and a new-and-improved Cinegrill supper club on the ground floor. $$ 7000 Hollywood Blvd. (N. Orange Dr.), 323-466-7000 / 800-950-7667, hollywoodroosevelt.com

Inn at Playa del Rey • Playa del Rey • Timeless (21 rms)

You'd expect the beach-going masses to have found Playa del Rey by now. The fact that they're still bypassing this sleepy community tucked between LAX, Marina del Rey, and 300 acres of wetlands lends even more charm and romance to this grand B&B, an unlikely piece of Cape Cod perfection just three blocks from the Pacific. Sitting in the sunny yellow breakfast area, out in the rose garden hot tub, on the back deck facing a channel of passing sailboats, or in the cozy living room stocked with books about birds, it seems impossible that one of the world's biggest international airports is just down the road. Especially in vast L.A., it's always a nice surprise when great escapes like this New England–style beach house are so close. Twenty-one guest rooms and suites are individually designed for couples, corporate travelers, and families. Romantic Suites include a king canopy bed, a fireplace, and marvelous views from two-person Jacuzzis. View Rooms provide balconies overlooking the marina or the wetlands. Standard rooms might feature not-so-standard accoutrements like pine sleigh beds and handmade Amish quilts. Rooms facing the Ballona Wetlands have their own private balcony. All come with a full hot breakfast, afternoon tea, evening wine and hors d'oeuvres, and peaceful sunsets. A small exercise room is on the property, and bicycles are available for an even quicker commute to the beautiful nearby beach. $$ 435 Culver Blvd. (Pershing Dr.), 310-574-1920, innatplayadelrey.com

Mondrian • West Hollywood • Trendy (237 rms)

Best Hotel Pools Some 12-story apartment buildings have all the luck. If not for its location smack in the middle of the Sunset Strip, this once-drab bit of '50s architecture probably wouldn't have won the attention of über-hotelier Ian Schrager and designer Philippe Starck about a decade ago. As it stands, a total makeover turned it into a chic magnet for celebrities, industry power players, and the people who love being near them. Enter the Mondrian's lobby with its diaphanous curtains and almost ridiculously attractive and radiant clerks, and you can practically smell Hugh Grant's cologne. The guest rooms are spare—or perhaps you'd say minimalist, depending on how you view your half-glasses. The white, beige, and gray color scheme and a sparsity of furnishings are just part of the design team's "uncomplicated sophistication" approach, which is as deliciously pretentious as it sounds. But with oversized bathrooms, kitchenettes (in the suites), and floor-to-ceiling glass walls offering excellent views, who's complaining? Best rooms have both a balcony and a pool view. Two of L.A.'s hottest destinations, Skybar (see *Hot & Cool Nightlife,* p.83) and Asia de Cuba (see *Hot & Cool Restaurants,* p.63), are right here—and if you're a privileged hotel guest, you're as good as in. $$$$ 8440 W. Sunset Blvd. (Olive Dr.), 323-650-8999 / 800-525-8029, mondrianhotel.com

The Standard Downtown • Downtown • Trendy (207 rms)

What's life without risks? The Standard, which already had such a good thing going at its trendy West Hollywood flagship, took a big leap in reimagining this former Superior Oil company headquarters as a haven for young, hip suits stuck down in the financial district. Has it paid off? We haven't looked at the books, but the Rooftop Bar crowds alone seem to indicate yes. The guest rooms are playfully grouped into nine Standard-esque subcategories, ranging from "Cheap" (260 sq. ft.) to "Huge" (420 sq. ft.), "Gigantic" (460 sq. ft.), "Humongous" (580 sq. ft.), and "Wow!" (710 sq. ft.). All of them come with multipurpose "Living" Platform Beds, designed for every other imaginable bed-friendly activity besides sleeping; oversized down pillows and duvets; cordless two-line speaker phones with data ports; fully-loaded stereos; stocked minibars; and welcome little details like extra-strength travel candles and a full supply of aromatherapy products. For Downtown views, get a Huge room facing east. Entry-level digs are on the lower floors, with queen-sized beds, big glass-enclosed showers (no tub), and little else to write home about. Medium rooms get you farther off the ground and large rooms provide some extra space and a king-sized bed. Guests who want a tub have to go up to at least XL and can spring an extra $20-$40 for a vanity area and extra closet space. What do the Wow! rooms have that the others don't? Emperor-sized beds, separate lounging areas, and big-screen TVs. There's also a Big Penthouse and Bigger Penthouse. Hotel facilities include a 24-hour restaurant, a comprehensive fitness center, and an indoor lobby lounge with billiard tables. $$$ 550 S. Flower St. (Sixth St.), 213-892-8080, standardhotel.com

The Standard Hollywood • West Hollywood • Trendy (129 rms)

Don't worry, you haven't had that much to drink, the hotel sign is upside down. Maybe this converted retirement home will one day return to its roots and house a bunch of drooling old Gen-Xers remembering the days when they read *Details* and William Burroughs books sitting on beanbag chairs in hotel lobbies. Until then, it's a motel-ish pleasure playground right on the Strip, devoted entirely to virtual youth. Everything about this place is calculatingly cool, retro, and over-the-top image conscious, from the bubble swings and human vitrine in the lobby to the blue AstroTurf pool deck. If you can deal with a first-floor "Sunset View" (as in Blvd.), rooms start as low as $99—a steal if you don't plan on sleeping anyway. All the guest rooms include balconies, cordless phones, CD players, VCRs, and spare motel-style furnishings that are so much cooler than anything "nice." First-floor Extra Large rooms have balconies and face the pool to the south. If you'd rather stay near your banking buddies, check into the Standard's new Downtown location (550 S. Flower St.). $$$ 8300 W. Sunset Blvd. (N. Sweetzer Ave.), 323-650-9090, standardhotel.com

Sunset Marquis Hotel & Villas • West Hollywood • Timeless (115 rms)

Sequestered below Sunset on a leafy cul-de-sac, the Sunset Marquis is about as far as you can get from the Strip in half a block. Secure, beautifully laid-out grounds offer the sort of cool gentility that reels in famous country singers, aging rock stars, and a steady roster of special guests—musical or otherwise—who no doubt appreciate the onsite recording studio and the fact that the hotel's velvety Whiskey Bar is puny enough to keep out most of the groupie riffraff. The main draw is the Mediterranean-inspired setting with its lush gardens, cobblestone walkways, lovely pools, and homey living quarters. One hundred and two one-bedroom or junior suites occupy the main building, and a dozen self-contained villas are planted out in the garden. King beds, marble bathrooms, empty fridges (and separate minibars), balconies, high-speed internet connections, twice-daily maid service, and tasteful modern furnishings are standard. If you check into a villa, you also get a butler. The poolside Patio Cafe provides light bites and the hotel's elegant Room restaurant serves Cal-Pacific cuisine. $$$$ 1200 N. Alta Loma Rd. (Holloway Dr.), 310-657-1333 / 800-858-9758, sunsetmarquishotel.com

Viceroy • Santa Monica • Modern (162 rms)

Full of retro-whimsy and suave British-style decor, this hip $15 million reinvention of the Pacific Shore Hotel is just the sort of place where Austin Powers and James Bond might fight each other for a penthouse suite. Scene-questers who want an ocean view with their chic boutique digs will find the vibe at the Viceroy and its slick Cameo Bar (See *Hot & Cool Nightlife,* p.78) to be Santa Monica's closest relation to a city place like the Mondrian—but still a distant cousin. In fact, the rooms here are nicer and more interesting, the attitude isn't in the same league, and other guests won't care as much if you aren't impossibly young and beautiful and dressed in black. Furnished in the Viceroy's signature palette of soft whites, parrot greens, and driftwood grays, with lots of chrome and glassy accents, boldly designed guest rooms and suites offer balconies (most with ocean views), Frette linens and bathrobes, custom beds with down comforters and pillows, and marble baths with seated vanities and deep soaking tubs, as well as flat-screen TVs, CD-DVD players, and high-speed internet access. For the best view, try the Grand rooms on the 7th floor. A pair of outdoor pools are also on the property along with a fully equipped fitness center and massage and in-room spa service by Fred Segal Beauty. Santa Monica's Third Street Promenade, Main Street, and the beach are all just steps away. $$$ 1819 Ocean Ave. (Pico Blvd.), 310-260-7500 / 800-670-6185, viceroysantamonica.com

W Los Angeles Westwood • Westwood • Modern (258 rms)

While Westwood isn't exactly breaking the hip meters these days, this cyber-age makeover of the old Westwood Marquis is one very chic exception. Hiding behind frosted glass doors on a leafy residential street, the L.A. chapter of Starwood's boutique hotel chain is what those pimply UCLA undergrads guzzling microbrews down the road may aspire to when they land their first expense accounts. Blurring the line between work and play, the W's stylish, modern lobby is also its living room, filled with funky chairs, cozy couches, stocked bookshelves, and W-brand board games. On weekends, this open area becomes a nerve center for the stylin' crowd over at the bar and the suave Latin restaurant, Mojo. Two hundred fifty-eight large one- and two-bedroom suites are fitted with cozy sofas, custom-designed African wood furnishings, and Westin Heavenly beds. They also come wired for high-speed internet and offer a full entertainment system with 24-hour access to the hotel's extensive CD and video library. If you need a printer, scanner, fax machine, Dodger tickets, or anything else, W's Whatever/Whenever desk is at the ready. Add two outdoor pools, a fitness center, and the full-service AWAY Spa—and suddenly this corner of Westwood is where it's at. Two Wonderful suites are located on the hotel's rarified penthouse floor (room numbers 17 and 8) overlooking the Wilshire Corridor. $$$ 930 Hilgard Ave. (Le Conte Ave.), 310-208-8765 / 888-625-4988, whotels.com

Hip Los Angeles:
The Restaurants

Alcove Cafe & Bakery • Los Feliz • Cafe/Bakery
This fairly recent addition to the Los Feliz scene has quickly become a neighbor-hood institution—mostly because of its gracious brick patio that wraps around for lots of private nooks and crannies. It attracts industry worker bees, hip moms with strollers, actors, and anyone who wants breakfast ... at two in the afternoon. Food, from sandwiches to dinner items and even a nice wine list, is ordered at the count-er. It's good—but not great, with the exception of excellent cakes. This place's big draw is atmosphere—if you're not that hungry but need an excuse to people-watch, order a pastry and a cup of coffee and take your seat out in the California sunshine. *Mon-Wed 6am-11pm, Thu-Sat 6am-midnight, Sun 7am-11pm.* $ ≣ 1929 Hillhurst Ave. (Franklin Ave.), 323-644-0100, alcovecafe.com

Alegria on Sunset • Silver Lake • Mexican
Far better than its strip mall location would indicate, this family kitchen is the place to go for wonderful Mexican food that brings back your childhood—if you grew up in Oaxaca. The single nod to the aging boho Silver Lake crowd that flocks here is a vegetarian burrito—which comes with chicken or steak if you want to bend the rules. Otherwise, go for the best sellers: tacos a la crema, tacos de pescado, or a carne asada burrito stuffed with lemon-marinated grilled skirt steak, rice, cilantro, and refried beans. When owner and chef Nadine Trujillo's mole sauce is bubbling in the back, you should at the very least order some on the side. *Mon-Thu 10am-10pm, Fri-Sat 10am-11pm.* $ ≣ 3510 W. Sunset Blvd. (Golden Gare Ave.), 323-913-1422, alegriaonsunset.com

Beacon • Culver City • Asian Fusion
Chef Kazuto Matsusaka spent a lot of time in other people's kitchens—includ-ing Wolfgang Puck's Chinois on Main for eight years—before finally opening Beacon, a high-ceilinged Asian cafe in the old Helms Bakery. The menu is all over the place—soy-glazed burger and a Rice Krispies sundae, anyone?—but when Beacon opened in early 2005, *Los Angeles* magazine called it the best restaurant in Los Angeles, and a crowd of chic young-to-old Culver City denizens began pouring in. No wonder the seats at the bar fill up lightning-fast. The servers can be a bit scattered, but as long as they keep bringing those small plates of sashimi, noodles, and maki rolls, you'll be just fine. *Mon-Sat 11:30am-2pm; Tue-Wed 5:30-9pm, Thu-Sat 5:30-10pm, Sun 5:30-9pm.* $ Ⓑ≣ 3280 Helms Ave. (Washington Blvd.), 310-838-7500, beacon-la.com

BLD • Los Angeles • American
BLD stands for breakfast, lunch, and dinner—so you'll find mid-city's most stylish set noshing here at every meal. They sit on red leather stools at the bar, or tuck into blond wood tables to enjoy New American comfort food with a decidedly California twist—all set in a clean, open, modern coffee shop setting. Menu items include yummy offerings like brioche French toast and Wagyu burgers. *Daily 8am-11pm.* $$ Ⓑ≣ 7450 Beverly Blvd. (Vista St.), 323-930-9744, bldrestaurant.com

The Bowery* • Hollywood • Fusion
Take a trip to the Big Apple at this New York-style bistro with French-American cuisine. See *Hip Nightlife*, p.113, for details. *Mon-Fri noon-2am, Sat-Sun 6pm-2am.* $ ≡ 6268 Sunset Blvd. (Vine St.), 323-465-3400, theboweryhollywood.com

Cha Cha Cha • West Hollywood • Cuban
This Cuban sleeper in West Hollywood recently joined the ranks of this eccentric chainlet (other members are a colorful bungalow in Los Feliz, 656 N. Virgil Ave., and a location down in Long Beach, 762 Pacific Ave.). Mojitos were a bar specialty here long before the whole fad started—lovingly made with real limes squashed with a pestle. A long starter list of spicy Nuevo Latino tapas could serve as a menu on its own. Some of these items, like the sweet-peppery camarones negros, come in generous entree portions too. Steer clear of the jerky-ish jerk pork and opt instead for the succulent chuleta al limon. Or go whole hog with the seafood. *Sun-Thu 5-10pm, Fri-Sat 5-11pm.* $ ≡ 7953 Santa Monica Blvd. (N. Hayworth Ave.), 323-848-7700, theoriginalchachacha.com

Ciudad* • Downtown • Latin
Started by Mary Sue Milliken and Susan Feniger, aka Too Hot Tamales—their nickname, not ours—Ciudad in Downtown hosts a buzzy crowd of young professionals during weekday lunch and on Friday evenings, when a tired workforce somehow finds the strength to lift mojitos and caipirinhas while talking about anything but work. Yellow walls and modernist art play backdrop to the Pan-Latin menu, which covers a great variety of South American countries, from Brazil (seafood stew) to Argentina (empanadas) to Bolivia (sweet corn tamales). On Sundays, the burgeoning Downtown populace flocks here for the tapas menu and Spanish wines by the glass. If you have tickets to an event at Staples Center or a concert in the Walt Disney Music Hall, Ciudad offers free shuttle service, so drink up. *Mon-Fri 11:30am-2:45pm, Sun-Tue 5-9pm, Wed-Thu 5-10pm, Fri-Sat 5-11pm.* $$ ≡ 445 S. Figueroa St. (Fifth St.), 213-486-5171, ciudad-la.com

Cobras & Matadors • Los Feliz • Spanish
Before the arrival of this smart addition to Hollywood Boulevard in Los Feliz, anyone craving Spanish tapas around here usually had to settle for linguini primavera or a ticket to Barcelona. You'll want to make advance reservations at this lively little hive because, as it turns out, lots of people like the idea of drinking Malvasia and nibbling on mini-plates of grilled octopus and patatas fritas in a charming little cafe with a wood-burning oven. It draws a steady crowd of hip, low-pretension locals who come in groups and as couples for a fun night out. Start by sampling some of the 25 or so tasty tapas selections and move on to the bigger plates—for instance, Catalan-style Cornish game hen or skirt steak. Save room for crema caramela. A handful of outdoor tables are first-come, first-served—but someone's usually come first. There's also a branch at 7615 Beverly Blvd., but it's BYOB, so purchase one from the connected wine shop. *Sun-Thu 6-11pm, Fri-Sat 6pm-midnight.* $ B≡ 4655 Hollywood Blvd. (N. Vermont Ave.), 323-669-3922

Duke's Malibu* • Malibu • American
Surfing memorabilia and Polynesian thatching decorate this busy oceanfront satellite of a popular Hawaiian restaurant chain. The fish is fresh (if best suited to tacos), the mai tais at the Barefoot Bar are rum-soaked (and cheap on

Fridays), and the servers are chipper surfer dudes and babes. But the best thing here is the location. The views through 300 feet of picture windows are some of the most beautiful on the Malibu coast. The patio is a dream at sunset and gets sprayed at high tide. And the parking lot, of course, is full. *Mon-Thu 11:30am-9pm, Fri-Sat 11:30am-9:30pm, Sun 10am-9pm.* $$ B= 21150 Pacific Coast Hwy. (Las Flores Canyon Rd.), 310-317-0777, dukesmalibu.com

Dusty's Bistro • Silver Lake • American
There are essentially two sections to Dusty's. The banquette seating on the brighter left side has a community feel, and across from that sit large but cozy booths of green corduroy and brown leather where conspiracies might be hatched if everyone wasn't busy talking about their screenplays. Three meals and a varied menu of pasta, steak, and seafood are served to a very hip, very industry clientele—this is Silver Lake, after all. Weekends are the optimal time for dinner and an adventurous trip through the wine list, which will have something you've never tried ... maybe a South African petit chenin blanc or ice wine from Quebec? *Sun-Thu 8pm-midnight, Fri-Sat 8pm-1am.* $$$ B= 3200 W. Sunset Blvd. (Descanso Dr.), 323-906-1018, dustysbistro.com

El Guapo Mexican Cantina* • Los Angeles • Mexican
This is a sports bar and Mexican cantina mix, with an open interior floor plan centered around a bar, and an outdoor deck. See *Hip Nightlife*, p.114, for details. *Sun-Thu 11:30am-midnight, Fri-Sat 9am-2am.* $ ⊟ 7250 Melrose Ave. (Alta Vista Blvd.), 323-297-0471, elguapocantina.com

Father's Office* • Santa Monica • American
This lively upscale pub on tony Montana Avenue starts up at 5pm every night, but at 4:45pm an eclectic crowd of industry folk, Westside hipsters, and web entrepreneurs pretends to be disinterested while waiting on the sidewalk for Father's Office to open. People come for the beer list, which ranges geographically from Quebec to Alaska to Belgium, as well as the Office Burger—perhaps the best in the city—made with dry aged beef and topped with caramelized onions, applewood bacon compote, Gruyère, Maytag blue cheese, and arugula. Like the rest of the dishes, the burger's ingredients are nonnegotiable. The menu reads: "No substitutions, modifications, alterations, or deletions." And you wouldn't want to make any. *Mon-Wed 5-10pm, Thu 5-11pm, Fri 4-11pm, Sat 3-11pm, Sun 3-10pm; Bar: Mon-Thu 5pm-1am, Fri 4pm-2am, Sat 3pm-2am, Sun 3pm-midnight.* $$ ≡ 1018 Montana Ave. (Tenth St.), 310-393-2337, fathersoffice.com

Ford's Filling Station • Culver City • American
Harrison Ford's son Ben is the chef and owner at Ford's Filling Station, but the real star is his tasty American-pub food like fried Ipswich clams, flatbread pizzas, burgers, panini, and a selection of cured meats—Serrano ham, copa, prosciutto, bresaola—that dominate the left side of the menu. The brick-walled space has sumptuous rugs, a fireplace, and lots of polished surfaces, making it a high-tech version of that loft apartment you dreamed about but never got around to owning. Make reservations, because this place is jumping, particularly during lunch, when industry folk from the nearby studios come here en masse. Side-patio dining is an option, but the inside tables are where the real action is. *Mon-Fri 11am-11pm, Sat 5-11pm.* $$ B= 9531 Culver Blvd. (Washington Blvd.), 310-202-1470, fordsfillingstation.net

410 Boyd • Downtown • American

Live slightly on the edge by venturing into a mildly intimidating pocket of Downtown and reward your palate at this cool New American bistro. Highlights include the grilled ahi club sandwich, blackened chicken salad, an assortment of excellent pasta dishes, and the signature one-pound gorgonzola-crusted New York steak. The lively art bar scene here feels about as New York as Downtown L.A. gets, with revolving local art exhibits to boot. You'll find a mix of Downtown (an eclectic and adventurous lot) and white-collar types from the courthouses, government buildings, and law offices. *Mon-Fri 11am-midnight, Sat 4pm-midnight.* $$ B≡ 410 Boyd St. (San Pedro St.), 213-617-2491

Fred 62 • Los Feliz • American

Depending on which side of Hollywood they happen to be on, L.A.'s proverbial crowds of struggling actors, writers, drummers, and anyone else looking for a better agent or band can be found eating (or serving) upscale diner fare at either Swingers (8020 Beverly Blvd., 323-653-5858) or this 24-hour scene in Los Feliz. The food is adequate—with burgers being a draw. More important, ham on rye is called a "Charles Bukowski," Poptarts are homemade, eggs can be scrambled with tofu, the noodles are soba, and the retro-green ambience includes a toaster at every table and a Pachinko machine in the restroom. Meat loaf and Raisin Bran never tasted so L.A. *24/7.* $ ≡ 1850 N. Vermont Ave. (Russell St.), 323-667-0062, fred62.com

Gingergrass • Silver Lake • Vietnamese

Gingergrass gets a rather eclectic clientele at lunch, but in the evening a younger, hipper crowd gathers for some of the cheapest appetizers in the city. Reservations aren't taken, but just give the hostess your cell phone number and have a glass of something across the street at Silver Lake Wine. (You'll be called soon enough.) Once you do get seated, try a noodle bowl with beef, chicken, tofu, or pork, then follow it up with the fried banana spring rolls for dessert. It all washes down nicely with a glass of ginger limeade. *Sun-Thu 11:30am-3pm, 5-10pm, Fri-Sat 11:30am-3pm, 5-10:30pm.* $$ ≡ 2396 Glendale Blvd. (Brier Ave.), 323-644-1600, gingergrass.com

House of Blues* • Los Angeles • Southern

Dine on authentic Cajun and Creole cuisine at The Porch Restaurant upstairs and come for the Sunday gospel brunch. See *Hip Nightlife,* p.115, for details. *Nightly 5:30-10pm, bar until 2am.* $$ ≡ 8430 Sunset Blvd. (Kings Rd.), 323-848-5100, hob.com

The Hungry Cat • Hollywood • Seafood

Best Seafood Occupying a smallish space set in the new mixed-use Sunset & Vine complex, The Hungry Cat is a lively modernist restaurant with the soul of an East Coast seafood shack. After downing a dozen oysters, move on to the "Pride of Baltimore" crab cake or the lobster roll, two of the signature dishes of chef David Lentz. Drinks made with fresh-squeezed, seasonal juices are a big hit with the industry types and fashionistas who use The Hungry Cat as a launching pad to one of nightlife spots within walking distance. If it's too loud, you can always request a table on the patio, but don't show up here without a reservation. *Tue-Fri 11:30am-2:30pm, Mon-Sat 5:30pm-midnight, Sun 11am-3pm and 5-10pm.* $$ B≡ 1535 N. Vine St. (Sunset Blvd.), 323-462-2155, thehungrycat.com

Jar • Los Angeles • American

It's hard to say upscale Jar has "updated" its look with its recent redo, since it went from a modern interior with pastels to walnut-colored walls and a 1940s supper club feel, but it is a more appropriate setting for the pot roasts, Kansas City steaks, and other comfort meats chef Suzanne Tracht prepares for an upscale, sophisticated crowd. A good night to stop by is Monday, when visiting celebrity chef Nancy Silverton puts her special spin on mozzarella cheese dishes. Reservations are accepted one month in advance, and for good reason. The place is usually packed. Be warned—this room can get very loud, no matter where you are sitting. *Sun 10am-2pm; Sun-Tue 5:30-10pm, Wed-Sat 5:30-11pm.* $$$ Ⓑ≡ 8225 Beverly Blvd. (Harper Ave.), 323-655-6566, thejar.com

Joe's Restaurant • Venice Beach • American

There was no dining scene in Venice Beach before Joe Miller opened his self-named restaurant in the early '90s. Pretenders have come and gone, but this is still the place to go for well-prepared fish, a lively brunch, and a prix fixe lunch that is considered one of the best deals in town. Joe's has become a symbol of the Venice Beach good life, and its loyal mix of artsy folks and sophisticates guarantees that reservations are hard to come by. But keep trying. *Tue-Fri noon-2:30pm, Sat-Sun 11am-2:30pm; Tue-Thu, Sun 6-10pm, Fri-Sat 6-11pm.* $$ Ⓑ≡ 1023 Abbot Kinney Blvd. (Broadway St.), 310-399-5811, joesrestaurant.com

Jones Hollywood* • West Hollywood • Italian

The main event at this industry hangout near the Warner Hollywood lot is the youngish crowd flirting at the bar and ordering cocktails named after rock stars (like Sid Vicious) who'd probably never drink here—but you never really know at a place like this. Usually seated at secluded booths in the surrounding dining room is a more eclectic crowd that, on one night, included a couple of local TV news anchors and Vegas's Siegfried Fischbacher. Thin-crust pizzas, vegetarian spring rolls, ahi sandwiches, wasabi mashed potatoes, and other smart comfort foods are served until 1:30am. *Daily noon-2am.* $ Ⓑ≡ 7205 Santa Monica Blvd. (Formosa Ave.), 323-850-1726

Kate Mantilini • Beverly Hills • American

Before Beverly Hills gets out of bed and long after it lies back down, this stylish neighborhood diner is wide awake, serving reliably tasty upscale breakfasts, salads, pastas, and sandwiches to the town's movers and shakers. The famous calves' brains have recently been pulled from the menu, either in honor of regular lunch guest Billy Wilder's passing or because he was the only one who ordered them. Highlights include seared ahi medallions, a perfect chicken breast sandwich with basil and aioli, and the turkey Cobb—and regular celebrity sightings. *Mon 7:30am-midnight, Tue-Thu 7:30am-1am, Fri 7:30am-2am, Sat 11am-2am, Sun 10am-midnight.* $$ Ⓑ≡ 9101 Wilshire Blvd. (Doheny Dr.), 310-278-3699

King's Road Cafe • Los Angeles • American

A super-strong bowl of coffee perked with espresso beans is the most popular item on the menu, best digested with an omelet, pancakes, or breakfast risotto in the am, or with an assortment of salads and gourmet sandwiches in the pm. The best time to be at this always-trendy corner cafe is during packed weekend brunch hours when at least a few sunny sidewalk tables are occupied by TV or movie personalities whose faces you recognize. *Mon-Sat 7:30am-10pm, Sun 6:30am-7pm.* $ ▣ 8361 Beverly Blvd. (King's Rd.), 323-655-9044, kingsroadcafe.com

Le Velvet Margarita Cantina* • Hollywood • Mexican
The award-winning, calorie-conscious yet authentic menu consists of cantina classics made from traditional family recipes. *See Hip Nightlife, p.116, for details. Mon-Thu 11am-12:30am, Fri 11am-2am, Sat 6pm-2am, Sun 6pm-12:30am.* $$ ▣ 1612 Cahuenga Blvd. (Hollywood Blvd.), 323-469-2000, velvetmargarita.com

Madame Matisse • Silver Lake • French
Paris meets Silver Lake at this sweet ten-table sidewalk cafe run by a classically trained French chef. Fresh-squeezed juices and custom-made omelets satisfy a local clientele accustomed to eating its first meal at around 3pm. The lunch menu includes a variety of salads, pastas, and sandwiches. On weekend evenings, out comes the coq au vin and steak au poivre and the place moonlights as a charming French bistro—but be sure to bring your own wine. *Thu-Sat 7:30am-3:30pm, 5-9:30pm, Sun-Tue 7:30am-3:30pm.* $ ▣ 3536 W. Sunset Blvd. (Maltman Ave.), 323-662-4862

Magnolia* • Hollywood • American
Just down the street from the famed intersection of Hollywood and Vine, Magnolia is where older people can go to feel not middle-aged again. For the crowd of mostly 20-somethings, carefully coiffed bedhead is the reigning hairdo. The late-night menu has more comfort food than the dinner menu, which offers everything from Asian-inspired dishes to grilled artichoke to arugula salad. It's a young person's place run by young people, but with Bowie and The Ramones playing on the sound system, you don't have to be 25 to feel young and hip here. The front room is the loudest (and trendiest), but the second room has two sought-after corner booths, and the back patio offers the most quiet—and the option of smoking. *Daily 11am-2am.* $$ B▣ 6266½ W. Sunset Blvd. (Argyle Ave.), 323-467-0660, magnoliahollywood.com

Memphis* • Hollywood • Southern
Memphis is set about 50 yards back from Hollywood Boulevard, but it's more like 2,000 miles away. While you're here, forget the word "fusion." This menu isn't Southern-inspired, it's Southern. When you order fried chicken and mashed potatoes, you get fried chicken and mashed potatoes. When you order macaroni and cheese, you get macaroni and cheese. Set in a historic Queen Anne, Dutch Colonial Revival home, Memphis has large, chintz-covered armchairs—squeezing is required to get to your table—blood-red silk walls, and New Orleans jazz playing in the background. You almost think you're in the South, except for the sightings of celebs and hangers-on that remind you exactly where you are. *Nightly 6-11pm, bar until 2am.* $$ B▣ 6541 Hollywood Blvd. (Hudson Ave.), 323-465-8600, memphishollywood.com

Michelangelo's Pizzeria Ristorante • Silver Lake • Italian
The second you walk into the tiny but stylish Italian joint on Silver Lake's trendiest street, you'll be treated like a regular by the family of owners. About a dozen simple wood tables, some with banquettes along the wall, are filled with a strictly-local clientele, which around here means a casually hip set, some with kids,

HIP

some on dates. Out front are a half-dozen tables on the sidewalk, tucked amid potted plants and little white lights. The menu covers territory from chicken marsala to pastas to pizza—but the spaghetti and meatballs is an absolute standout. The wine list isn't great, but it does the trick, and you can always bring your own bottle. *Mon-Sat 11:30am-2pm, 5:30-10pm.* $ ▤ 1637 Silver Lake Blvd. (Effie St.), 323-660-4843

Newsroom Café • West Hollywood • American/Vegetarian

While folks across the street at The Ivy (see *Hot & Cool Restaurants,* p.69) invest in their fancy-pants salads and bisque, you can read a magazine, open a laptop, and take a seat at this tasty and healthy lunch scene featuring Indonesian gado gado, grilled vegetable chop-chop, smoked tofu with mixed organic field greens, and—our personal favorite—homemade soup in a big ol' multigrain bread bowl. While the menu takes its health consciousness seriously enough to include several vegan items and a message right at the top to "stop poisoning your body with bad food," it's not all about organic oatmeal, wheatgrass, and basmati rice pudding here. The Newsroom's smart menu includes lots of "fun" stuff for people without yoga mats too—think grilled ahi burger, house-smoked chicken quesadilla, spicy noodles diablo, and a chocolate espresso brownie served with cappuccino crunch ice cream. It would be wrong not to mention the fire-grilled artichoke appetizer, which is simple and great. Lunch can be a wait, and midday reservations aren't taken, so prepare to put your name on the list and browse the restaurant's in-house magazine rack for awhile. *Mon-Thu 8am-9pm, Fri 8am-10pm, Sat 9am-10pm, Sun 9am-9pm.* $ B▤ 120 N. Robertson Blvd. (Beverly Blvd.), 310-652-4444

Nyala • Los Angeles • Ethiopian

Using your hands as utensils can lighten any mood, making this exotic restaurant on a commercial strip of Fairfax Avenue (aka Little Ethiopia) the perfect place for gatherings from group dinners to first dates. Amidst African music and earthy colors, diners eat family style on a single plate, using a piece of injera (pancake) to smother, pinch, and lift—this is the only workable method—your citrusy chunks of marinated chicken, sautéed beef, and split pea dishes. Order an African beer or wine to complete the effect. *Mon-Sat 11:30am-10:30pm, Sun noon-10:30pm.* $ B▤ 1076 S. Fairfax Ave. (Whitworth Dr.), 323-936-5918, nyala-la.com

Palms Thai • Hollywood • Thai

Palms Thai recently moved from its Thai Town location on Hollywood Boulevard to a larger, strip-mallish spot about seven blocks east. For that you can blame Thai Elvis. Groups of Thai families, Hollywood hipsters, and LAPD officers share community tables and chow down on green curry with tofu and frog with pepper and garlic while the coiffed Asian look-alike—sort of—sings subdued versions of "Love Me Tender" and "Return to Sender." The über-spicy food at Palms Thai is well regarded but often takes a back seat when the jumpsuit-wearing King is performing, which happens at 7:30pm and 10pm from Wednesday to Sunday. *Mon-Thu 11am-midnight, Fri-Sat 11am-1:30am.* $ ▯▤ 5900 Hollywood Blvd., Suite B (Bronson St.), 323-462-5073, palmsthai.com

Primitivo Wine Bistro • Venice Beach • Spanish

At Primitivo Wine Bistro you can't just walk in and start ordering pinot grigios left and right. Without reservations, the wait might be an hour or more before you're noshing on a Mediterranean-inspired menu of hot and cold tapas dishes like the foie gras sandwich, bacon-wrapped Medjool dates, and selection of artisanal cheeses amongst an upscale crowd of artists, hipsters, and any other bohemian types who actually have jobs. The most sought-after tables are on the patio, where Primitivo's atmosphere is at its most festive, a mood helped along with a wine-by-the-glass selection covering the four corners of the globe. *Mon-Fri noon-2:30pm, Sun-Thu 5:30-10:30pm, Fri-Sat 5:30pm-midnight.* $$ B☰ 1025 Abbot Kinney Blvd. (Broadway St.), 310-396-5353, primitivowinebistro.com

R-23 • Downtown • Japanese

The hard part's over once you actually find this hip sushi hideaway tucked into a stylishly converted warehouse between Little Tokyo and the L.A. River, in what looks like a semi-deserted alley. Have a seat in a corrugated cardboard chair (designed by Frank Gehry) and feast on some of the best raw fish in the city. Other winning dishes from a long list of chef's specials include Dungeness crab salad, lobster tempura, grilled yellowtail collar, steamed bay scallops, and for vegetarians, a dish of sautéed shimeji mushroom with chili peppers. The scene here is as good as the food—hipsters mingle with in-the-know lawyers and other white-collar types at lunch, while at dinner, it's the stylish loft-dwelling locals who take over. *Mon-Fri 11:30am-2pm, Mon-Sat 5:30-10pm.* $$ ☰ 923 E. Second St. (Garey St.), 213-687-7178, r23.com

Sanamluang Café • Hollywood • Thai

Best Late-Night Eats This late-night Thai stop has been adopted by just about everyone in this East Hollywood neighborhood. Sanamluang is a bright, decor-less place, but it will feed you steaming noodle dishes and savory curries well after the bars in Hollywood and Silver Lake have squeezed out all their guests. Start with a big plastic cup full of sweet Thai iced tea and make it easy on yourself: Just say "General's Noodles, please." *Daily 10:30am-2am.* $ ☰ 5176 Hollywood Blvd. (Kingsley Dr.), 323-660-8006

Social Hollywood* • Hollywood • American

Best Trendy Tables The neighborhood's cool quotient has risen with this ultrahip restaurant in the historic Hollywood Athletic Club building, home to a former men's club that included founding members Charlie Chaplin and Cecil B. DeMille. It was host of the first Emmy Awards in 1949, and the place where Jean Harlow reportedly showed up wearing only a fur coat after being stood up by Errol Flynn. A new generation of Hollywood stars is now showing up—mostly clothed—with some heading straight to the invite-only Green Room on the second floor. But the huge main dining room with Moroccan architectural details is still a delightfully trendy scene. The eclectic cuisine, which runs the gamut from foie gras to Turks & Caicos conch, may not measure up to the surroundings, but what could? This is Hollywood history, and you're sitting in the middle of it. *Sun-Wed 6-11pm, Thu-Sat 6pm-1am; bar until 2am.* $$$ ☰ 6525 W. Sunset Blvd. (Schrader Blvd.), 323-462-5222, socialhollywood.com

Soot Bull Jeep • Koreatown • Korean

Decor is beside the point at this smoky, bustling Korean barbecue joint in the middle of Koreatown that ranks right up there with the city's tastiest food. Meats are cooked on a real grill over mesquite at your table, and the waitress makes sure that the myriad extras—three sides of kimchi, sesame spinach, garlic, and so on—come pronto. If you seem unsure while ordering, the waitress will point to the spencer steak, which she will throw on the grill and turn from time to time, unless she sees you ably manning the cooking tongs yourself. There are some tasty red-meat alternatives, including chicken and shrimp, or, if you're feeling adventurous, which might be the reason you came here in the first place, the octopus. Don't miss the soju—Korean wine. *Daily 11am-11pm.* $$$ ≡ 3136 W. Eighth St. (S. Catalina St.), 213-387-3865

Sushi Katsu-ya • Studio City • Japanese
Best Sushi While some sushi chefs insist on simplicity, Katsu-ya on Studio City's "sushi row" prefers to tempt your eyes as well as your tummy. The results are so stellar that crowds of stylish foodies cross into the valley for a taste. Menu items like salmon caviar sashimi and the spicy tuna plate are so photogenic, diners take pictures of them to post on their blogs. The decor is underwhelming, but so what? When the food tastes as good as it looks, interior design is a Katsu-ya customer's last concern. *Mon-Thu 11:30am-2:30pm, 5:30-10pm, Fri-Sat 5:30-10:30pm, Sun 5:30-9:30pm.* $$$ ≡ 11680 Ventura Blvd. (Colfax Ave.), 818-985-6976

Sushi Sasabune • Brentwood • Sushi
Signs telling you Sushi Sasabune does not serve California rolls or spicy tuna rolls almost make you feel guilty for having enjoyed them so often in the past. If you're a first-timer, sit at the counter and say "omakase," which allows chef Nobi Kusuhara to take you on a journey of redemption that includes impossibly fresh albacore tuna, maybe some toro, a little halibut, and perhaps some butter fish. To chef Kusuhara, timing is everything, and that extends to the warm rice that has been cooked only in the last 30 or 40 minutes (it will collapse in your hands, which is why you should use chopsticks). And just when you've had your fill, omakase time is over. *Mon-Fri noon-2pm, 5:30-9:30pm.* $$$$ B≡ 12400 Wilshire Blvd., Suite 150 (S. Carmelina Ave.), 310-820-3596

Toast • Los Angeles • American
For some reason, this perfectly good corner on busy Third Street has housed a few failed cafe attempts in the last several years. Then along comes Toast—the neighborhood's latest breakfast and lunch hot spot—with the winning combination of good food and better style. Is it the cool name? Are the coffees, pastries, waffles, eggs, granola, soups, salads, wraps, melts, quesadillas, and burgers really that much better this time around? Whatever the reason, brunch-seeking herds of 20-something fashionistas and entertainment industry up-and-comers now come in droves. *Daily 7:30am-11:30pm.* $ ≡ 8221 W. Third St. (Harper Ave.), 323-655-5018, toastbakerycafe.com

25 Degrees • Hollywood • American
Named for the difference in cooking temperatures between well-done and medium rare, this build-your-own burger bar is situated in the Roosevelt Hotel, which has become a hot spot for the young, sleek Hollywood crowd, many of whom come here after a night of partying at nearby clubs. Don't mind the fuschia wallpaper, which seems a bit out of place, even for a joint where you choose among ten artisanal cheeses with names like Big Woods Blue and Straus Family Jack. Try the 25 Degrees Red Ale microbrew or one of 50 half-bottles of wine. Or go old school with an egg cream, a whipped root beer, or a rhubarb "dry soda," just

like Grandpa used to do. *Mon-Wed 11:30am-1am, Thu-Sat 11:30am-3am, Sun 11:30am-10pm.* $ B≡ Hollywood Roosevelt Hotel, 7000 Hollywood Blvd. (Orange Dr.), 323-785-7244, 25degreesrestaurant.com

24/7 Restaurant at the Standard • West Hollywood • American
Standard guests and non-guests (it's often hard to tell the difference at this place) converge at the hotel's groovy all-hours staple eatery, featuring separate breakfast, lunch, dinner, weekend brunch, and "overnight" (midnight-6am) menus. An eclectic array of midday favorites includes yellowtail carpaccio, Japanese sweet potato soup, and oysters-on-the-half-shell appetizers, a free-range chicken club, "Moroccan" pizza with caramelized onions, merguez, and goat cheese, and an organic omelet. *24/7.* $ ≡ The Standard Hollywood, 8300 W. Sunset Blvd. (N. Sweetzer Ave.), 323-650-9090, standardhotel.com

Vermont • Los Feliz • American
Here's some tasty proof that Los Feliz is no longer monopolized by hip over-priced diners and aging supper clubs. A pair of talented first-time restaurant owners are behind this sophisticated New American favorite. Poached salmon, tender short ribs, roasted chicken, a mountain of fresh mussels, and filet mignon with blue cheese potato gratin are a few staples on the revolving menu. The flourless chocolate cake and old-style vanilla custard with caramel sauce are equally lauded. Tasteful modern decor is embellished with white columns, vaulted ceilings, and a lovely picture window looking out onto the restaurant's namesake street. Adding to the atmosphere is a slick lounge next door. *Mon-Fri 11:30am-3pm, Sun-Thu 5:30-10pm, Fri-Sat 5:30-11:30pm.* $$ B≡ 1714 N. Vermont Ave. (Prospect Ave.), 323-661-6163, vermontrestaurantonline.com

HIP

Hip Los Angeles:
The Nightlife

Acme Comedy Theatre • Los Angeles • Comedy

In L.A.'s ragtag world of sketch comedy, this perfectly nice 99-seat theater is the equivalent of Carnegie Hall. The highly acclaimed Acme Players and an emerging school of talented improv performers strut their twisted stuff on this inventive and always funny stage. One night's demented fare included a sketch centered on the ramblings of a fingerless shop teacher facing his first sex education class. *Fri-Sat 8pm and 10:30pm, Sun 7:30pm.* C≣ 135 N. La Brea Ave. (First St.), 323-525-0202, acmecomedy.com

Actors' Gang Theater • Culver City • Theater

One of the city's longest-running theater ensembles has collected more than 100 awards for its daring interpretations of classic plays and equally bold, politically charged new material—from a coproduction of Eric Bogosian's *Suburbia* to the recent in-house hit, *Bat Boy: The Musical*. Board members include actors Giancarlo Esposito and founding member and artistic director Tim Robbins. C≣ 9070 Venice Blvd. (Culver), 310-838-4264, theactorsgang.com

Ahmanson Theatre • Downtown • Theater

After a four-year-run of *Phantom of the Opera* in the early '90s, the Ahmanson formally apologized with a $17.1 million renovation and a grand reopening with Bernstein's *Candide*. A mix of big-name dramas and musical imports as well as productions from the resident Center Theater Group are presented in this large space, seating up to 2,000 people. Sight lines and acoustics have been improved, but it's still best to avoid the back half of the room. C≣ 135 N. Grand Ave. (Temple St.), 213-628-2772, taperahmanon.com

The Bar • Hollywood • Dive Bar

Best Dive Bars Known simply as The Bar, this secret Hollywood hideaway is a neighborhood favorite among local hipsters. The narrow, yellow-tinted interior is dark, yet inviting with its rich brown color scheme, sconce lamps, high ceilings and comfy wall-lined booths. Nightly DJs (including Frodo himself—Elijah Wood) mix everything from the Who to Madonna, while a crowd of indie intellectuals sporting vintage band T-shirts and meticulously messed-up hairdos sing and dance to their flashback favorites. It's a rock 'n' roll joint, so the cocktails are stiff, last call is late, the music is loud, and the bartenders are usually the hottest chicks in the place. Poor ventilation inside makes the expanded, bamboo-lined back patio a breath of fresh air. *Nightly 8pm-2am.* ≣ 5851 Sunset Blvd. (Bronson St.), 323-468-9154

Beauty Bar • Hollywood • Theme Bar

Let your hair down at this kitschy-cool beauty "saloon" along the Cahuenga Corridor. Owner Paul Devitt's chain of glamour bars (New York, San Francisco, Las Vegas, San Diego) doesn't fit into any conventional category, much like the MySpace generation of indie rockers it attracts. The retrofitted '60s salon interior is a pink and white pastiche of chrome-dome hair dryers, tile floors, vanity mirrors, and a vintage photo booth. The pasty-faced, tattooed crowd consists of

SuicideGirls, floppy-haired aspiring artists, and Hollywood bar hoppers. Celebrity DJs from the Yeah Yeah Yeahs, Interpol, and the Moving Units spin a flash-forward mix of NWA, Blur, and the Rolling Stones. Early birds come out for the $10 martini and manicure happy hour (Thu-Sat 6-11pm), where you can sip on specialty drinks like the Platinum Blonde while getting your nails done. *Sun-Wed 9pm-2am, Thu-Sat 6pm-2am.* ▤ 1638 N. Cahuenga Ave. (Hollywood Blvd.), 323-464-7676, beautybar.com

The Bigfoot Lodge • Atwater Village • Dive Bar

"Rough it" in the Eastside's kitschiest drinking scene—a forest theme complete with logs and owls. Order a Toasted Marshmallow (Stoli vanilla, butterscotch liqueur, Frangelico, half and half, and an ignited Bacardi-dipped marshmallow) or a Girl Scout Cookie (crème de menthe, Irish Cream, half and half) in this fake-log barn of a bar favored by the wallet-chain crowd and decorated with stuffed rodents and forest fire messages. Camping was never this fun. *Nightly 5pm-2am.* ▤ 3172 Los Feliz Blvd. (Glen Feliz Blvd.), 323-662-9227, bigfootlodge.com

The Bowery* • Hollywood • Bar/Restaurant

Best Date Spots This New York–style bar and bistro takes a bite out of Big Apple charm and chutzpah. This gutsy little Sunset Strip hang is more metropolitan than cosmopolitan. With black and white checkered subway tile walls, tin ceiling, wall-mounted booths, and an oversized chalkboard announcing the daily specials, it feels straight out of Lower East Side Manhattan. The democratic first-come, first-served seating policy make it the perfect place to catch a bite or a buzz before heading to the nearby Arclight Cinemas or the Cahuenga Corridor a block away. The Bowery Burger headlines a moderately priced French-American lunch and dinner menu that's both filling and flavorful. The cozy, cramped neighborhood feel and impressive bar attract a chic clientele that knows a good trend when it sees one. *Mon-Fri noon-2am, Sat-Sun 6pm-2am.* ▤ 6268 Sunset Blvd. (Vine St.), 323-465-3400, thebowryhollywood.com

The Brig • Venice • Bar

Cruisin' for a boozin'? Make a pit stop at this Venice landmark that dates back to the 1950s. A major makeover has transformed it from a washed-up dive bar to a contempo cool lounge. The revamped Art Deco design brings a cutting-edge look while retaining its endless-summer sensibility. A retractable garage-door front converts the narrow interior into an open-air affair, while the bustling pool table is the center of attention. Smooth, down-tempo grooves set a laid-back, unpretentious tone as the suntanned and sandaled talk surf and turf. On weekends, the limited space gets packed tighter than a *Baywatch* bikini, so come early and claim your spot. *Nightly 6pm-2am.* ▤ 1515 Abbot Kinney Blvd. (Palms Blvd.), 310-399-7537, thebrig.com

Ciudad* • Downtown • Restaurant/Bar

A spicy bar scene heats up after work and on Sunday nights at this Cuban favorite. *See Hip Restaurants, p.103, for details. Mon-Fri 11:30am-2:45pm, Sun-Tue 5-9pm, Wed-Thu 5-10pm, Fri-Sat 5-11pm.* ▥ 445 S. Figueroa St. (Fifth St.), 213-486-5171, ciudad-la.com

The Derby • Los Feliz • Restaurant/Lounge

The swingin' happy ending of the movie *Swingers* happened right on the dance floor of this '40s-era supper club, launching the '90s fad that's come and gone.

If you miss those Lindy Hop days, The Derby's beautiful brass-railed bar, curtained wood booths, and smooth live bands haven't lost their luster. Nor have the folks on the compact dance floor, who don't need those free swing lessons. The club's Italian-ish menu is from Louise's Trattoria next door. *Nightly 8pm-1:30am.* C≣ 4500 Los Feliz Blvd. (Hillhurst Ave.), 323-663-8979, clubderby.com

The Dresden Room • Los Feliz • Restaurant/Lounge
The last stop on the *Swingers* film location tour is most importantly the home of the inimitable husband-and-wife duo, Marty and Elayne, who've been crooning in this time warp of a lounge six nights a week for the last 23 years. Like a living-and-breathing museum set with its gorgeous bar, tuxedoed drink mixers, Bob Hope *Road* movie–era photos, and creamy white banquettes in the dining area, the Dresden at first seems above the flighty crowd it draws. That thought goes out the window when the Munster-ish house band opens its next set with "Rudolph the Red-Nosed Reindeer" even though it's late May. *Mon-Sat 10am-2am, Sun 4-10pm.* C≣ 1760 N. Vermont Ave. (Melbourne Ave.), 323-665-4294, thedresden.com

Duke's Malibu* • Malibu • Bar
Fresh fish and mai tais are served at a seaside setting. See *Hip Restaurants,* p.103, for details. *Mon-Thu 11:30am-10pm, Fri-Sat 11:30am-10:30pm, Sun 10am-10pm.* ≣ 21150 Pacific Coast Hwy. (Las Flores Canyon Rd.), 310-317-0777, dukesmalibu.com

El Carmen • Los Angeles • Lounge
This stylishly campy cantina with its odd mix of imported Mexican wrestling posters and Asian mushroom lamps is another winning invention from L.A.'s Midas of late-night life, Sean McPherson (Swingers, Jones, Good Luck, Bar Marmont). On weekends (which include Thursdays here), the boxy room is stuffed with a young, attractive crowd of tequila swillers who appreciate the humongous selection of rare brands, until it's time to figure out how the hell to get home. Tacos, guacamole, and other quick Mexican snacks take the edge off. *Mon-Fri 5pm-2am, Sat-Sun 7pm-2am.* C≣ 8138 W. Third St. (Crescent Heights Blvd.), 323-852-1552, committedinc.com

El Coyote Mexican Cafe • Los Angeles • Restaurant/Bar
Some L.A. traditions shouldn't be questioned. One of them is parking yourself at this '30s-era dive, gulping down stiff, cheap margaritas, and delaying the aftershock with plates of lard cleverly disguised as rice, refried beans, and mystery meat rolled in a tortilla and topped with a warm blanket of Day-Glo cheese. If you start seeing Christmas lights and large, frowning waitresses in gaudy folk dresses, you're actually not hallucinating. *Sun-Thu 11am-10pm, Fri-Sat 11am-11pm.* ≣ 7312 Beverly Blvd. (La Brea Ave.), 323-939-2255, elcoyotecafe.com

El Guapo Mexican Cantina* • Los Angeles • Restaurant/Bar
Daytime fun-in-the-sun spot is the ideal location to catch a buzz and the big game. This sparse, yet spirited Melrose place is a sports bar and Mexican cantina halfbreed. The atypical open-spaced interior features a center bar, 20-plus TVs, dining tables, and an indoor deck area overlooking the bustling shopping strip. A breezy outdoor patio in back is a fan favorite during the football season. The extensive margarita menu is more appealing than the gringo-flavored Mexican dishes so satisfy

your inner Chupacabra with a 42-ounce Monster Margarita or the fresh and fruity Sangria. The crowd is a random mix of weary shoppers, jersey wearing jocks, and trendy locals in trucker hats. *Sun-Thu 11:30am-midnight, Fri-Sat 9am-2am.* ⊟ 7250 Melrose Ave. (Alta Vista Blvd.), 323-297-0471, elguapocantina.com

Father's Office* • Santa Monica • American
The beer list spans the globe from Alaska to Belgium at this upscale pub. See *Hip Restaurants*, p.104, for details. *Mon-Thu 5pm-1am, Fri 4pm-2am, Sat 3pm-2am, Sun 3pm-midnight.* ≣ 1018 Montana Ave. (Tenth St.), 310-393-2337, fathersoffice.com

4100 Bar • Silver Lake • Bar
Garnished with flying dragons and a phat candlelit Buddha at the back, the Eastside's hippest new lounge proves that opium-den designs are tough to resist even in this gimmick-cautious part of town. An eclectic bunch of Silver Lakers, straight and gay, come here and leave that other, better-known Far East–themed hot spot (the Good Luck Bar) to trendoids and tourists. *Nightly 8pm-2am.* ©≣ 4100 W. Sunset Blvd. (Manzanita St.), 323-666-4460

Golden Gopher • Downtown • Bar
This Downtown L.A. dig was given a Victorian glam rock makeover by the same nightlife visionaries who lie behind nearby Broadway Bar, Hollywood's Three of Clubs, and Silver Lake's 4100 Bar. The formerly rundown '30s-era speakeasy's first-rate face-lift features deep brown decor, gleaming gold fixtures, sparkling glass chandeliers, plush wraparound couches, and wide panel windows. Gopher lamps, vintage arcade games and an eclectic jukebox blasting everything from the Scissor Sisters to Neil Diamond keep things kickback and kitschy. An alley-like outdoor patio and an in-house take-home liquor store only add to its unique charm. It's become a favorite afterwork spot for 9 to 5 suits and a trendy nighttime spot for loft-dwelling artist types who appreciate the $3 Pabst Blue Ribbons. If you can't find street parking on either side of Eighth, try the Paragon Parking Lot by the rear of the bar on Hill Street for $2. *Tue-Fri 5pm-2am, Sat-Mon 8pm-2am.* ⊟ 417 W. Eighth St. (Olive St.), 213-614-8001, goldengopher.com

Good Luck Bar • Los Feliz • Bar
This trend-setting singles lounge next to a vacuum store in Los Feliz takes the Far East theme about as far as it can go. You'll find just about every clichéd piece of decor here: paper lanterns—check; bamboo stools and dragons on the ceiling—check-check; opium-den–style lounge in the back—check; plus some nifty extras like a last-call gong. After a few Singapore Slings it all somehow works. The house special is The Good Luck—Amaretto, Midori, juice, and milk, served by women with chopsticks in their hair—check. *Sun-Thu 7pm-2am, Fri-Sat 8pm-2am.* ©≣ 1514 Hillhurst Ave. (Hollywood Blvd.), 323-666-3524

House of Blues* • Los Angeles • Live Music
The House that the Blues Brothers built ironically hosts every kind of music but its namesake. Touring hip-hop, pop, reggae, punk, indie, and classic rock tours have been coming through these rustic barnyard doors since the music chain venue broke ground on the Sunset Strip in 1994. The venue's charming Deep South sensibilities, intimate concertgoing experience, and stellar sound system are what keep the crowds coming. Dine on authentic Cajun and Creole cuisine at The Porch

HIP

restaurant upstairs. The Foundation Room is a plush VIP bar often reserved for industry types or private parties. The popular Sunday gospel brunch is a rich, soulful treat for the body and soul. *Nightly 5pm-2am, dinner 5:30-10pm, Sun brunch 10am-1pm.* C≣ 8430 Sunset Blvd. (Kings Rd.), 323-848-5100, hob.com

Ivan Kane's Forty Deuce • Los Angeles • Dive Bar

Best Theme Bars Nightlife auteur Ivan Kane's masterpiece is undoubtedly this back alley burlesque bar that puts the tease back into striptease. This retrofitted speakeasy oozes sensuality with its smoky lighting, plush lounge chairs, and intimate seating. The horseshoe-shaped bar top doubles as a stage for the strutting femme fatales, who slow-strip down to the bump-and-grind beat of a live jazz trio. The Roaring '20s revelry regularly draws A-list voyuerists like Nicole Kidman, Jennifer Aniston, and Sting as well as a cathartic congregation of "behind closed doors" bad girls. The limited space, strict door policy, and expensive drinks make it more of a special occasion destination than a regular hangout, so make a reservation if you plan on going. *Wed-Sat 9pm-2am.* C≣ 5574 Melrose Ave. (Gower St.), 323-465-4242, fortydeuce.com

Jones Hollywood* • West Hollywood • Restaurant/Bar

A youngish, industry-heavy crowd flirts at the bar and orders cocktails named after rock stars. See *Hip Restaurants,* p.106, for details. *Daily noon-2am.* ≣ 7205 Santa Monica Blvd. (Formosa Ave.), 323-850-1726

L'Scorpion* • Hollywood • Theme Bar

Best Theme Bars "The spirit of Mexico" undeservedly gets a bad name, but if done right (not mixed, sipped), tequila drinking doesn't have to result in a needless bar fight, foolish table dance, or nameless morning bedfellow. The nightlife gurus behind nearby Rokbar and Table 8 prove that fact with their tantalizingly fun and smart tequila bar and taqueria. Sconce candlelight, exposed brick, cowhide walls, an elongated bar, wrought-iron chandeliers, and black-laced bar girls give the Latin-Goth decor a sultry, hot, and dangerous feel with mass sex appeal. Rhythmic iPod sounds abound throughout the bustling bar area, while the rear dining lounge through the stone archway offers more private booth seating. The savvy staff will help you navigate through the 160-plus selection of tequilas and mescals that's complemented by an authentic Mexican tapas menu. *Nightly 6pm-2am.* ⊟ 6679 Hollywood Blvd. (Las Palmas Ave.), 323-464-3026, lscorpion.com

Le Velvet Margarita Cantina* • Hollywood • Restaurant/Lounge

Best Theme Bars Cultures clash as American pop meets Mexican pulp. This ultra lounge and restaurant's delightfully devilish, dimly lit interior is straight out of Robert Rodriguez's *From Dusk Till Dawn.* Red velvet booths and leopard print furnishings dot the dining area where strolling mariachi bands play between the DJ's grooves. Black-lit Elvis and Frank Sinatra pictures dot the velvet walls, while Mexican cult classics screen behind Dante's Inferno bar. The mature hipster crowd (Vince Vaughn is a regular) consists of weekend warriors and nestling lovebirds. The award-winning calorie-conscious, yet authentic menu consists of cantina classics made from the owners' traditional family recipes. *Sun-Thu 11:30am-2am, Fri-Sat 11:30am-3am.* ≣ 1612 Cahuenga Blvd. (Hollywood Blvd.), 323-469-2000, velvetmargarita.com

Los Angeles Neon Tour • Downtown • Tour

Best Guided Tours Every Saturday night throughout the summer and early fall, three dozen people gather at the Museum of Neon Art (MONA) for wine or beer and cheese. They then board a bright red open-air double-decker bus for an evening's exploration of L.A.'s coolest, brightest neon signs—rolling through Downtown, Chinatown, midtown, and Hollywood with an informative, entertaining host who knows his neon and his L.A. cultural history. If this sounds like your kind of party, book ahead. It's regularly ranked as L.A.'s top tour and gets booked up long in advance. Don't forget to bring a jacket—it can get cold up there. *Tours run 7:30-10:30pm.* C▭ Museum of Neon Art, 501 W. Olympic Blvd. (Grand Ave.), 213-489-9918, neonmona.org

Lucky Strike Lanes • Hollywood • Bowling Alley

Let the good times roll at this rocking Hollywood bowling alley. Located at the Hollywood & Highland complex, Lucky Strike Lanes proves that the bald and beer-bellied aren't the only ones who like to play a little tenpin. A dozen neon-lit lanes with plasma TV scoring and retractable video screens are state-of-the-art, while the wooden bar top is lane 16 from legendary Hollywood Star Lanes of *Big Lebowski* fame. As this is Hollywood, there of course is a VIP area, where you will find closet kingpins like Jessica Simpson or *Wedding Crashers* Owen Wilson and Vince Vaughn on four private lanes. The casual American menu is more than just standard grease grub, while the steep drink prices will remind you that this isn't your grandpappy's bowling alley. *Daily 11am-2am.* ▤ 6801 Hollywood Blvd. (Highland Ave.), 323-467-7776, bowlluckystrike.com

Magnolia* • Hollywood • Restaurant/Lounge

Mostly 20-somethings flock here for the Asian-inspired cuisine and Ramones on the sound system. See *Hip Restaurants,* p.107, for details. *Daily 11am-2am.* ▤ 6266½ W. Sunset Blvd. (Argyle Ave.), 323-467-0660, magnoliahollywood.com

Mark Taper Forum • Downtown • Theater

For more than 35 years, this distinguished drama stage has chalked up just about every theatrical award in the book and launched many a play bound for Broadway and beyond. With just under 800 seats, the Taper is by far the smallest venue in Downtown's four-part Performing Arts Center, which includes the Ahmanson Theatre, the Dorothy Chandler Pavilion, and the Walt Disney Concert Hall. Along with the Ahmanson, the Taper is operated year-round by the Center Theatre Group, one of the country's largest and most active theater production companies. *Box office Tue-Sun noon-8pm.* C▤ 135 W. Grand Ave. (First St.), 213-628-2772, taperahmanson.com

Memphis* • Hollywood • Restaurant/Lounge

New Orleans jazz sets the backdrop for hearty plates of Southern-fried food. See *Hip Restaurants,* p.107, for details. *Nightly 6pm-2am.* ▤ 6541 Hollywood Blvd. (Hudson Ave.), 323-465-8600, memphishollywood.com

Mood • Hollywood • Nightclub

Best Single Scenes Hollywood's young and restless migrate to this exotic party paradise when they want to get hot and bothered. Paparazzi line up out front midweek for the likes of Lindsay Lohan, Nick Lachey, and the stars of *The OC*, while the weekends feature just as beautiful but not-so-famous faces. The lush

Bali-inspired interior features carved bamboo and teak fixtures, authentic Shiva sculptures, copper-lined walls, and sultry candle lighting. Plush brown booths surround a sunken dance floor as DJs turn up the hip-pop to the accompaniment of a live drum and horn section. The velvet rope mafia in front pays favorites to those with cleavage or cash, so groups of guys would be advised to reserve a bottle-service table. *Wed-Sun 10pm-2am.* C▤ 6623 Hollywood Blvd. (Cherokee Ave.), 323-464-6663, moodla.com

The Roost • Atwater Village • Bar

Silver Lake's trendy bar scene has sent some of its most talented young boozers sailing to find a divier safe harbor in neighboring Atwater Village. If the tacky "Big TV" sign outside doesn't send the caramel-apple-martini crowd running, the fake-wood paneling, the old dartboard, the jukebox full of Eagles and Johnny Cash, and the empties strewn everywhere will finish the job. If this sounds good to you, however, don your best Goodwill hipster garb and—welcome home. *Daily 10am-2am.* ▤ 3100 Los Feliz Blvd. (Edenhurst St.), 323-664-7272

Spaceland • Silver Lake • Live Music

This funky concert space continues to be L.A.'s top alternative music venue, showcasing artists—famous and fringe—in a loud, intimate setting that's as laid-back and purely music-oriented as all those moneyed halls aren't. Covers are cheap when local bands rock the house. Spaceland productions are also held at Hollywood's Henry Fonda Theatre (6126 Hollywood Blvd.) and at The Echo (1822 Sunset Blvd.). *Nightly 8pm-2am.* C▤ 1717 Silver Lake Blvd. (Effie St.), 323-661-4380, clubspaceland.com

Social Hollywood* • Hollywood • Restaurant/Lounge

This Moroccan-themed lounge with a private club on top has become the hip mecca for those looking for old Hollywood glamour. See *Hip Restaurants,* p.109, for details. *Sun-Wed 6-11pm, Thu-Sat 6pm-1am; Bar until 2am.* ▤ 6525 W. Sunset Blvd. (Schrader Blvd.), 323-462-5222, socialhollywood.com

Temple Bar • Santa Monica • Live Music

Bohemian beat junkies flock to this Westside music sanctuary to give thanks and praise. This funky, intimate live music lounge keeps it real by shunning mainstream hype in favor of a rootsy underground vibe. The incense-laden "Eastern-meets-urban" interior has a Downtown Chinatown feel with its red and black color scheme, stone Buddha statues, papier-mâché lanterns, and local artwork. National and international jazz, Latin, indie rock, hip-hop, world, reggae, soul, and spoken word artists take the stage nightly, while resident DJs keep the head-nodding, shoulder-shrugging melting pot of peeps on their toes. The fruit-flavored specialty drinks are tasty, while the multicultural menu is nothing more than glamorized bar food. *Nightly 8pm-2am.* C▤ 1026 Wilshire Blvd. (Eleventh St.), 310-393-6611, templebarlive.com

Tropicana Bar at the Roosevelt Hotel • Hollywood • Hotel Bar

Best Celebrity Hangouts Acclaimed designer Dodd Mitchell's renovation oozes laid-back glamour harkening back to the days of Marilyn Monroe (who once lived here) and Clark Gable. An illuminating pool, private bungalows, swaying palm trees, linen-covered chaise longues, and coquettish cocktail waitresses give it a retro Palm Springs vibe, while the sizzling nights are like an *Entourage* episode come to life. Indulge in Miami-style vices during the summer season weekend pool parties featuring live DJs, tasty barbecues, and lots of hot bikini bods. You'll have to take out a loan to buy a round of drinks and show a room key or name-drop to get in, but no one said living in La-La land was cheap. *Pool: daily 8am-8pm; Bar: Thu-Sat 8pm-2am.* ⊡ Hollywood Roosevelt Hotel, 7000 Hollywood Blvd. (Orange Dr.), 323-466-7000, hollywoodroosevelt.com

The Well • Hollywood • Lounge
Most Hollywood lounges are as loud and frantic as any other old bar. This lounge is a lounge, right down to its sedate entrance on the side of a office building. If it's late, you're tired, and you suddenly find yourself older than 25, dropping into this dark, sleek room with its smooth centerpiece bar, comfy nooks, unchallenging jukebox (James Brown, Bob Marley), and good vibes is like sneaking into business class. Being in the right company is important here, as you'll actually be able to carry on a conversation. *Mon-Fri 5pm-2am, Sat 8pm-2am, Sun 9pm-2am.* ☰ 6255 W. Sunset Blvd. (Argyle), 323-467-9355

Ye Rustic Inn • Los Feliz • Bar
This is a dive bar, pure and simple. Guys in Dickies get beers from bartenders past their stripping age, while music and sports blare simultaneously. The chicken wings are good, and the raucous vibe even better. On weekends, it's jampacked with hipsters from Silver Lake and Los Feliz. *Mon-Fri 11am-2am, Sat-Sun 9am-2am.* © 1831 Hillhurst Ave. (Melbourne Ave.), 323-662-5757

Zanzibar • Santa Monica • Lounge
The resident DJs at Zanzibar would be welcome at any dance club in town. The fact that they're spinning nu-jazz, future-soul, electro-dub, and Afro-beat at a hot new lounge brought to you by the creators of Temple Bar means that Santa Monica must have a club scene worth knowing about—even if it's only at this stylish Indian and African dance mecca. *Nightly 9pm-2am.* © 1301 Fifth St. (Arizona Ave.), 310-451-2221, zanzibarlive.com

Hip Los Angeles:
The Attractions

Arclight Cinemas • Hollywood • Movie Theater
Best Movie Theaters An electronic board listing theaters and movie times gives the voluminous main room of the Arclight theater the feel of a train station. Ticket prices here are higher than those at your average cineplex, but the bathrooms are immaculate, seating is assigned, and the front row is a comfortable distance from the screen. Including the separate geodesic-domed theater, Arclight has 15 screens, so if your movie is sold out, another interesting option should be starting soon. While you're waiting, grab a cocktail at the Arclight cafe. $$ 6360 W. Sunset Blvd. (Vine), 323-464-4226, arclightcinemas.com

Bergamot Station • Santa Monica • Site/Shopping
Get your art fix all in one place at this unique complex, an agglomeration of 33 local galleries, ten shops, and a museum. As the converted warehouses might indicate, this site did time as an industrial wasteland before becoming an eclectic forum for local painters, sculptors, photographers, jewelers, and a variety of other skilled artisans. Contemporary exhibits can be found at the Santa Monica Museum of Art in building G-1. When everything starts to look the same, it's time for a break at The Gallery Cafe, where tasty specials change daily. *Tue-Fri 10am-6pm, Sat 11am-5:30pm (most galleries).* 2525 Michigan Ave. (Cloverfield Blvd.), 310-829-5854, bergamotstation.com

Bliss • Westwood • Spa
Best Spas At long last this superhot New York spa company has opened in Los Angeles, much to the delight of the West Coast faithful who have been buying Bliss products for years. On the second floor of the W, Bliss is not huge, but is well laid out. Individual steam showers are a luxurious touch in the changing areas, along with a shared sauna. The quiet room comes complete with a bar of sweet treats like brownies to go along with the usual fruit and tea. Be warned: Bliss is a scene on weekends and not even the treatment rooms are immune from the noise of chattering socialites. Come during the week or in the morning for more calm. *Daily 9am-9pm.* $$$$ W Hotel, 930 Hilgard Ave. (Weyburn Ave.), 323-930-0330, blissworld.com/spa/location/la

Crunch Fitness • West Hollywood • Gym
Best Workouts Fitness is about as hip, high-tech, and hyper-social as it gets in this two-level gym. You may need a buff trainer to navigate your way through the curriculum here, which includes Thai boxing boot-camp classes, ballet Pilates, yoga, and an ice-breaker called "cardio striptease." Hammer Strength and Icarian machines are state-of-the-art. Multitaskers will enjoy the stationary bikes with Web access. *Mon-Fri 5am-midnight, Sat-Sun 7am-10pm.* $ 8000 W. Sunset Blvd. (Crescent Heights Blvd.), 323-654-4550, crunch.com

Dtox Day Spa • Los Feliz • Spa
This little gem on the far side of Los Feliz is the first true spa in the area—and it's setting a high bar. Inside the Zen space, you'll find compact but graceful facilities including sauna and steam for both men and women. There's a com-

bined waiting lounge with high ceilings and a Buddha statue guarding a fountain. Treatment rooms are off of this main space. The facility also offers yoga. *Mon-Fri 10am-8pm, Sat-Sun 10am-6pm.* $$$$ 3206 Los Feliz Blvd. (Glenfeliz Blvd.), 323-665-3869, dtoxdayspa.com

The Geffen Contemporary • Downtown • Art Museum

MOCA's satellite art hall in Little Tokyo (helped by a $5 million donation from David Geffen) lives on as the institution's coolest, funkiest wing. Larger exhibits and interactive installations that need their space are housed in this former LAPD garage retooled by Frank Gehry, who kept its essential warehouse feel intact. Popular displays include works by Rauschenberg, Warhol, and Oldenburg. Tickets issued at either MOCA or the Geffen include entrance to both. *Mon 11am-5pm, Thu 11am-8pm, Fri 11am-5pm, Sat-Sun 11am-6pm.* $ 152 N. Central Ave. (First St.), 213-621-2766, moca.org

Jet Rag • Los Angeles • Shop

This unique building with the rockets sticking out of its windows houses affordable vintage clothing from the '60s through the '80s. Unlike so many other vintage stores in L.A., Jet Rag sells regular-guy jeans for regular-guy prices, '80s rock T-shirts that won't blow your wallet away, and enough household items, children's clothes, and evening wear to practically make it a one-stop shop. If the clothes still aren't cheap enough, stop by on Sundays after 9:30am, when the store holds an everything-for-a-dollar sale out in the parking lot. *Daily 11am-7:30pm.* 825 N. La Brea Ave. (Waring Ave.), 323-939-0528

Little Tokyo • Little Tokyo • Site

Between First and Third Streets (to the north and south) and Alameda and Main Streets (to the east and west), this cultural pocket was first settled by Japanese immigrants in the late 19th century, and effectively wiped out during the mass internments of WWII. While the majority of L.A.'s Japanese population has spread to the 'burbs, these blocks remain a firm socioeconomic and cultural hub for the community at large. It doesn't take much time to explore the area on foot. Highlights include an assortment of craft and earthenware shops, ramen and sushi counters, and the excellent Japanese American National Museum (369 E. First St.).

Los Feliz Municipal Golf Course • Los Feliz • Golf

Cheap and easy in every way, Griffith Park's little-league course (1,065 yards, flat as a pancake) would be a great place to impress a six-year-old stepkid if only you had one. This nine-hole playground is frequented by 20-somethings who are cash tight and feeling better about their game than they should. There's a coffee shop, and rental clubs are available. No tee times or jackets required. *Daily 7am-sundown.* $ 3207 Los Feliz Blvd. (Glenfeliz Blvd.), 323-663-7758, golflink.com

Mulholland Highway • Santa Monica Mountains • Site

Not to be confused with Mulholland Drive, this even longer and windier road through the Santa Monica Mountains is a beautiful escape for stressed-out Angelenos, running between Malibu and Woodland Hills in the west San Fernando Valley. On weekends, you'll see (and hear) far more motorcycles than cars buzzing around this network of cliffs, canyons, and country roads. From Los Angeles, take the Pacific Coast Highway (Hwy. 1) west for about 30 miles.

Museum of the American West • Griffith Park • Cultural Museum

Just how was the West won? This enormous collection of artifacts, artwork, histori-cal documents, film footage, and—let's not forget—firearms tackles that question largely from the perspective of the white male winners. Founded by "Singing Cowboy" Gene Autry, the expanded museum now includes seven permanent gal-leries and two revolving exhibition areas that explore historical and contemporary topics relating to the development of the American West. *Tue-Sun 10am-5pm.* $ 4700 Western Heritage Way (Zoo Dr.), 323-667-2000, autrynationalcenter.org

Museum of Contemporary Art (MOCA) • Downtown • Art Museum

L.A.'s main modern art hub houses permanent and revolving exhibits from 1940 to the present in an arresting East-meets-West building from architect Arata Isozaki. More than 5,000 largely American and European works include abstract master-pieces as well as more recent additions from emerging names. Gallery tours (free) run on the hour between noon and 2pm. Celebrity chef Joachim Splichal is behind the menu at Patinette, MOCA's Mediterranean cafe. Entrance includes admission to the Geffen. *Mon 11am-5pm, Thu 11am-8pm, Fri 11am-5pm, Sat-Sun 11am-6pm.* $ (Free Thursdays.) 250 S. Grand Ave. (First St.), 213-626-6222, moca.org

Museum of Neon Art (MONA) • Downtown • Art Museum

Los Angeles was filling tubes with argon gas and hanging them all over town before the rest of the country caught on to this novel advertising—and, yes, art—form. The neon tradition is honored in this small gallery's revolving collection of electric media, along with classes that teach you to make your own. To get a taste of what's still out hanging around town, book a Neon Tour on MONA's open-air, double-deck-er bus for an evening's exploration of L.A.'s coolest, brightest, gaudiest signs (tours run between April and October). *Wed-Sat 11am-5pm, Sun noon-5pm.* $ 501 W. Olympic Blvd. (Grand St.), 213-489-9918, neonmona.org

Petersen Automotive Museum • Los Angeles • Museum

Dragging yourself to this monolith on Wilshire Blvd.'s "Museum Row" doesn't require a rainy day (as LACMA across the street may). Founded by publishing mogul Robert Petersen, it's a most appropriate homage to a city that evolved around wheels and engines. Four floors of permanent, revolving, and interactive exhibits include more than 150 rare and classic cars, trucks, and motorcycles spanning a century, with special exhibitions like life after petroleum. All the cool hot rods and celebrity vehicles are one flight up. *Tue-Sun 10am-6pm.* $ 6060 Wilshire Blvd. (Fairfax Ave.), 323-930-2277, peterson.org

Polkadots & Moonbeams • Los Angeles • Shop

If you're looking for something trendy and girly, chances are you'll want to look in on one of two stores that share the same name. The vintage portion of Polkadots & Moonbeams opened about 20 years ago and has one-of-a-kind frilly fashions and costume jewelry to match. The younger sister a few doors north is equally trendy and girly, with contemporary dresses running the gamut on pricing. It's the rare sort of ego-less store where fellow shoppers feel secure enough to com-pliment each other on their ensembles. *Mon-Sat 11am-7pm, Sun 11am-5pm.* 8367 W. Third St. (Kings Rd.), 323-651-1746, polkadotsandmoonbeams.com

Pure Surfing Experience • Manhattan Beach • Sport

Now entering its seventh year, Manhattan Beach's official surf school has helped thousands of people learn how to safely ride the waves, from kids as young as five to adults as old as seventy. Founded by a former L.A. County lifeguard and run by pro-level instructors, the school offers private lessons (usually 90 minutes) as well as weekend group clinics at Manhattan Beach's Rosecrans break and at two other reliable spots nearby. Boards and wet suits are included, safety is emphasized, and nearly everyone stands up in the first or second class. $$$$ Parking lot at 40th St. and Rosecrans Ave., 310-374-5902, campsurf.com

Runyon Canyon Park • Hollywood • Park

Best Hikes There may be much nicer trails farther afield in the Santa Monica Mountains, but for sheer convenience and star power it's hard to beat this one-mile ramble (uphill) to the top of Hollywood. On a clear day, views stretch to Catalina Island. On a not so clear day, views will make you want to write a sympathy card to your lungs. For a quieter trailhead (one that starts at the top), use the Mulholland entrance. And note: If you don't like dogs, lots of dogs, this place isn't for you. *Daily until sundown.* 2000 N. Fuller Ave. (Franklin Ave.), 323-644-6661, runyon-canyon.com

Satine • Los Angeles • Shop

This boutique is so hot, its owners Jeannie Lee and Sophia Banks are "it girls" in their own right. It's a great place to try on a straight-from-the-runway size 2 Stella McCartney dress or contoured silk camisoles. (That explains why petite Kirsten Dunst shops here.) Not everything is hip-hugging, so the twig-challenged won't go away empty-handed. *Mon-Fri 11am-7pm, Sat 10am-7pm, Sun noon-6pm.* 8117 W. Third St. (Crescent Heights Blvd.), 323-655-2142, santineboutique.com

Venice Beach and Ocean Front Walk • Venice Beach • Beach/Walk

Best Beaches Venice Beach's carnivalesque Strand has received some clean-up funds over the last few years. Thankfully, it hasn't lost its essential grit. Buy some incense or ten pairs of sunglasses for a steal. Get a massage from a homeless chiropractor. Check out the dudes pumping iron, shooting hoops, banging drums, or spouting off on some nutty subject. Here, the circus is always in town. From Rose Ave. to Washington St.

Wilson and Harding Golf Courses • Griffith Park • Golf

Golfers of all levels have been populating Griffith Park's two regulation-size courses almost from the time Wilson and Harding were in office. Well-staffed and maintained, they share all facilities, including a pro shop, lockers, a cart and club rental, a snack bar, and a driving range that's open until 10pm. Which course is more challenging? The jury's been out on that for the last 70 or 80 years. Wilson (par 72, 6,947 yards) is longer and has more trees. Harding (par 72, 6,536 yards) has tighter fairways. Walk-ons are easier during the week. On weekends especially, be sure to get a reservation card from the pro shop or by calling the City of Los Angeles Golf and Tennis Reservation Office (213-473-7055). *Sunrise-sunset.* $$ 4730 Crystal Springs Dr., 323-664-2255, laparks.org/dos/sports/golf.htm

Classic Los Angeles

Los Angeles is the town of perpetual reinvention—so it's no surprise that fresh and young always seem to trump old and classic here. That's a shame, because tucked between all those Chinese food and donut shops and spray-tan parlors is an elegant, historical LaLa Land just longing for someone to notice. There's a few old-school places you may have heard of—Grauman's Chinese Theater or the Hollywood Walk of Fame—but true Classic L.A. will take you to stretches of the area most visitors miss, from Downtown to Pasadena. Along the way, there are plenty of sophisticated spots to eat, lively haunts for a cocktail, and maybe even a pastrami sandwich or a slice of pie—because old-fashioned doesn't always mean played out. These Los Angeles relics are still ready for their close-ups, daahling.

*Note: Venues in bold are described in detail in the listings that follow the itinerary. Venues followed by an * asterisk are those we recommend as both a restaurant and a destination bar.*

Classic Los Angeles:
The Perfect Plan (3 Nights and Days)

Perfect Plan Highlights

Thursday

Lunch	**Patrick's Roadhouse**
Afternoon	**Getty Villa**
Cocktails	**Pig 'n Whistle*, Musso & Frank Grill***
Dinner	**Musso & Frank*, Mr. Chow, Il Cielo**
Nighttime	**Pig 'n Whistle*, Formosa Café, Burgundy Room**
Late-Night	**Pink's, Kibbitz Room**

Friday

Breakfast	**Brighton, Farmers Market**
Morning	**LACMA, Msm. Tolerance**
Lunch	**The Ivy, Spago**
Afternoon	**Pen. Spa, Warner Bros.**
Cocktails	**Peninsula, Polo Lounge**
Dinner	**Hotel Bel-Air Restaurant, Giorgio Baldi's, La Scala**
Nighttime	**Egyptian, Grauman's**
Late-Night	**Bar at Chateau Marmont**

Saturday

Breakfast	**Raymond, Pantry Café**
Morning	**Huntington Botanical, Norton Simon Museum**
Lunch	**Pie 'n Burger, Water Gr.**
Afternoon	**Hollywood & Highland, Griffith Observatory**
Cocktails	**Sunset Trocadero, Yamashiro's***
Dinner	**Morton's, Dan Tana's**
Nighttime	**Troubadour, Laugh Factory, Hollywood Bowl**
Late-Night	**Lola's, Ivar**

Hotel: **Beverly Hills Hotel and Bungalows**

Thursday

1pm Lunch What's more Classic L.A. than a long drive? Head up the PCH (Pacific Coast Highway) for a lunch of burgers and fries at **Patrick's Roadhouse**—it's on the way to your next stop.

3pm The **Getty Villa** is L.A.'s newest old treasure—not just because of its famous (or infamous) collection of antiquities, but also for its stellar setting off the Pacific Coast Highway. Of course, you've reserved your tickets well in advance, but if not, check the website for last-minute offerings—it's limited admission here.

6pm Tonight is about old Hollywood. A couple rounds of Bass beer at the restored **Pig 'n Whistle*** in Hollywood will start the evening nicely—this old-school spot used to be a hangout for Clark Gable. For a dry martini in one of the city's most beloved bars, wander down the block to **Musso & Frank Grill***. Park yourself at the bar, and imagine Sam Spade on the next stool.

8pm Dinner Slide into a booth and order a steak at **Musso & Frank*** to dine with the ghosts of Hollywood past. The ghosts of Hollywood present are in **Mr. Chow** eating

Chinese (lettuce cups are a favorite) and figuring out how to avoid the paparazzi out front—or not. If romance is what you want, there's no better spot than the charming patio at **Il Cielo**.

10pm Both **Pig 'n Whistle*** and **Musso & Frank*** have great bar scenes, but **Formosa Café** has a classic pedigree with a younger crowd. For a taste of Hollywood's alluring seedy side, the **Burgundy Room** has a jukebox with everything from Johnny Cash to the Sex Pistols. Non-tattooed bodies are rare here, but people are friendly enough, and it's good the lighting is so dark, because this is one beat-up bar. Just remember to dress down before showing up.

Midnight When dinner is a distant memory, line up for a chili dog at **Pink's**, where you'll probably see a few familiar faces from your night on the town.

1am **The Kibbitz Room** is anything but grand. That doesn't stop this tiny bar from filling up with night-crawlers—many of whom will soon stumble next door to **Canter's** for a pastrami sandwich.

Friday ————————————

9am Start with a hearty breakfast and some gourmet coffee at the **Brighton Coffee Shop**. Breathe in the small-town atmosphere. Is this Beverly Hills or Peoria? Let the diamond-drenched gals at the next table help you make up your mind. The **Farmers Market** might also beckon for breakfast—you can get anything from beignets to barbecue in the open-air restaurants.

10am Get an art fix at **LACMA** (Los Angeles County Museum of Art), with its varied collection in the heart of the city, close to the La Brea Tar Pits. To explore one of Los Angeles' most unique and respected museums, check out the **Museum of Tolerance**. It has drawn world leaders like the Dalai Lama.

1pm Lunch Head to **The Ivy** or **Spago**. Both offer glimpses of the city's notorious power lunch scene, with tables packed with A-listers, agents, and managers.

3pm **The Peninsula Spa** is the perfect place to indulge in some R&R. But if you're still looking for action, head to Burbank and a behind-the-scenes tour at the **Warner Bros.** lot.

6pm **The Bar at the Peninsula** is a refined scene to start the night with elegant company, as is the **Polo Lounge**. For a livelier vibe, head over to **Cabo Cantina** and grab a margarita.

8pm Dinner No one said L.A. was an easy town to traverse—tonight's fun means a drive, but it's worth it. Up in the hills, you'll find the lush, romantic patio at **The Hotel Bel-Air Restaurant**. Come early to wander the grounds, which are teeming with swans, fragrant flowers, and ancient oaks, not to mention the occasional couple getting engaged. Farther west, there's **Il Ristorante di Giorgio Baldi's**, the dim, packed, and very A-list Italian joint that's way off the tourist track, just the way locals like it. If the drive is just too daunting, a bit closer to Beverly Hills is **La Scala**, a gem for both romance and cuisine.

10pm In the town that makes movies, how can you resist seeing one? **The Egyptian Theater** will be showing something quirky and/or classic, like *Godzilla* or *Easy Rider*. If you absolutely have to see a movie at **Grauman's Chinese Theatre**, buy tickets to the latest blockbuster and get a good look at the over-the-top faux-Oriental interiors before the movie starts. Of course, you could always catch a live show at the **Key Club** over in West Hollywood.

Midnight **The Bar at Chateau Marmont** is sure to be a stylish late-night scene, and you really never know who will wander in.

Saturday

10am **The Raymond**, housed in an old Craftsman bungalow in Pasadena, serves a mean eggs Benedict—not to mention some of the best Bloody Marys in town. Make a reservation. Or stop in Downtown at the **Original Pantry Café**. This eight-decades-old breakfast joint serves up to 3,000 people daily—despite having only 85 seats.

11am Flora fans can check out the **Huntington Botanical Gardens**. Wander through 150 acres of themed foliage, including Australian, desert, palm, and rose gardens. Pasadena is also home to the Gehry-renovated **Norton Simon Museum**, with impressive collections of Masters, impressionists, and South Asian art. But if you're a golfer, consider a round at **Brookside Golf Course**, near the Rose Bowl.

1pm Lunch Check out the formica counters at **Pie 'n Burger**, where the patties come with Thousand Island dressing. For a meal to remember, head to Downtown and take a table at **Water Grill**.

2:30pm The shopping at Hollywood & Highland is pretty much what you'll find in any mall—except for the **Kodak Theatre**, where the Oscars take place—so head to level 2 and take a guided tour on the half-hour. Then stroll along the nearby **Hollywood Walk of Fame**, a tourist must. Along the way, check out props from *Ben-Hur* or *Your Show of Shows*, an authentic *Star Trek* set, and other industry artifacts at the **Hollywood Entertainment Museum**. If such celebrity-mongering isn't your style, then grab the shuttle at Hollywood & Highland that takes you up to the recently renovated **Griffith Observatory**, whose copper dome is a new landmark.

CLASSIC

6pm The Sunset Trocadero has sex appeal and some of the best cocktails in town. It's laid-back—not exactly the norm on this part of the Strip. For a memorable start to the night, head up the hill to **Yamashiro's*** for a drink with a view over the city.

8pm Dinner If you're in the mood for a juicy New York strip, you've got two choices: **Morton's** or **Dan Tana's**. Morton's is known for hosting the *Vanity Fair* Oscar party, but Dan Tana's is decidedly less pretentious. There aren't many view restaurants in L.A., but **Yamashiro's*** is one of the best. The food won't wow, but the stellar gardens and hilltop locale make up for it. In summer, you could also pack a picnic and take advantage of the **Hollywood Forever Cemetery's** outdoor screenings. No joke, you get to watch your flick projected on the side of a tomb, while enjoying whatever bottle and snack you brought along.

10pm The **Troubadour** is one of the best places in Los Angeles for live music, but you can't always just show up and gain entrance. Get your tickets online, just to be sure. For some live comedy, yuk it up at the **Laugh Factory**, where Richard Pryor used to perform. Funnymen Jon Lovitz and Bob Saget appear here regularly. If it's a summer night, though, check out what's happening at the **Hollywood Bowl**—some shows start early, so plan ahead.

Midnight Lola's is a cozy little bar filled with a young crowd—a great place to continue the fun. **Ivar** in Hollywood is another option, for a glamorous club scene with a packed dance floor.

The Morning After
Campanile does a very refined brunch with a crowd that's both lively and sophisticated.

Classic Los Angeles:
The Key Neighborhoods

Beverly Hills has long been dominated by palm trees, high-end shopping, classic hotels, valet parking, and famous residents from Bob Hope to Merv Griffin. If you're not driving a nice car, you can always try to find parking on the street.

Downtown features a long list of historic gems like the Grand Central Market, Chinatown, and Union Station. It's popular belief that nobody goes Downtown, but the area is home to dozens of old-school spots, along with an influx of hot new places.

Hollywood occupies a significant amount of L.A.'s history, from the Egyptian and Chinese theaters to the Walk of Fame, the Hollywood Bowl, and the infamous sign. It's an area in transition—lots of tourist shops and homeless are mixed in with new live-work spaces, clubs, and restaurants.

Malibu symbolizes the California way of life, mainly because of its 27 miles of beaches, history as a surfing paradise (as documented in *Gidget* and numerous surfing movies), and longtime reputation as the playground of celebrities. All this coastal prestige has prices to match.

Pasadena is its own city—an enclave of charming Arts & Crafts bungalows mixed with happening shopping and dining areas.

CLASSIC

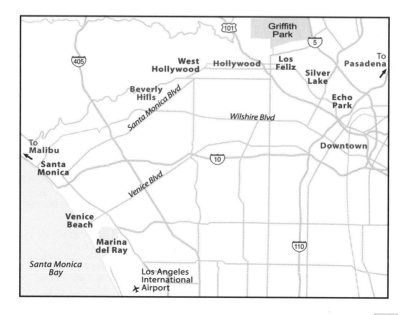

Classic Los Angeles: The Shopping Blocks

Rodeo Drive

Window-shopping on this quintessential not-in-your-price-range street tends to be a lot less stressful than actually going inside and having your pocketbook status judged by pretentious salespeople. Should that deter you from entering one of these stores and plunking down $100 for a T-shirt? No, but then again, mere window-shopping never broke anyone's bank.

Chanel The place to go for elegant two-piece suits and irresistible jewelry. 400 N. Rodeo Dr. (Brighton Way), 310-278-5500, chanel.com

Gucci Just buying loafers or sandals here can set you back a few bills. 347 N. Rodeo Dr. (Dayton Way), 310-278-3451, gucci.com

Louis Vuitton These go-to travel bags for the rich are some of the most counterfeited products ever made. 295 N. Rodeo Dr. (Dayton Way), 310-859-0457, louisvitton.com

Madison Shoes from Dolce & Gabbana, Jimmy Choo, and Valentino are as stylish as they are pricey. 9630 Brighton Way (Bedford Dr.), 310-273-4787, madisonstyle.com

Prada Beverly Hills Three whopping stories of smart luggage and equally smart men's and women's clothes and shoes. 343 N Rodeo Dr. (Dayton Way), 310-278-8661, prada.com

Rose Bowl

The best shopping in Pasadena takes place in a parking lot.

Rose Bowl Flea Market A shopping extravaganza of antiques, collectibles, and new merchandise takes place the second Sunday of every month. 1001 Rose Bowl Dr. (N. Arroyo Blvd.), 323-560-7469, rgcshows.com

Sunset Plaza

As good a place as any to spot celebrities, this two-block collection of upscale stores in West Hollywood represents one of L.A.'s oldest shopping areas. This little slice of browsing paradise comes with an unexpected bonus: free parking.

Billy Martin's Before heading to their Santa Barbara ranches, the stars load up on shirts and boots at L.A.'s Western-wear staple. 8605 W. Sunset Blvd. (Sunset Plaza Dr.), 310-289-5000, billymartin.com

Laura Urbinati Upscale clothes that perfectly suit the career woman. 8667 W. Sunset Blvd. (Sunset Plaza Dr.), 310-652-3183, lauraurbinati.com

Tracey Ross Catch the aroma of scented candles while poring over a mix of designer extravagance and T-shirt simplicity. 8595 W. Sunset Blvd. (Sunset Plaza Dr.), 310-854-1996, traceyross.com

Classic Los Angeles:
The Hotels

Beverly Hills Hotel and Bungalows • Beverly Hills • Timeless (204 rms)
Best Hotel Pools Chances are at least a few of the stars immortalized on the Hollywood Walk of Fame showered in your room before cutting a deal in the Polo Lounge or the pool. Built in 1912 (and purchased, 75 years later, by the Sultan of Brunei for a cool $185 million) on 12 acres of prime real estate covered in palms and hibiscus, the "Pink Palace" has been an institution for Hollywood's rich and famous from the get-go. Rooms are all accented in the hotel's signature palette of pinks, greens, apricots, and yellows. Custom furnishings include English-style sofas, canopied beds, '40s-style oval desks, and plush marble bathrooms. Most rooms also have fireplaces and balconies or patios. For the utmost privacy, a Bungalow guest room has its own individual entrance and a private porch. Recreation facilities include a full fitness center, an Olympic-size swimming pool, and tennis courts. $$$$ 9641 Sunset Blvd. (Crescent Dr.), 310-276-2251 / 800-283-8885, beverlyhillshotel.com

Beverly Wilshire Four Seasons Hotel • Beverly Hills • Timeless (395 rms)
Best Presidential Suites Elvis once called Suite 850 home. Warren Beatty crashed here for more than a decade. And on it goes. For 75 years, a celestial roster of celebs, dignitaries, and Hollywood location scouts have naturally gravitated to this icon of Beverly Hills opulence—now in Four Seasons hands—on the extortionate corner of Wilshire and Rodeo. Having received more face-lifts than most of its guests, the Beverly Wilshire is everything you've seen in *Pretty Woman* or *Beverly Hills Cop*, right down to the Italian tile bathrooms, sumptuous terry robes, silk hangers, and a new 5,000-square-foot, three-bedroom penthouse suite (a bargain $7,500 a night). This is the way Beverly Hills will always want to be seen. Large and lavish rooms (120 of them suites) are divided between the hotel's classical-style Wilshire Wing and the more contemporary Beverly Wing. Some larger deluxe rooms have views of Rodeo Drive. Impeccable facilities include a full-service health spa, an Italian villa–style pool, and world-class dining. $$$$ 9500 Wilshire Blvd. (El Camino Dr.), 310-275-5200 / 800-332-3442, fourseasons.com/beverlywilshire

Hotel Bel-Air • Bel-Air • Timeless (92 rms)
Set on 12 acres of gorgeous grounds in L.A.'s most exclusive neighborhood, the Hotel Bel-Air's quiet reputation as the loveliest, most romantic hideaway in the city hasn't much budged in the last 50 years. Back in the day, folks like Cary Grant, Grace Kelly, and Jackie Gleason checked in here for some "me" time. Today's bigwigs are just as drawn to this dreamy Mission-style property with its cobbled paths, bubbling fountains, swan lake, and floral overload. Privacy is guaranteed in uniquely designed rooms and suites, all with private entrances from the garden or courtyard. Exquisite furnishings include romance enhancers like canopy beds, wood-burning fireplaces, and French doors opening onto intimate tiled patios. Garden rooms have the most privacy. The oval-shaped pool and surrounding terrace with its spry attendants proffering premium waters, fresh fruits, and pink swan towels is an oasis within an oasis. The nearby fitness

center, housed in a former cottage frequently checked into by Marilyn Monroe and Joe DiMaggio, is now filled with top-of-the-line cardio and muscle-toning equipment (open 24 hours). A destination unto itself, the hotel's bougainvillaea-engulfed restaurant terrace will be forever considered one of L.A.'s most romantic spots for any meal. (See *Classic Restaurants*, p.136). $$$$ 701 Stone Canyon Rd. (Sunset Blvd.), 310-472-1211 / 800-648-4097, hotelbelair.com

Maison 140 • Beverly Hills • Timeless (43 rms)

Silent movie star Lillian Gish would no doubt approve of the intimate and stylishly offbeat B&B that her old Beverly Hills residence has been transformed into (at least that's what the management—the same visionaries who reworked the nearby Avalon and Santa Monica's Viceroy—assures you). Lots of opposites attract at this warm pied-à-terre, a few doors down from the frosty Creative Artists Agency building and a quick zig-zag from Barneys and Saks. Though its exterior is unassuming, its ornate interior is a bold blend of French chandeliers; Far Eastern red, white, and black; and breezy California touches—all for the right price, by Beverly Hills standards. Individually designed rooms include overstuffed French Bergère chairs, Frette Egyptian cotton linens, Philosophy toiletries, plus cordless phones, data ports, and media centers that somehow manage to gel nicely with the antiques. Mandarin Kings in the corners of the hotel are larger and have four-poster beds. $$$ 140 S. Lasky Dr. (S. Santa Monica Blvd.), 310-281-4000 / 800-432-5444, maison140beverlyhills.com

Millennium Biltmore Hotel • Downtown • Grand (683 rms)

Since 1923, L.A.'s grand dame of hotels has hosted kings, presidents, dignitaries, the Beatles, generations of celebrities, and businesspeople milking their corporate expense accounts for all they're worth. A treasured landmark right in the heart of Downtown's central business district, this 11-floor Italian Renaissance–style beauty is the only hotel in town with its own separate walking tour hosted by the Los Angeles Conservancy. It has also received more facelifts over the years than Joan Rivers, the latest being in 2002 from new owners Millennium Hotels and Resorts. In a city where urban improvement has often meant tearing something old and in-the-way down only to replace it with a monstrosity or parking lot, the Biltmore, with its frescoed lobby and stately guest rooms, remains the city's most reliable Old World fixture. Classic Rooms, occupying the third through ninth floors, feature warm gold, cream, and ivory color schemes with rich woods, plush drapery, French shutters, and rather small but well-appointed marble bathrooms. Newly modeled Club Rooms on the 10th and 11th floors offer extra space, personalized butler service, and access to the exclusive Club Lounge, where a complimentary continental breakfast is served. For the best views overlooking Downtown, try the Club Rooms on the 11th floor. Just past the lobby, the handsome Gallery Bar is Downtown's most dignified retreat for a premium cocktail. One floor down, the Biltmore's venerable health club is also something to see, offering full spa facilities and a gorgeous Roman-style pool. $$ 506 S. Grand Ave. (W. Fifth St.), 213-624-1011 / 800-245-8673, millenniumhotels.com

The Peninsula Beverly Hills • Beverly Hills • Timeless (196 rms)

Best Presidential Suites A spectacular French Renaissance–style property hiding on the edge of the Golden Triangle, the Peninsula by most accounts is tied with the Hotel Bel-Air (see p.131) for the title of top hotel. Never mind the courtesy Rolls-Royce service—a quick zigzag on foot leads you straight to Rodeo Drive for that emergency trip to Tiffany's or Louis Vuitton. Best of all, the hotel's secluded grounds are near all the glitz yet feel far removed. Lose a day up at the rooftop pool and spa, luxuriate over afternoon tea and superb Cal cuisine at the Belvedere Restaurant, and revel in the fact that all those Hollywood agents infesting the Club Bar will have to go home at some point. One hundred ninety-six lavish guest rooms (36 suites and 16 private villas) include custom and antique furnishings, marble bathrooms with oversized tubs, Italian linens, and French doors looking out on lovely gardens. For the most relaxing setting, get a Villa bungalow in the garden courtyard, complete with its own patio. A 24-hour check-in, check-out policy means there's really no such thing as arriving late here. $$$$ 9882 S. Santa Monica Blvd. (Wilshire Blvd.), 310-551-2888 / 866-382-8388, peninsula.com

Sunset Tower • West Hollywood • Timeless (74 rms)

Saved from several hare-brained plans for demolition in the late '70s and early '80s, this 1929 Art Deco gem on the Sunset Strip was known as the Sunset Tower Hotel when John Wayne, Elizabeth Taylor, and Marilyn Monroe stayed here. It's been through a few name changes and renovations since, but it's back to being known as the Sunset Tower Hotel. Striped chairs and wood-paneled walls fill out the renovated lobby area, while the rooms are decorated in a suave brown palette. The two 15th-floor penthouses have eye-popping views, but so do the rest of the guest rooms, all of which have floor-to-ceiling windows. Rooms on the north side of the hotel look out over the Sunset Strip—chocolate curtains can block out the bright, flashing lights—and the south section overlooks the L.A. basin. Bathrooms are done up in limestone, and every room has an iPod station and a flat-screen television—now standard issue in all boutique-type hotels. If the smallish but cozy guest rooms aren't large enough, spring for the junior suites, or go big and pop for the deluxe. Corner guest rooms offer an encompassing view of Downtown and the ocean. $$$ 8358 Sunset Blvd. (N. Sweetzer Ave.), 323-654-7100 / 800-225-2637, sunsettowerhotel.com

CLASSIC

Classic Los Angeles:
The Restaurants

Apple Pan • West Los Angeles • American
This no-nonsense burger joint probably hasn't changed much since it opened in 1947. Same U-shaped counter, same cash register, same no-nonsense service. Celebrities don't get special treatment over anybody else—for the plumbers, students, and businesspeople that flock here for lunch, it's strictly first-come, first-served. You can try to eat your burger (try it with hickory sauce) and fries at the packed counter or take it to go. The line is sometimes long, but it moves quickly. *Tue-Thu, Sun 11am-midnight, Fri-Sat 11am-1am.* $ ▣ 10801 N. Pico Blvd. (Glendon Ave.), 310-475-3585

Arnie Morton's of Chicago • Downtown • Steakhouse
Until a few years ago, anyone craving the Morton's experience (which includes the whole tableside treatment) had to journey west to La Cienega Boulevard. Now you can sit in this rough-hewn boys' club and enjoy first-rate chops just three blocks north of the Staples Center. Fresh fish, lobster, and chicken entrees are nice but come in second to the signature beef cuts, including the house specialty, a 24-ounce porterhouse. Save room for the chocolate velvet cake or the hot upside-down apple pie. *Mon-Fri 11:30am-11pm, Sat 5-11pm, Sun 5-10pm.* $$$ ▣ 735 S. Figueroa St. (W. Seventh St.), 213-553-4566, mortons.com

Brighton Coffee Shop • Beverly Hills • American
All-day breakfast, killer meatloaf, and good honest cups-a-joe. We're talkin' real food served on real honest-to-god Formica, and not an iota of attitude. Sometimes it just don't get no better in them glitzy Beverly Hills. *Mon-Sat 7am-5pm, Sun 9am-3pm.* $ ▣ 9600 Brighton Way (Camden Dr.), 310-276-7732

Cabo Cantina* • Los Angeles • Mexican
The cheap Mexican food menu takes a backseat to the two-for-one happy hour. See *Classic Nightlife*, p.141, for details. *Mon-Fri 4pm-midnight, Sat-Sun noon-midnight.* $ Ⓑ▣ 8301 W. Sunset Blvd. (Sweetzer Ave.), 323-822-7820

Campanile • Los Angeles • Cal-Med
Long before chef-duo Mark Peel and Nancy Silverton turned this dramatic building into a James Beard Outstanding Restaurant, Charlie Chaplin scouted it as an office. Simply arriving at this heavenly setting with its towering ceilings, cloistered patio, and signature bell tower feeds you even before you sit down. So does the rustic Cal-Med menu, which changes daily, and the inspired wine list. At lunch, it's packed with industry types casually checking out who else is there. At dinner, the crowd is upscale and sophisticated. *Mon-Fri 11:30am-2:30pm, Sat-Sun 9:30am-1:30pm; Mon-Wed 6-10pm, Thu-Sat 5:30-11pm.* $$$$ Ⓑ▣ 624 S. La Brea Ave. (Sixth St.), 323-938-1447, campanilerestaurant.com

Canter's • Los Angeles • American
Best Late-Night Eats Like any deli worth its sodium, this famous landmark hasn't changed in decades, and whether you park yourself in a booth at 4am or 4pm, they won't treat you any better or worse, even if you happen to be Matt Damon

behind those shades. Star sightings are common here at any hour of the day or night, which just proves that matzo balls and salty meats served on rye are some of the world's great equalizers. *24/7.* $ ≣ 419 N. Fairfax Ave. (Oakwood Ave.), 323-651-2030, cantersdeli.com

Dan Tana's • West Hollywood • Steakhouse
Best Steakhouses with Atmosphere The maître d's name is Jimmy. The pricey menu's got a 16 ounce slab of meat named after Dabney Coleman. Jerry Seinfeld celebrated his 45th birthday here. So you know the place is first rate. The chicken parmigiana and lasagna are too, but what this West Hollywood fixture has always been known for are its steaks and its red leather booths crammed with bloodthirsty locals and Beverly Hills goodfellas. There's just one kind of cow on the menu, Bub—the New York strip. Just decide whether it'll be the 12- or 16-ounce. *Nightly 5pm-1am.* $$$$ Ⓑ≣ 9071 Santa Monica Blvd. (Doheny Dr.), 310-275-9444, dantanasrestaurant.com

Dar Maghreb • Hollywood • Moroccan
You'll find this exotic 27-year-old venue on a relatively quiet patch of Sunset Boulevard in Hollywood. Enter through large doors into a compact greeting area where monastic robed hosts lead you into a dark dining room that might be a set from *Arabian Nights.* Seat yourself at a cushioned knee-high table, where a bowl of water is brought for a traditional hand-washing. Choose from one of several prix fixe meals and prepare for a course-by-course Moroccan-style feast that you eat with your hands (hence the mandatory hand-washing). Specials of the evening include couscous and sweet eggy b'stilla, savory lamb and squab dishes, and frequent appearances by a young, writhing belly dancer who appreciates having bills tucked into her apparel. Gape for a few moments at the bill, then remember that part of what you're paying for here is the experience. *Mon-Fri 6-11pm, Sat-Sun 5:30-11pm.* $$ ≣ 7651 W. Sunset Blvd. (Stanley Ave.), 323-876-7651, darmaghrebrestaurant.com ·

Du-Pars • Farmers Market • American
The menu is unnecessarily long at this beloved restaurant/bakery at the gates of the Farmers Market. A piping hot stack of pancakes and a bottomless cup of joe are the only things you really need to know. Homemade pies are a close second. *Mon-Fri 6am-10:30pm, Sat-Sun 6am-11pm.* $ ≣ 6333 W. Third St. (Fairfax Ave.), 323-933-8446, dupars.com

Empress Pavilion • Chinatown • Chinese
The weekend dim sum experience at this classic Cantonese banquet hall at the top of Chinatown is its strong suit (ignore the forgettable decor and perfunctory service, which you didn't come here for in the first place, so don't bother sweating the small stuff). Crowds are heaviest in the early afternoon, when a good portion of the city seems to be here waiting for the carts of steamed prawns, delectable dumplings, stewed chicken feet, and fried turnip cakes. Bring the Sunday paper along and take a number. Or come in the off-hours for a variety of excellent Hong Kong–style seafood dishes and a garlicky steamed Dungeness crab worth driving miles for. *Mon-Fri 10am-2:30pm, Sat-Sun 9am-2pm; Nightly 5:30-9pm.* $ ≣ Bamboo Plaza, 988 N. Hill St. (Bamboo Ln.), 213-617-9898, empresspavilion.com

Hotel Bel-Air Restaurant • Bel-Air • Cal-French (G)

Best Patio Dining This Cal-French beauty wins the blue ribbon for romantic dining, and you'll find lots of very well-heeled, mature diners taking advantage of it. Seasonal tasting menus change every Friday and are in the hands of executive chef Douglas Dodd, who spent years at Aspen's Little Nell before becoming something of a California purist—using only fresh indigenous herbs and produce in his exceptional dishes. There's a formal dining room inside, but the casual terrace gets you closer to Bel-Air's version of the great outdoors, where a profusion of flowers fills the foreground and a pretty little pond with swans (not on the menu) the background. Sunday brunch ($48 per person) is a weekly highlight, featuring a page of exquisite appetizers and main courses. *Daily 7am-9:30pm.* $$$ ▣ Hotel Bel-Air, 701 Stone Canyon Rd. (Chalon Rd.), 310-472-5234, hotelbelair.com/terrace.html

Il Cielo • Beverly Hills • Italian

Best Romantic Dining If there's a greater aphrodisiac than rose crème brûlée with candied rose petals on a bed of white chocolate and raspberry sauce, we don't know about it. That's just the coup de grace at this ultraromantic Italian charmer tucked away in a low-hype section of Beverly Hills, which draws savvy, sophisticated locals who prefer ambience over a buzzing scene. Ceiling frescoes, private nooks, and a fireplace in the cozy main dining room are upstaged by the alfresco settings—a pair of vine-shrouded patios in the front and back. Thankfully, the food is just as heart-warming as the ambience. Best sellers include fresh Maine lobster with hand-rolled fusilli from Calabria, and a whole grilled branzino filleted at tableside. *Mon-Sat 11:30am-3pm, 5:30-10pm.* $$$ ▣ 9018 Burton Way (Wetherley Dr.), 310-276-9990, ilcielo.com

The Ivy • Beverly Hills • American

Best Celebrity-Spotting Restaurants It would be hard to invent a more contrived movie set than the raised front porch at The Ivy, with its white picket fence, chintz-covered chairs, conspicuous cars by the curb, and celebrity guests stopping by to make an entrance and pay big money for crab cakes or a chopped salad. Don't expect the star treatment when you walk in, however. You might get a bit of a cold shoulder, and doubtfully a seat on that high-profile patio, but this is still one of the city's most buzzing scenes, especially at lunch. However you play it on this tasty New American stage, it's a jolly good show. *Mon-Thu 11:30am-10:30pm, Fri 11:30am-11pm, Sat 11am-11pm, Sun 10:30am-10pm.* $$$ ▣ 113 N. Robertson Blvd. (Alden Dr.), 310-274-8303

Michael's • Santa Monica • Californian (G)

Best Patio Dining Belying its adobe and stucco nightmare of a façade, the traditional white-tablecloth decor of Santa Monica mainstay Michael's features original art works by Richard Diebenkorn, Robert Graham, David Hockney, and even chef and owner Michael McCarty's wife. Lunch on weekdays sees a slew of business heavyweights, but at night the celebs are drawn here for its built-in discretion. Sit out in the Eden-like garden and order the prawn carpaccio or the foie gras followed by the 28-day dry-aged New York steak or the rack of lamb. You might even try a pinot noir that McCarty produces at his small Malibu vineyard. Finish it all up with the warm chocolate cake, one of the only confections to survive a recent dessert-menu makeover. *Mon-Fri noon-2:30pm, Mon-Thu 6-10pm, Fri-Sat 6-10:30pm.* $$$ ▣ 1147 Third St. (Wilshire Blvd.), 310-451-0843, michaelssantamonica.com

Morton's • West Hollywood • Steakhouse

One of the city's great power grills, this classy, skylit room and veteran Cal-Continental hot spot run by Arnie (of the steakhouse chain) Morton's kin, Pam and Peter, is a reliable place to see stars and an even better place to dine like one. Service and food are just plain flawless, from Caesar salad to chocolate truffle cake. What's in between? Lots more good stuff, like sesame-crusted ahi with shiitake mushrooms, basmati rice, bok choy, and ponzu sauce, free-range lime-grilled chicken with shoestring potatoes. *Mon-Fri noon-2:30pm, Mon-Sat 6-10pm.* $$$ ≡ 8764 Melrose Ave. (Robertson Blvd.), 310-276-5205, mortons.com

Mr. Chow • Beverly Hills • Chinese

Best Celebrity-Spotting Restaurants Celebrities know how to separate themselves from the hoi polloi: Eat at restaurants with decent food and obscene prices. How else to explain Mr. Chow's enduring success? This is where dressed-to-the-nines stars like Gwyneth Paltrow and James Caan fill up from a never-changing Beijing-style menu that will feature Peking duck and green prawns long after the sun has burned out. The stark decor consists of hanging screens and images of the owner, bit-part actor Michael Chow, who you may or may not have seen in *Lethal Weapon IV* (he was Uncle Benny's assistant). Incidentally, you won't actually need the menu, because the waiter will pick for you. It's just the way things are done here. *Mon-Fri noon-2:30pm, 6-11:30pm, Sat-Sun 6-11:30pm.* $$$ ≡ 344 N. Camden Dr. (Wilshire Blvd.), 310-278-9911, mrchow.com

Musso & Frank Grill* • Hollywood • American

Best Steakhouses with Atmosphere Hollywood's oldest restaurant (established 1919), with its cavernous booths, red-jacketed waiters, swivel-chair barstools, and dusty lamb chops, will hopefully outlive us all. The hallowed dual dining rooms have hosted the guzzling of regulars like Faulkner, Fitzgerald, and Nathanael West, and the restaurant has watched its peers (like the Brown Derby and Mocambo) come and go. Musso's tough old flannel cakes are a popular breakfast item (served until 3pm), and a couple of Bloody Marys makes for a nice lunch, thank you. Don't be surprised if you're drawn back for martinis and steak at sundown. *Tue-Sat 11am-11pm.* $$ Ⓑ≡ 6667 Hollywood Blvd. (Highland Ave.), 323-467-7788

Original Pantry Café • Downtown • American

There may be more facts and figures attached to this classic 24-hour steak and slaw greasepit than to any other restaurant in the city—including that it's owned by a former L.A. mayor, that it grinds through about 20 cows a day, and that it's been keeping cardiologists in business since 1935. Of course, none of these stats much matter when you're buzzed and craving short ribs and a mountain of corn niblets at 3am (definitely the most sensible time to line up for a table or fryer-facing counter stool). Cash only. *24/7.* $ ≡ 877 S. Figueroa St. (Ninth St.), 213-972-9279, pantrycafe.com

Pacific Dining Car • Downtown • Steakhouse

Best Steakhouses with Atmosphere You'd think a railcar-themed restaurant on the edge of Downtown that never closes would frighten most people away. Not so at this classy 83-year-old icon, which features USDA prime Eastern corn-fed, dry-aged, mesquite-grilled beef and a wine list that would be tough to bench-press. In fact, it's a favorite of politicos and other white-collar types from the nearby high-rises. Get here around 5pm for one of L.A.'s best happy-hour spreads—

baby back ribs, broiled chicken wings, and shrimp. Attention, eggs Benedict fans—y'all come back for breakfast, y'hear? *24/7.* $$$$ ▣ 1310 W. Sixth St. (Whitmer St.), 213-483-6000, pacificdiningcar.com

Patrick's Roadhouse • Pacific Palisades • American
One look at this funky green building emblazoned with a shamrock, filled with all sorts of old junk lining the walls, and you know there's a long story behind it. Patrick's is friendly, family-run, and full of character. Best of all, when you're craving fried, this place has it all in big, tasty portions. *Mon-Fri 7am-3pm, Sat-Sun 8am-3pm.* $ ▣ 106 Entrada Dr. (Pacific Coast Highway), 310-459-4544

Philippe the Original • Downtown • American
Nostalgia at this 1908 landmark comes in the form of warm 'n' chubby French rolls packed with a lean pile of pork, ham, beef, lamb, or turkey, dipped in jus, and set on a plastic tray with a ten-cent cup-a-joe (and a purple pickled egg, if you like). Yes, there's sawdust on the floor and a slew of L.A. memorabilia on the walls. There's also spicy homemade mustard on the family-style tables and one of the most varied lunch crowds you'll find anywhere. Cash only. *Daily 6am-10pm.* $- ▣ 1001 N. Alameda St. (Ord St.), 213-628-3781, philippes.com

Pie 'n Burger • Pasadena • American
One Formica counter, a few tables, and reliably perfect heartland food. That's good enough for the motley crew of suits, Pasadena soccer moms, and Cal Tech physics majors that have been keeping this place going for the last 40 years. Lovingly created burgers are spiked with homemade Thousand Island dressing. Sodas are hand-mixed from syrup and soda water, just like in the old days. And of course, pies are made right here. *Mon-Fri 6am-10pm, Sat 7am-10pm, Sun 7am-9pm.* $- ▣ 913 E. California Blvd. (S. Lake Ave.), 626-795-1123, pienburger.com

Pig 'n Whistle* • Hollywood • American
Clark Gable, Judy Garland, Shirley Temple, Loretta Young, and others held court here after their movie premieres next door at the Egyptian. Shuttered for years, a full restoration has granted this establishment its old Art Deco good looks. There's a full Continental menu (but it still steers the eye toward a cheeseburger and pint of Bass) and a late-night bar scene. *Sun-Thu 11:30am-10pm, Fri-Sat 11:30am-11pm; bar until 2am most nights.* $ ▣ 6714 Hollywood Blvd. (Las Palmas Ave.), 323-463-0000, pignwhistle.com

Pink's • Hollywood • American
Best Late-Night Eats You can't leave Los Angeles before tasting a Pink's chili dog. It's a law. Politicians come here to schmooze, and celebrities come here to be seen with "the people," who constitute an egalitarian mix of tourists and locals. The menu has expanded over the years and includes everything from Brooklyn pastrami and Swiss cheese dogs to a Polish dog named after rocker, icon, and nagging husband Ozzy Osbourne (it's smothered with nacho cheese, American cheese, grilled onions, guacamole, and chopped tomatoes). Pink's is famous for its perennially long line, but things can get pretty social while you wait. It's when people finally get their hot dogs that words seem beside the point. *Sun-Thu 9:30am-2am, Fri-Sat 9:30am-3am.* $ ▣ 709 N. La Brea Ave. (Melrose Ave.), 323-931-4223, pinkshollywood.com

Polo Lounge* • Beverly Hills • American

Celebs, schmoozers, and deal makers come for the divine Continental cuisine and premium cocktails. See *Classic Nightlife,* p.144, for details. *Daily 7am-11pm (appetizers until 1:30am).* $$$ B▤ Beverly Hills Hotel, 9641 Sunset Blvd. (Beverly Dr.), 310-887-2777, thebeverlyhillshotel.com

The Raymond • Pasadena • American

This unique converted bungalow in Pasadena has seen a thousand special-occasion dinners, and exudes romance with its polished, homey interior and tiny patios filled with flowers and fruit trees. The straightforward menu changes weekly but might include a tender rack of lamb with Grand Marnier sauce or a perfectly grilled sea bass topped with fresh papaya and jalapeno relish. The brunch here is one of the best in the city with stellar options like crab cakes Benedict. Booth 2 in the side room is one of the most requested for romance, as is the patio table under the wisteria. *Tue-Fri 11:30am-2:30pm, Sat 11am-2:30pm, Sun 10am-2:30pm; Tue-Thu 6-9:30pm, Fri-Sat 5:45-10pm.* $$ ▤ 1250 S. Fair Oaks Ave. (Columbia St.), 626-441-3136, theraymond.com

Il Ristorante di Giorgio Baldi • Santa Monica • Italian

Best Celebrity-Spotting Restaurants Giorgio Baldi is set on a nondescript street off the Pacific Coast Highway, and that's just how the A-list celebs like it. The Italian trattoria food is highly lauded—even if the high prices aren't—but people come here mostly for the scene. Seating is tight, on simple wood chairs in a dim main room or a plastic-covered front patio, but that could be a good thing if you picture yourself chowing down on mushroom risotto while overhearing Nicole Kidman talk about her next juicy role. *Tue-Sun 6-10pm.* $$$ ▤ 114 W. Channel Rd. (Pacific Coast Hwy.), 310-573-1660, giorgiobaldi.com

La Scala • Beverly Hills • Italian

Twenty or thirty years ago, this time-honored Italian-lite restaurant was arguably the snooty power lunch spot in Beverly Hills. Age and a recent move (just a few doors up the street) has softened the place into a friendly local hangout for regulars who no longer bother lying about their age. The bread is warm, the pastas are tasty, but the place is still most famous for its chopped salads. *Mon-Sat 11:30am-10pm.* $$ ▤ 434 N. Canon Dr. (Brighton Way), 310-275-0579

Smoke House • Burbank • Steakhouse

Across the road from Warner Bros. Studios, this classic steakhouse is way older than anyone you know—although the façade gives a clue. It's said that both Gable and Bogart, on occasion, liked to order the liver here. Good food on a fairly priced traditional American menu still makes this an off-Hollywood nerve center in the most nostalgic sense. Go easy on the garlic bread. *Mon-Thu 11:30am-10:30pm, Fri-Sat 11:30am-11pm, Sun 10am-9pm.* $$ ▤ 4420 Lakeside Dr. (Olive Ave.), 818-845-3731, smokehouse1946.com

Spago • Beverly Hills • American

Best Power Lunches Everyone knows Spago, at least as a synonym for the Hollywood high-life. It's also the epicenter of Wolfgang Puck and wife Barbara Lazaroff's culinary empire, and the same hallowed spot that half of L.A.'s glitterati will be fighting over for patio reservations come dinnertime. Go for the tasting menu or choose from a broad selection of American, Asian, and European entrees. Outdoor courtyard seating is the most coveted, but for action-packed views into the open kitchen, head to the back tables inside. *Mon-Fri 11:30am-2:15pm, Sat noon-2:15pm; Mon-Thu 5:30-10pm, Fri-Sat 5:30-11pm, Sun 5:30-10pm.* $$$ ≡ 176 N. Cañon Dr. (Wilshire Blvd.), 310-385-0880, wolfgangpuck.com

Sunset Trocadero* • Los Angeles • Tapas
The Nueva Latina tapas menu is one of the best in town, as is the martini selection. See *Classic Nightlife*, p.144, for details. *Nightly 6pm-2am.* $ ⊟ 8280 Sunset Blvd. (Sweetzer Ave.), 323-656-7161

Valentino • Santa Monica • Italian (G)
Best Wine List Italian restaurant extraordinaire Valentino recently went to a tasting menu, which means you can now splurge on the wine pairings and save yourself the headache of a) choosing among 2,500 wines, and b) trying to pronounce any of them. Spend the rest of your time staring into the eyes of your significant other, as you look forward to the veal tenderloin with black summer truffles followed by the osso buco, or perhaps the spaghetti alla chitarra and the Angus beef filet. The two booths in the sumptuous main dining room are the most sought after, but if you're trending romantic, try a table along the window that separates the garden room and the patio, or a half-booth in one of the alcoves just off the main dining room. *Mon-Fri 5:30-10:30pm, Sat 5-11pm.* $$$$ ⊟ 3115 Pico Blvd. (31st St.), 310-829-4313, valentinosm.com

Water Grill • Downtown • Seafood (G)
Best Seafood Welcome to L.A.'s seafood mecca. The oyster and roe selections alone in this formal wood, leather, and brass dining room will move any raw bar aficionado to tears. New American–style entrees like steamed mahi mahi with peppercorns and roasted bluefin tuna are subtly prepared without much aid from heavy crusts or sauces—no need when you've reeled in the best raw materials in town. A perfect choice before an evening at the Performing Arts Center, a few blocks up the street. *Mon-Fri 11:30am-9pm, Sat 5-9:30pm, Sun 4:30-8:30pm.* $$$ B≡ 544 S. Grand Ave. (Fifth St.), 213-891-0900, watergrill.com

Yamashiro* • Hollywood • Japanese
Best Romantic Dining Originally built to house a private Asian art collection, this 90-year-old hilltop mansion remains one of classic Hollywood's most storied properties, having done time as an exclusive club for silent movie idols like Lillian Gish and Ramon Novarro. It's the kind of place you come to spend a couple of hours, wandering the gardens, enjoying a sunset cocktail, and dining with the stellar view as a backdrop. Sadly, the food here is not nearly as stellar as the view, and the sushi has been accused of being less than fresh. But with a bit of wise ordering—sticking to the basics—you'll have one of the most memorable dining experiences in the city. Of course, you could also come up just for a drink. *Nightly 5-9:45pm, bar until 2am.* $$ ⊟ 1999 N. Sycamore Ave. (Franklin Ave.), 323-466-5125, yamashirorestaurant.com

Classic Los Angeles:
The Nightlife

The Bar at Hotel Bel-Air • Bel-Air • Lounge

You might half-expect one of Nancy Reagan's neighbors to ask to see your membership card at L.A.'s most refined hotel bar. In fact, this genial drinking den in the heart of Bel-Air is open to anyone who can behave themselves in polite, snifter-sipping society among visiting British gentry and others who look pretty in tweed. You'll get the whole leather armchair, peaty-scotch-by-the-fire, humidor-on-the-premises, suave-gent-tickling-the-ivories deal here. But don't bother to bring your bathing trunks unless you're checking in as a guest—a smashing idea, what? *Sun-Thu 11am-12:30am, Fri-Sat 11am-1:30am.* ☐ Hotel Bel-Air, 701 Stone Canyon Rd. (Tortuoso Way), 310-472-1211, hotelbelair.com

Bar Marmont • West Hollywood • Bar/Lounge

Chateau Marmont's stylish neighbor is now a famous destination in its own right for its dark, cozy lounge, popular patio, butterfly-painted ceilings, and specially prepared drinks priced to attract young celebrities and whispering fans. Seeing as you'll be forking over close to ten bucks for the privilege of drinking a beer here, you might as well go large and get the highly recommended Marmont Cosmo or the #9 Mint Martini. By the by, one of the city's best filet mignon cheeseburgers in town is served here into the late hours. *Mon-Sat 6pm-2am, Sun 7pm-2am.* ☐ 8171 W. Sunset Blvd. (Marmont Ln.), 323-650-0575, chateaumarmont.com

The Burgundy Room • Hollywood • Dive Bar

Best Dive Bars Never mind the bollocks at this dingy, burgundy-tinted dive bar along the Cahuenga Corridor. Smudged mirrored walls, shaky ceiling fans, sticky floors, a dinged-up tabletop bar, and hanging red Chinese lanterns give the narrow interior a Vietnam-era G.I. bar look, while the *Sid and Nancy*-type crowd and punk rock aesthetic give it a CBGB's vibe. Take advantage of the infamous jukebox, which features punk rock classics from the Sex Pistols and the Ramones as well as Johnny Cash. A typical night will include *Jackass* behavior like broken glass, random nudity, puking, and an appearance by Johnny Knoxville or Steve-O. The crowd of local cronies might seem a bit intimidating with their tattoos, piercings, sneered lips, and penchant for whiskey shots, but are quite accommodating, especially if you look like one of them. *Nightly 8pm-2am.* ☐ 1621½ Cahuenga Blvd. (Selma Ave.), 323-465-7530

Cabo Cantina* • Los Angeles • Restaurant/Bar

Best Daytime Drinking Spots Relive your spring break daze at this Sunset Strip staple where two-for-one equals tons of below-the-border fun. Blaring cock rock, tequila shots, and drunken debauchery establish "a party till you puke" premise—beer bong not included. An open-roofed front and back patio bookend a main bar area covered in beer propaganda and mid-sized TVs broadcasting games. The Abercrombie-looking staff is both friendly and flighty. The low-priced Mexican food menu serves its purpose, but the daily happy hour (4pm to 8pm) is the reason why this watering hole is always packed with party animals. *Mon-Fri 4pm-midnight, Sat-Sun noon-midnight.* ☐ 8301 W. Sunset Blvd. (Sweetzer Ave.), 323-822-7820

Club Bar at the Peninsula Beverly Hills • Beverly Hills • Bar/Lounge

Peaty scotch just tastes better at this classy, birch-paneled drinking den housed in what is commonly called the city's finest hotel. If the Peninsula's Club Bar took memberships as the name suggests, Hollywood agents would buy it out. As it stands, you're welcome to sink into a red leather chair, order a Millionaire Margarita (double reserve Cuervo tequila, 150-year-old Grand Marnier, Cointreau, and fresh lime juice) and listen to this congregation of schmoozers have at it. Better yet, sit by the fire where there's less of a chill in the air. *Sun-Thu 1pm-midnight, Fri-Sat 1pm-1am.* ⊟ 9882 S. Santa Monica Blvd. (Charleswille Blvd.), 310-551-2888, peninsula.com

Formosa Café • Hollywood • Bar/Restaurant

This famed showbiz watering hole was saved from the wrecking ball and made an L.A. landmark in the late '90s. Nearly every glamorous Hollywood star has wined and dined here since it opened in 1925, as evidenced by the countless auto-graphed celebrity photos (Humphrey Bogart, James Dean, Frank Sinatra) on the walls. The converted trolley car has been featured in many films itself including *L.A. Confidential* and *The Misfits* starring Marilyn Monroe and Clark Gable. The red and black Asian-noir motif still attracts industry insiders and movie buffs who appreciate its authenticity and storied past. The Chinese menu is passable, while the mai tais are legendary. *Mon-Fri 4pm-2am, Sat-Sun 6pm-2am.* ⊟ 7156 Santa Monica Blvd. (N. Formosa Ave.), 323-850-9050, formosacafe.com

Greek Theatre • Griffith Park • Live Music

Rock, R&B, classical, Kenny G.—everything under the stars has been played at the Greek over the last 70-odd years. Nestled in the foothills of Griffith Park, the legendary 6,162-seat amphitheater has recently hosted The Black Crowes, The Gipsy Kings, Elton John, Patti LaBelle, Pearl Jam, the Russian National Ballet, Sting, and many other big-ticket shows that people will gladly navigate one of the worst parking bottlenecks in the city to hear. Acoustics are a distant second to the open-air ambience. *Season runs May-Oct.* ⓒ≡ 2700 N. Vermont Ave. (Los Feliz Blvd.), 323-665-5857, greektheatrela.org

Hollywood Bowl • Hollywood • Live Music

Former boxholders at this world-famous amphitheater include Mr. and Mrs. Cecil B. DeMille, Sid Grauman, and Charlie Chaplin. Vladimir Horowitz played here. Sinatra sang here. Fred Astaire danced here. Abbott and Costello and Monty Python did their shticks here. The Bowl is now home to its own res-ident orchestra and a stacked summer concert calendar. Come with a bottle of wine (and a seat cushion). Or, for the whole shebang, reserve box seats, and have a gourmet meal delivered straight to you by the doting staff. *Box office: Tue-Sun noon-6pm (July-Sept).* ⓒ≡ 2301 N. Highland Ave. (S. Dixie Way), 323-850-2000, hollywoodbowl.com

Ivar • Hollywood • Nightclub

Inside these tall frosty doors is the Cadillac of nightclubs in Hollywood—a stark, futuristic landscape with four bars, several VIP pods, a roster of top DJs, and a large pulsing dance floor packed with beautiful young things. Despite its 14,000-square-foot size, it can still be pretty hard to get into, so dress to impress. *Fri-Sat 9:30pm-2am.* ⓒ≡ 6356 Hollywood Blvd. (Ivar Ave.), 323-465-4827, ivar.com

Laugh Factory • Los Angeles • Comedy

Nearly every famous funnyman from Richard Pryor to Dave Chapelle has graced the stage at Jamie Masada's legendary comedy club since it opened in 1979. Masada's sharp eye for breaking in up-and-coming talent is a big reason why you will find long lines outside the neon-lit marquee every night of the week. The long-running Latino Night (Mon), Asian Night (Thu), and Chocolate Sundaes (Sun) are the stuff of urban legend, while the sold-out weekend nights feature multiple shows by all-star *Tonight Show* talent. Reservations are encouraged and be aware that sitting in the front row puts you in the direct firing line—making you a marked target for the butt of many jokes. *Hours vary.* ⒸＥ 8001 Sunset Blvd. (Crescent Heights Blvd.), 323-656-1336, laughfactory.com

Lola's • West Hollywood • Bar

Anyone coming to this unassuming block of Fairfax above Melrose is either dropping off a broken VCR or, hopefully, checking into Lola's—a cottagey bar/restaurant with an aspiring sitcom-cast crowd, an antique pool table, a leopard-skin sofa, and a menu of 50 or so martinis. It all hangs together well after a few candied cups of gin or vodka. *Nightly 5:30pm-1:30am.* Ｅ 945 N. Fairfax Ave. (Romaine St.), 213-736-5652, lolasla.com

Musso & Frank Grill* • Hollywood • Bar/Restaurant

This joint opened in 1919, and the old wood bar here is still a great place for a martini—then slip into a booth for a steak. See *Classic Restaurants,* p.137, for details. Ｅ 6667 Hollywood Blvd. (Highland Ave.), 323-467-7788

The Music Box @ The Henry Fonda Theatre • Downtown • Live Music

Best Live Music Venues This classic theater where legends like Marlene Dietrich and Al Jolson once performed has seen many incarnations since it opened in 1926. Extensive renovations have recaptured the luster of the vintage venue's Art Deco design, while a state-of-the-art sound and light system has brought it into modern times. The multifaceted venue has hosted everything from the Pussycat Dolls burlesque show to monthly boxing matches. As for live music concerts (Kanye West, the Yeah, Yeah, Yeahs, KCRW-sponsored events), it's one of the best in terms of intimacy because of its unique and wide-open standing-room-only concert hall. Voyeurs can relax in the mezzanine, while those in need of fresh air or a nicotine fix can watch the on-stage antics from plasma TVs at the rooftop terrace overlooking Hollywood Boulevard. *Hours vary.* ⒸＥ 6126 Hollywood Blvd. (Gower St.), 323-464-0808

Pantages Theatre • Hollywood • Theater

A $10 million restoration has revived this stunning Art Deco structure—home to the Academy Awards throughout the '50s—turning it into a top venue for Broadway musicals. Recent productions include *The Lion King* and *The Producers. Showtimes vary.* ⒸＥ 6233 Hollywood Blvd. (Argyle Ave.), 323-468-1700, broadwayla.org

Pig 'n Whistle* • Hollywood • Restaurant/Bar

The Continental menu at this fully restored spot entices mostly for its cheeseburger and pint of Bass. See *Classic Restaurants,* p.138, for details. *Sun-Thu 11:30am-10pm, bar until 2am most nights.* Ｅ 6714 Hollywood Blvd. (Las Palmas Ave.), 323-463-0000, pignwhistle.com

CLASSIC

Polo Lounge* • Beverly Hills • Lounge

Even if you're not staying at the Beverly Hills Hotel, you can simply pretend that you are at this definitive leisure room for schmoozers and deal makers. Savor divine Continental cuisine, sip premium cocktails, and—don't look now, but guess who's sitting over there. In this world-famous lounge, you're always in good—and usually recognizable—company. For an even steeper tab, visit the hotel's opulent new-comer, the Polo Grill. *Daily 7am-11pm, appetizers until 1:30am.* ▤ Beverly Hills Hotel, 9641 Sunset Blvd. (Beverly Dr.), 310-887-2777, beverlyhillshotel.com

Sunset Trocadero* • Los Angeles • Restaurant/Bar

This cozy and casually cool Sunset Strip hangout is located just a few blocks away from its legendary Hollywood namesake. The intimate, living room–like space is nothing more than a pair of comfy couches, a flat-screen TV, and two tiny book-end patios overlooking the boulevard of broken dreams. The dimly lit, low-key vibe makes it a perfect place to chill for an afterwork martini or pre-party cocktail. The hip-pop tunes turn up as nomadic party people mix in with canoodling couples later in the night and the mood shifts from laid-back to getting laid. The martini selection is one of the best in town, as is the Nuevo Latino tapas menu. *Nightly 6pm-2am.* ▤ 8280 Sunset Blvd. (Sweetzer Ave.), 323-656-7161

Tiki Ti • Los Feliz • Dive Bar

Best Dive Bars Size doesn't matter, at least not after a couple of stiff, blue-col-ored umbrella drinks. Such is the motto of this pint-sized tiki bar that dates back to the swinging '60s. The family-owned L.A. institution is the kind of place that you have to experience at least once. The wise-cracking Hawaiian shirt–clad bar-tenders concoct over 85 different cocktails, including the infamous Rey's Mistake. The jumbled, eclectic setting is littered with beat-up license plates, turtle lamps, a fluorescent waterfall, and Tiki figurines set against a molten lava backdrop. If all that doesn't put you in a tropical mood then Don Ho's *Tiny Bubbles* blasting out of the speakers will. *Wed-Thu 6pm-1am, Fri-Sat 6pm-2am.* ▤ 4427 W. Sunset Blvd. (Virgil Pl.), 323-669-9381, tiki-ti.com

Troubadour • Los Angeles • Live Music

Best Live Music Venues This beloved rocker shrine is as relevant today as it was when it broke iconic acts like Elton John and the Eagles in the '70s. While most of the surrounding "Boystown" area has changed dramatically, the Troub is still nothing more than a crusty, creaky sweatbox of sound and fury. The balcony offers a bird's-eye-view of the tiny stage as does the VIP loft upstairs. The loud, no-frills forum continued to break bands like No Doubt and the Killers over the past decade, but continued to have more of a heavy metal mentality. Thankfully that has changed as it reestablishes itself as an indie rocker haven. The concert calendar showcases local talent, indie up-and-comers, and surprise appearances by crossover stars like Franz Ferdinand and the Yeah Yeah Yeahs. The venue is all ages, so bring a valid form of ID if you want to drink and smoke. *Nightly 8pm-2am.* ⓒ▤ 9081 Santa Monica Blvd. (Doheny St.), 310-276-6168, troubadour.com

The Wiltern LG • Los Angeles • Live Music

Best Live Music Venues Built in 1931 and renovated as recently as 2002, this historical cultural monument is a concert venue with more history than hype. The breathtaking Art Deco building has seen more face-lifts than the Jackson family, yet manages to retain its classic look with restorations that touched up its rich tradition rather than wipe it clean. Shiny gold-plated fixtures and the forest green, rose, and burgundy color scheme complement the opulent design and decor. The standing-room-only main area is layered into five-tiers, rising upward from the stage. The three service bars and two bathrooms are ill-equipped for the 2,300 capacity crowd, so expect long lines at both. Everyone from Bob Dylan to The Killers, Thievery Corporation, and comedian Eddie Izzard has played here, so check the vintage marquee out front for upcoming shows. *Box office noon-6pm.* ©☰ 3790 Wilshire Blvd. (Western Ave.), 213-380-5005

Yamashiro* • Hollywood • Restaurant/Lounge

Enjoy a walk in the gardens and a drink with one of the best views in the city at this Japanese hilltop hideaway. See *Classic Restaurants*, p.140, for details. *Nightly 5pm-2am.* ☐ 1999 N. Sycamore Ave. (Franklin Ave.), 323-466-5125, yamashirorestaurant.com.

Classic Los Angeles:
The Attractions

Beverly Hills Trolley Tours • Beverly Hills • Tour

Meet your docent at the trolley stop on the northwest corner of Dayton and Rodeo for one of two educational spins through Beverly Hills. The 40-minute Sites and Scenes Trolley Tour features the city's most prominent attractions including Rodeo Drive. The 50-minute Art and Architecture Trolley Tour includes the Gagosian Gallery, the Beverly Hills City Hall, CAA, and the Museum of Television & Radio. *Year-round tours every Saturday plus weekday tours (Tue-Sat) during summer and winter; All trolleys depart on the hour from 11am-4pm.* $ Rodeo Dr. and Dayton Way, 310-285-2438, beverlyhills.org

Bradbury Building • Downtown • Site

Looking at the unremarkable exterior of this 19th-century architectural masterpiece—L.A.'s oldest commercial building, built by a rookie one-hit-wonder architect—you'll wonder yourself what all the fuss is about. Then enter its shocking iron, oak, and marble core, bathed in sunlight, and suddenly you've been transported into a sort of Sam Spade–themed Escher painting. There's nothing like that first time—and saying any more here would spoil the surprise. *Mon-Fri 8am-5pm.* 304 S. Broadway (Third St.), 213-626-1893, bradburybuilding.info

Brookside Golf Course • Pasadena • Golf

Pasadena's lush Arroyo Seco grounds—home of the Rose Bowl—are also home to the neighborhood's most sophisticated public course, a distinguished former host of the Los Angeles Open. Pros and well-heeled amateurs flock to the Koiner course, a 7,037-yard, par 72 endurance test designed by Bobby Bell. The E.O. Nay course (or "Course Two") is a thousand yards shorter and easier to book. *Daily 6am-7pm.* $$$$ 1133 Rosemont Ave. (Rose Bowl Dr.), 626-796-0177, brooksidemensgolfclub.com

Chinatown • Chinatown • Site

Just north of the financial district, L.A.'s rather small and sedate Chinatown isn't New York's or San Francisco's, but a closer look reveals some great finds. Survey the first contemporary American Chinatown planned, built, and run by the local Chinese community by wandering north along its main thread, Broadway between Ord Street and Bernard Street and back down through Hill Street, Spring Street, and New High Street, where all the curio shops, galleries, jewelry stores, ginseng counters, and tempting eateries can easily fill up a few hours. It's hard to miss Central Plaza (947 N. Broadway), Chinatown's pedestrian court with its handful of shops and multitiered pagoda. Other attractions along the way include Wing Hop Fung Ginseng and China Products Center (727 N. Broadway), a clearinghouse of Asian herbs, teas, crafts, and tableware. Farther north, the Chinese Historical Society of Southern California (411 and 415 Bernard Street) houses a bookstore and gallery open to visitors on Sunday from noon-5pm. Nearby Empress Pavilion (988 N. Hill Street) is dim sum headquarters, and the venerable Phoenix Bakery (969 N. Broadway) has been serving dessert since 1938. 213-680-0243, chinatownla.com

Egyptian Theatre • Hollywood • Movie Theater

Best Movie Theaters The Egyptian Theatre got a badly needed $14 million surgery in 1998, and now the place looks at least as good as it did when Sid Grauman was hosting screenings here of *Robin Hood* (the one starring Douglas Fairbanks Sr.). Predating Grauman's better-known Chinese Theatre (just down the block) by five years, this equally themey and ornate movie palace started into a tailspin right after premiering Barbra Streisand's *Funny Girl* (coincidence?). Mothballed for years, the new home of the American Cinematheque screens a wide range of generally non-Hollywood films. For the full experience, book a guided afternoon tour of the theater. An hour-long house documentary, *Forever Hollywood*, plays on Saturdays and Sundays at 2pm and 3:30pm. $ 6712 Hollywood Blvd. (Las Palmas Ave.), 323-466-3456, egyptiantheatre.com

Epicurean School of Culinary Arts • West Hollywood • Activity

The CIA grads (that's Culinary Institute of America) who started this delicious school nearly 20 years ago believe that actual food, not music, is the "food of love." Fall back in amore by taking a class with your partner here. Beginners and aspiring chefs alike come here for intensive programs that can run several weeks, but many one-day workshops are also offered that focus on just about anything you and your beloved haven't yet made together—Punjab-style chicken curry, spicy tuna rolls, or chocolate soufflé with crème anglaise—whatever tickles your taste buds. Classes are usually three hours long and, of course, some kind of a meal is always included. *Call for class times.* $$$$ 8500 Melrose Ave. (La Cienega), 310-659-5990, epicureanschool.com

Farmers Market • Los Angeles • Market

The apples aren't cheap and the east side of the market might be mistaken for a glorified geriatric ward on any given Wednesday afternoon. That said, here's one of those few places in L.A. that tourist buses and devout locals (who hate tourist buses) descend upon with equal enthusiasm—unlike, say, the La Brea Tar Pits. Just how time-honored a hangout is this casual maze of fruit mongers, open-air restaurants, and souvenir stalls? Walt Disney allegedly sat at a table here working on a design for Disneyland. For a sanitized browse, check out The Grove, an outdoor shopping center next door. *Mon-Fri 9am-9pm, Sat 9am-8pm, Sun 10am-7pm.* 6333 W. Third St. (Fairfax Ave.), 323-933-9211, farmersmarketla.com

Getty Villa • Pacific Palisades • Museum

Best Cool Museums The nine-year renovation of the Getty Villa was completed for the low, low price of $275 million. The redesign changes the way visitors approach the Villa. Instead of taking an elevator up into the garden, you walk a scenic pathway and arrive at the entrance after descending the stairs of the outdoor theater. It's a bit overdone, but the walk is an appropriately dramatic lead-in for antiquities like the *Sarcophagus with Scenes of Bacchus*, the fully intact mummy, and the controversial kouros statue that may or may not be fake—your guess is as good as theirs. These works are now bathed in natural light thanks to the installation of several skylights and windows. The self-guided audio tour is worth the wait for headphones, although the word "wait" is deceiving—with a limited number of daily passes, the Villa is much less crowded than its sister museum, the Getty Center. If you failed to book ahead, check the website for last-minute availability. *Thu-Mon 10am-5pm.* 17985 Pacific Coast Hwy. (Sunset Blvd.), 310-440-7300, getty.edu

Gold's Gym • Venice Beach • Gym

Best Workouts Even though Gold's Gym in Venice is synonymous with Arnold Schwarzenegger, Franco Columbo, and myriad other champions who have worked out at the "Mecca of Bodybuilding," this isn't the bare-bones Gold's of yesteryear, where you'd need a weight belt and some serious ego to even think of entering the place. There is no separate room for Mr. Olympia hopefuls who are still drawn to this legendary gym en masse. The main room has machines, free weights, and an egalitarian mix of muscleheads, babes, and regular folks like you just looking to stay in shape. *Mon-Fri 4am-midnight, Sat-Sun 5am-11pm.* $$ 360 Hampton Dr. (Rose Ave.), 310-392-6004, goldsgym.com

Grand Central Market • Downtown • Market

Unlike the pricey Farmers Market at Third and Fairfax, the true bazaar experience is still going strong at L.A.'s oldest and largest open-air market. In its 87th year, Grand Central is still bursting with cheap produce, meat, poultry, pupusas, warm tortillas, ceviche, fish tacos, chow mein, mango concoctions, fruit drinks you can't pronounce, and some of the best people-watching this side of the L.A. River. *Mon-Sun 9am-6pm.* 317 S. Broadway (Fourth St.), 213-624-2378, grandcentralsquare.com

Grauman's Chinese Theatre • Hollywood • Movie Theater

Landmarks don't get more "must-visit" than Hollywood's number one tourist destination. After measuring your digits against the handprints of Clark Gable or Katharine Hepburn, you can actually go in and watch a movie, something countless stars have done during countless world premieres of countless movies from time immemorial ... or 1927, when this faux-Oriental movie house opened with a premiere of Cecil B. DeMille's *The King of Kings*. The option of getting your own hands forever recorded in cement—a keepsake you must take with you—helps make this the kitschiest of all Hollywood attractions, which is saying something. To see this shrine in all of its fake-Orient glory, take the half-hour tour, which covers the main lobby, auditorium, VIP balcony, and backstage area. *Tours: Daily every 30 minutes between 10:30am and 5pm. Several screenings daily.* $ 6925 Hollywood Blvd. (Orange Dr.), 323-461-3331, manntheaters.com

Greystone Park & Mansion • Beverly Hills • Park/Site

Believe it or not, you can actually pull into the driveway of the largest home ever built in Beverly Hills and not draw a squad of security cars. Sitting gray, empty, and most likely haunted on 16 acres of public grounds, the 55-room Greystone Mansion was built by oil baron Edward L. Doheny as a housewarming gift to his son, who lived here for all of six months before dying in a bizarre murder-suicide in 1929. The house (which has starred in many movies) is closed to the public, but the grounds are wide open, with nice hilltop views, plenty of grassy picnic space, and a labyrinth of old stairways, stone walkways, and secluded courtyards. Admission is free and parking is available within the gates. *Daily 10am-5pm.* 905 Loma Vista Dr. (Robert Ln.), 310-550-4796, greystonemansion.org

Griffith Park Observatory • Los Feliz • Park/Site

Originally opened in 1935, Griffith Park Observatory has evolved into one of Los Angeles' most enduring icons. Perched high atop Mount Hollywood, the classical building has been a landmark on the skyline and the backdrop for numerous films, including, of course, *Rebel Without a Cause*. The Observatory only recently reopened after years of renovations, including the addition of the copper dome. Because of the high interest of visitors, taking a shuttle up the hill or hiking up are the only ways to visit—no private cars allowed. Shuttle bus pickup is either at Hollywood & Highland on the west side of the complex, or at a satellite parking lot at the zoo. And timed reservations, best made online, are an absolute necessity—you will not be admitted without your printout. Also, your entrance ticket only gets you so far: If you want to see the planetarium show, you need to purchase an additional ticket at the Observatory—but there is limited space, meaning that once you get off that shuttle bus, its a rush to the ticket counter. But for athletic types, some tickets are available for free 48 hours before the visiting time. For these tickets, you get to park at the Greek Theater and either take a shuttle bus or walk up. *Tue-Fri noon-10pm, Sat-Sun 10am-10pm.* $- Griffith Park, 888-695-0888, griffithobs.org

Hollywood Entertainment Museum • Hollywood • Museum

A museum on Hollywood Boulevard about movies and TV? Go figure. It's also the only one on this street to be taken more than half-seriously, going so far as to call its subject matter "the entertaining arts." About a century of film, television, and radio art is showcased here, including a number of memorabilia exhibits, multi-screen video presentations, and interactive displays demonstrating various facets of production, and a Foley room where you can create your own sound effects. A reconstruction of a studio lot in the back includes famous sets from *Star Trek: The Next Generation* and *Cheers.* Visit the museum gift shop for old stage props and clothes worn by the stars. *11am-6pm, closed Wed during the winter.* $ 7021 Hollywood Blvd. (Orange Dr.), 323-465-7900, hollywoodmuseum.com

Hollywood Forever Cemetery • Hollywood • Cemetery

Best Graveyards of the Stars Where are they now? Some of Tinseltown's biggest ex-living legends are resting in these peaceful old grounds in full view of the Hollywood Sign. Want some names? Rudolph Valentino, Douglas Fairbanks, Peter Lorre, Clifton Webb, Jesse Lasky, Janet Gaynor, and Darla and Alfalfa from *The Little Rascals.* For a truly unusual night out, check out a movie screened on the grounds by looking over the summer schedule at cinespia.org. *Daily 8am-5pm.* 6000 Santa Monica Blvd. (Gower St.), 323-469-1181, hollywoodforever.com

Hollywood Walk of Fame • Hollywood • Site

Part publicity stunt, part tribute to great entertainers like Bob Hope and Big Bird, and part sorry-but-no-cigar to rejected applicants like Suzanne Somers—Hollywood's most famous roll of credits stretches along the sidewalks of Hollywood Boulevard between La Brea and Gower, and along Vine Street between Sunset and Yucca. More than 2,100 illustrious names in film, television, radio, recording, and live theater are emblazoned on these bronze-and-marble stars, and it's amazing how many do not ring a bell. This year's new arrivals include Anthony Hopkins, Britney Spears, and Journey. Hollywood Blvd. and Vine St., hollywoodchamber.net

Holy Cross Cemetery • Culver City • Cemetery

Best Graveyards of the Stars Two hundred acres of rolling hills house the remains of everyone from Ann Miller and Rita Hayworth to Fred MacMurray and John Candy. Most of the celebrities rest in peace in a section to the southwest called The Grotto. *Daily 8am-5pm.* 5835 W. Slauson Ave. (Bristol Pkwy.), 310-670-7697

Huntington Botanical Gardens • San Marino • Gardens

Founded by railroad and real estate tycoon Henry Huntington, the 150-acre grounds include three art galleries and a library filled with rare stuff. But unless a really old volume of *The Canterbury Tales* excites you, head for the gardens. An array of more than 15,000 plant species is immaculately arranged into a variety of themed landscapes, including Japanese, Australian, palm, desert, jungle, and subtropical, plus a separate rose garden with about 1,500 varieties of plants. *Tue-Fri noon-4:30pm, Sat-Sun 10:30am-4:30pm.* $ 1151 Oxford Rd. (E. Union St.), 626-405-2100, huntington.org

Leo Carillo State Beach • Malibu • Beach

Nearly 30 miles upcoast from Santa Monica at the county line, Malibu's last stop attracts surfers, sailboarders, and beachcombers to its one-and-a-half-mile sandy beach speckled with sea caves and some nice tide pools. Hikers and campers can cross the highway to the adjoining state park filled with hilly trails and sycamore-sheltered campgrounds. Between December and April, keep a lookout for gray whales. *Daily 8am-10pm.* 35000 Pacific Coast Hwy. (Mulholland Hwy.), 818-880-0350

Los Angeles Conservancy Walking Tours • Downtown • Tour

Best Guided Tours Hook up with volunteer guides from this large nonprofit organization for one of several excellent Saturday morning Downtown walking tours. The Broadway Theaters walk is a runaway favorite, showcasing the ornate remains of Movietown's first Main Street before Hollywood Boulevard took over in the '20s. A rotation of ten other tours includes close-ups of Union Station, the Biltmore Hotel, and Little Tokyo. *Most tours begin at 10am and last 2.5 hours, but start times (and meeting places) do vary, so call ahead for reservations.* $ 523 W. Sixth St. (S. Olive St.), Suite 826, 213-623-2489, laconservancy.org

Los Angeles County Museum of Art (LACMA) • Los Angeles • Museum

Best Cool Museums When you want to see a Winslow Homer, a Rembrandt, a Diego Rivera, and a Chinese sculpture from the Tang Dynasty all in one go, this big gray edifice on Wilshire Boulevard's Miracle Mile is the place to do it. Permanent exhibits at LACMA—one of the country's largest art museums with over 250,000 holdings—cover a huge scope of American, European, and Asian works from the moderns to the ancients. Major traveling exhibitions almost always wind up here, too. The facility includes a cafe, a Rodin sculpture garden, and a lecture hall and special screening theater, plus extensive grounds shared with the oozing La Brea Tar Pits. Free outdoor jazz concerts on the museum's open-air plaza are a Friday evening ritual between April and December (5:30-8:30pm). Free chamber concerts are held in the Leo S. Bing Theater on Sunday evenings (6pm). *Mon, Tue, Thu noon-8pm, Fri noon-9pm, Sat-Sun 11am-8pm.* $ 5905 Wilshire Blvd. (Fairfax Ave.), 323-857-6000, lacma.org

Madison • Beverly Hills • Shop

Women don't come here to get deals on shoes, they come to to feed the Imelda Marcos disease that causes closets to fill to capacity. With a selection of footwear that includes Jimmy Choo, Sigerson Morrison, and Marc Jacobs, among other budget-breaking styles, Madison is the kind of place where you don't plan on paying several hundred dollars for a pair of black pumps, it just sort of happens. *Daily 10am-7pm.* 9630 Brighton Way (Bedford Dr.), 310-273-4787, madisonstyle.com

Malibu Country Club • Malibu • Golf

Los Angeles has a ton of golf clubs open to the public, but none with names like this. High above the coast of Malibu, the gates of this William F. Bell–designed, par 72 course are surprisingly wide open to nonmembers. There aren't any ocean views on these canyon-encased fairways, but they are lovely, secluded grounds in their own right. There's no driving range either, so warm up in the shower before you come. *Daily 6:30am-sunset.* $$$$ 901 Encinal Canyon Rd. (Mulholland Hwy.), 818-889-6680, malibucountryclub.com

Manhattan Beach • Manhattan Beach • Beach

Best Beaches Hard-to-please visitors tend to cheer up when they're taken to this yuppie backyard in the South Bay. The rents have skyrocketed since the Beach Boys hung out here, but there's still a plethora of people hanging out—bikini babes, volleyball players, rollerbladers, sand wastrels—who seem unamble to afford much in the way of clothing. It's one of the more active, outdoorsy parts of Greater Los Angeles, but the simple act of laying out on a towel hasn't gone out of fashion. End of Manhattan Beach Blvd.

Mann's Village Theatre • Westwood • Movie Theater

Best Movie Theaters Thanks to the cineplex craze, they truly don't make movie theaters like the Mann's Village Theatre anymore. From the historic Fox Tower to the whimsical 1,400-seat space, this is the perfect spot to see a modern-day epic. $ 961 Broxton Ave. (Weyburn Ave.), 310-248-6266, manntheaters.com

Museum of Tolerance • Los Angeles • Cultural Museum

In its ten years, this unique educational arm of the Simon Wiesenthal Center has welcomed nearly 4 million people, including nine heads of state and the Dalai Lama. Visits begins with a brief orientation, during which guests are prompted to choose between two doors, labeled "Prejudiced" and "Unprejudiced," which lead to the main exhibition room. Self-guided tours in the Tolerancenter lead through a floor of interactive exhibits that provoke self-examination while offering an objective exploration of contemporary and historic issues centering on race and prejudice in America, from the Civil Rights movement to the L.A. riots. Reserve an hour and five minutes for the extensive Holocaust Section, which takes visitors back in time and walks them room by room through a pre-taped chronicle of events during World War II. The museum also houses a multimedia learning center and a temporary exhibition gallery, and offers daily seminars hosted by Holocaust survivors. *Mon-Thu 11am-6:30pm (last entry 4pm), Fri 11am-3pm (last entry 1pm), Sun 11am-7:30pm (last entry 5pm), closed Sat.* $ 9786 W. Pico Blvd. (Roxbury Dr.), 310-553-8403, museumoftolerance.com

Norton Simon Museum • Pasadena • Art Museum

Best Cool Museums The late industrialist Norton Simon ranks among the world's greatest art patrons and collectors. His staggering collection is best known for its European holdings, which showcase over five centuries of masterpieces, from Botticelli and Raphael to Toulouse-Lautrec and Picasso. A huge cache of French Impressionist work includes an entire gallery devoted to Degas. Simon's later art interests leaned toward India and Southeast Asia, and are represented here by a remarkable Asian sculpture collection spanning 2,000 years. A recent $6 million renovation by Frank Gehry brightened the place and improved the lovely gardens, which are modeled after Monet's Giverny. Norton Simon's life is encapsulated in

CLASSIC

a half-hour documentary, screening daily in the museum's theater. Award-winning audio tours highlight more than a hundred works and allow you to view them in whatever order you choose. *Wed-Thu, Sat-Mon noon-6pm, Fri noon-9pm.* $ 411 W. Colorado Blvd. (Orange Grove Blvd.), 626-449-6840, nortonsimon.org

Paramount Pictures • Hollywood • Tour/Site
Take a two-hour behind-the-scenes look through the very recognizable Bronson or Melrose gates of this famous studio. You can also attend a television taping. It'll get tedious once the novelty wears off, but at least you'll be standing inside the last major studio in Hollywood. Reservations—required—can be made up to 30 days ahead by calling guest relations at 323-956-1777. For a great margarita in a local scene, head across the street to Lucy's El Adobe (5536 Melrose Ave., 323-462-9421). *Shows usually start around 5pm and run for 3-4 hours.* $$$ 5555 Melrose Ave. (Van Ness Ave.), 323-956-5000, paramount.com

Paramount Ranch • Agoura Hills • Site
In the 1920s, Paramount purchased this set piece of mountains, canyons, and creeks in the Santa Monica Mountains and turned it into a bustling Western movie factory—home of *Gunsmoke*, *Gunfight at the OK Corral*, and *The Adventures of Tom Sawyer*. Walk through the property's old Western Town façade and follow the chaparral-covered Coyote Canyon Trail to a quiet picnic ground with nice vistas. *Daily 8am-sunset.* Paramount Ranch Rd. (Cornell Rd.), 818-597-9192, paramount.com

Red Line Tours • Hollywood • Tour
Best Guided Tours A small fry on the Hollywood tour circuit, Red Line leads one of the most personalized and informative walks through historic Hollywood. The standard tour includes inside access to Grauman's Egyptian Theatre, Disney's El Capitan Theatre, the Roosevelt Hotel, and Hollywood's last remaining speakeasy, hiding in a place you'd otherwise never find. Guides point out architectural highlights, spout local trivia, and provide good updates on Hollywood's billion-dollar resuscitation effort. Customized walks and tours of Downtown are also available. *Four Historic Hollywood tours daily between 10am and 4pm.* $ 6773 Hollywood Blvd. (Highland Ave.), 323-402-1074, redlinetours.com

Rose Bowl Flea Market • Pasadena • Market
On the second Sunday of every month, more than 2,000 vendors descend on the Rose Bowl parking lot with a million-plus items, including but not limited to vintage and contemporary clothes, antiques, furnishings, electronics, collectibles, novelty items, and beauty products—just about everything but animals, guns, ammunition, and pornography. Bring some sunscreen and a hat, because this can be an all-day affair. *9am-4:30pm.* $ 1001 Rose Bowl Dr. (N. Arroyo Blvd.), 323-560-7469, rgcshows.com

Silent Movie Theatre • Hollywood • Movie Theater
Hollywood's first generation of movie stars gets its due at this little gem that hails itself as "the last fully operational silent cinema in America." Sit back, give the live organist a warm welcome, enjoy some *Felix the Cat* cartoon openers, and gain an appreciation for pre-talkie legends like Rudolph Valentino, Mary Pickford, and Buster Keaton. *Tue-Sat 8pm, Sun matinees at 1pm.* $ 611 N. Fairfax Ave. (Melrose Ave.), 323-655-2520, silentmovietheatre.com

Southwest Museum of the American Indian • Los Angeles • Cultural Museum
Slightly off the radar in Mt. Washington, L.A.'s oldest museum dedicates itself to the people who were already here when the Europeans arrived to wreak havoc and build museums. The lovely 90-year-old hilltop hacienda contains one of the best collections of American Indian art and artifacts in the U.S. Four main exhibit halls focus on the Southwest, California, the Great Plains, and the Northwest Coast. Highlights include a Chumash rock-art site replica and an 18-foot Cheyenne summer tipi. Loads of pre-Columbian pottery, textiles, baskets, paintings, and other relics cover Native groups from Alaska to South America, but note: Renovations mean that much of the collection is in storage. Check the website for updates. *Sat-Sun noon-5pm.* $ 234 Museum Dr. (Marmion Way), 323-221-2163, autrynationalcenter.org/southwest

Sunset Strip • West Hollywood • Site
The Sunset Strip has sported various personalities, from that of celebrity nexus in the '20s, '30s, and '40s to that of rocker mecca in the '70s. Recently, though, the celebrated 17-mile stretch of Sunset Boulevard has gone uptown, with high-rises and chichi nightclubs dotting the landscape where edgy rock havens and gritty nightclubs once stood. The vibe may be more martini than Budweiser these days, but the essentials of the last few decades—historic rock clubs, colorful billboards, and eye candy—have never really left. They're just waiting for the Strip's next incarnation. Sunset Blvd. (La Cienega Blvd.)

Temescal Gateway Park • Pacific Palisades • Park
Best Hikes This accessible park right off Sunset Boulevard in Pacific Palisades is one of the Westside's quickest and easiest escape hatches into the mountains, providing well-tended trails and some wonderful views of the coast at the top. Enter the parking lot from Sunset at Temescal Canyon Road (or save a few bucks by parking on the street). Temescal Ridge Trail and Temescal Canyon Trail form a five-mile loop up a moderate to steep grade—passing seasonal waterfalls, rocky outcrops, and sweeping ocean vistas. Watch out for poison oak (leaves grow three to a stem and each leaf contains three leaflets, which look like small oak leaves). Bring your own water. Temescal Gateway Park, 15601 Sunset Blvd. (Temescal Canyon Rd.), 310-454-1395, lamountains.com

3rd Street Dance • Los Angeles • Activity
Even if you're not getting hitched in two weeks, you need to know a few dance steps, just to be civilized. Moves of all kinds are taught at this top-notch dance school, which offers basic and advanced classes in salsa, swing, tango, ballroom, and other popular styles (if Viennese waltzes are your thing, the staff can usually accommodate special requests). Group classes usually run for several weeks, so book a private lesson, and one of the school's five professional dance studios plus an instructor is all yours for an hour. Cedars Sinai Hospital is right across the street if you twist something. *Classes Mon-Thu 10am-10pm, Fri 10am-6pm, Sat 10:30am-5pm.* $$$$ 8558 W. Third St. (La Cienega Blvd.), 310-275-4683, 3rdstreetdance.com

Tracey Ross • West Hollywood • Shop
Like the eponymous owner's innate sense of style, the store has a warmth that turns shopping celebrities into devotees. Must-have offerings run the gamut from Ross' own shoe line to Chloe dresses to snakeskin iPod cases to hundred-dollar

foot cream, not to mention the occasional item Ross picks up from her extensive travels abroad. If you need a break from all that shopping, there are comfy couches for resting. *Mon-Sat 10am-7pm, Sun noon-5pm.* 8595 W. Sunset Blvd. (Sunset Plaza Dr.), 310-854-1996, traceyross.com

Warner Brothers Studios • Burbank • Site/Tour

Best Studio Tours Long before it belonged to AOL, this 110-acre dream factory was churning out *Casablanca*, *Rebel Without a Cause*, *Bonnie and Clyde*, *Dirty Harry*, *Chariots of Fire*, and countless other movies and TV productions. And the show at this busy lot goes on. Get behind the scenes on a two-hour VIP tour, which offers a candid look at life on the lot without the aid of a theme park ride. Warner's Deluxe Tour (Wednesdays only, at the moment) is twice as long and includes lunch. Tickets are available online, or first-come, first-served on the lot. *Tours depart weekdays on the half hour, 8:30am-4pm, varied hours in summer.* $$$$ 4000 Warner Blvd. (Avon St.), 818-972-8687, wbsf.warnerbros.com

Will Rogers State Historic Park • Pacific Palisades • Park

This former home of the famous cowboy humorist Will Rogers is now the only state park in the Santa Monica Mountains featuring a 31-room mansion and polo grounds. Back in the day, Rogers and buddies like Walt Disney, David Niven, and Gary Cooper mounted their ponies and gallivanted around the 186-acre estate's regulation-size polo field before retreating to the Beverly Hills Hotel's Polo Lounge for grub—which is allegedly how the place got its name. Players and spectators still gather here for Saturday games, but the real prize is a rejuvenating mile hike up to Inspiration Point, with its wide-angle views of the Westside and the Pacific Coast. Picnic grounds are down the hill by the parking lot. Don't forget to pay respects at the old Rogers ranch house. *Daily 8am-sunset.* $ 1501 Will Rogers State Park Rd. (Sunset Blvd.), 310-454-8212, parks.ca.gov

Zuma Beach • Malibu • Beach

Best Beaches Malibu's best full-service beach borders quieter gems like Westward Beach and Point Dume's County Beach, which are slightly trickier to access. For a restful day on four miles of sand with restrooms, lifeguards, volleyball courts, gymnastic rings, and fry-shacks when you need them, start here. The water is clean, the surf's decent, the sand is beer-bottle-free, and Santa Monica is a relaxing 20 miles away. Save six bucks by parking for free on PCH. 30050 Pacific Coast Hwy. (Morning View Dr.)

PRIME TIME
LOS ANGELES

Everything in life is timing. Would you want to arrive in Pamplona, Spain, the day after the Running of the Bulls? Not if you have a choice and relish being a part of life's peak experiences. With our month-by-month calendar of events, there's no excuse to miss out on any of Los Angeles' greatest moments. From the classic to the quirky, the sophisticated to the outrageous, you'll find all you need to know about the city's best events right here.

Prime Time Basics

Eating and Drinking

Los Angeles starts lunch between noon and 1pm, dinner between 7:30pm and 9pm, and Sunday brunch at 10am. Some restaurants have a break between lunch and dinner, starting at about 2:30pm, with dinner service resuming at around 5pm. Cocktails before dinner are most popular at 7pm, but happy hour gets started around 6pm, when some exhausted workers, preferring to avoid L.A.'s intense rush-hour traffic, hit the bars near where they work. Most bars really get going by 9pm or 10pm, and last call is around 1:30am, though alcohol is served up until 2am. The Westside, Pasadena, and the Valley tend to go to sleep earlier, while Hollywood is the late-night king, continuing to rock well into the wee hours with a large offering of after-hours clubs.

Weather and Tourism

A touch of fog in the summer. A dash of rain in the winter. Nearly 300 days of at least partial sunshine and no humidity. Smog aside, it really is a lovely day just about every day in Los Angeles. That mildness doesn't necessarily extend to the Valley, which, unlike the rest of L.A., can be relied upon to hit triple digits in summer.

Dec–Feb: These are the coolest and rainiest months, though it's not uncommon to have a sudden heat wave in December, with temps hovering around 75 or 80 for a few days. For the past few years, rains have been especially heavy, with floods and mudslides.

Mar–May: Spring is perhaps the only discernible "season," as the jacaranda trees bloom in purple profusion and the poppies that give California the nickname "the Golden State" appear on hillsides everywhere.

Seasonal Changes

Month	Fahrenheit High	Low	Celsius High	Low
Jan	68	48	18	8
Feb	70	50	19	8
Mar	70	52	19	9
Apr	73	54	21	10
May	75	58	22	12
June	80	61	24	13
July	84	65	27	16
Aug	85	66	28	16
Sept	83	65	27	14
Oct	79	60	24	12
Nov	73	53	23	10
Dec	69	48	19	8

It can still be cool in the evenings, especially close to the coast. And although it doesn't happen often, rains can still hit in this season. Bring layers to be prepared.

June–Aug: The hottest months of the year see virtually no rain. June often brings with it a weather condition referred to as "June gloom," when the skies are known to stay overcast throughout the day. July gets the real heat, when it's warm even at night. With August comes some humidity, which tends to be felt more acutely here, since many homes and businesses don't have air-conditioning.

Sept–Nov: Early fall brings the hot Santa Ana winds, which blow in from the desert and push the smog out to sea, resulting in some spectacularly fiery sunsets—along with wildfires in the hills. Otherwise, it can be a fairly mild time of year.

National Holidays

New Year's Day	January 1
Martin Luther King Day	Third Monday in January
Valentine's Day	February 14
Presidents' Day	Third Monday in February
Memorial Day	Last Monday in May
Independence Day	July 4
Labor Day	First Monday in September
Columbus Day	Second Monday in October
Halloween	October 31
Veterans Day	Second Monday in November
Thanksgiving Day	Fourth Thursday in November
Christmas Day	December 25
New Year's Eve	December 31

Listings in blue are major celebrations but not official holidays.

PRIME TIME

The Best Events Calendar

January

- Tournament of Roses Parade and Rose Bowl Game

February

- The Academy Awards
- Chinese New Year and Golden Dragon Parade
- Nissan Open Golf Tournament

March

- Los Angeles Marathon

April

- Toyota Grand Prix of Long Beach

May

- Cinco de Mayo Festival
- Venice Art Walk

June

- Playboy Jazz Festival

July

- Festival of Arts and Pageant of the Masters
- Honda U.S. Open of Surfing

August

- Long Beach Blues Festival
- Nisei Week Japanese Festival

September

- Los Angeles County Fair
- Watts Towers Day of the Drum

October

- Halloween Carnaval

November

- AFI Fest
- Catalina Island Triathlon
- Doo Dah Parade
- Hollywood Christmas Parade
- L.A. Auto Show

December

- Holiday Light Festivals

Night+Day's Top Four Events are in blue.

The Best Events

January

Tournament of Roses Parade and Rose Bowl Game

626-449-7673, parade tickets 626-795-4171, tournamentofroses.com

The Lowdown: At 8am, Pasadena ushers in the New Year with its world-famous parade of floral floats, followed by one of the biggest football games of the year (in the top four of Bowl games, with teams chosen by computer ranking). The Rose Bowl is "The Granddaddy of Them All," and isn't sponsored by FedEx, Nokia, or Tostitos like some of the other big college bowls out there. Kick-off is usually at 2pm. For the parade, line up very early, or reserve VIP seating.

When and How Much: *January 1.* Parade Free, Rose Bowl ticket prices vary.

February

The Academy Awards

310-247-3000, oscars.org

The Lowdown: Formerly in March, Hollywood's biggest tribute to itself has been pushed forward to late February when dolled-up celebs congregate at Hollywood & Highland's new Kodak Theatre for Oscar Night. Don't expect to get anywhere near the entrance of this private, high-security event, but crowds will always flock here to catch a glimpse of their favorite stars outside. (For a savvy approach, book reservations at celebrity-friendly hotels and restaurants well in advance, as the days before the event are filled with parties.) Bleacher seats are traditionally offered on a lottery basis. But most important, there is no hotter weekend in L.A.

When and How Much: *Late February.* Free.

Chinese New Year and Golden Dragon Parade

213-617-0396, lagoldendragonparade.com

The Lowdown: L.A.'s Chinese community throws its own New Year's party, with floats, marching bands, and 100-foot dragons parading down North Broadway into the heart of Chinatown amidst more than 110,000 celebrants and a steady eruption of firecrackers. Famous guests of honor have included Bruce Lee, Hugh Hefner, Dr. Haing Ngor from *The Killing Fields,* Kieu Chinh from *The Joy Luck Club*, and actress Ming-Na. The good times carry on into the evening, so stick around for dinner in Chinatown.

When and How Much: *Takes place on Chinese New Year's Day, which falls in late January or early February.* Free.

Nissan Open Golf Tournament

800-752-6736, nissanopen.pgatour.com

The Lowdown: It's the oldest civic-sponsored golf competition on the PGA Tour. More important, this event that began in 1926 is the Tour's only stop in Los Angeles—and an excellent place to spy on celebrity golf fans. The ritzy Riviera Country Club in Pacific Palisades has been the tournament's primary host for eight decades.

When and How Much: *Mid-February.* Tickets from $25 to $180.

March

Los Angeles Marathon

310-444-5544, lamarathon.com

The Lowdown: While New York and Boston wait for the ice to thaw, L.A. hosts the nation's first big city marathon (and the world's seventh largest). The 26.2-mile course starts and ends Downtown, looping past 25 entertainment sites and about a million cheering spectators. The race usually begins just after 8am, starting with the world-renowned Wheelchair Division. More than 20,000 marathoners are expected. Other events held on this day include a 5K (3.1-mile) run-walk and a noncompetitive Bike Tour along the marathon route.

When and How Much: *Usually held the first Sunday of March.* Free to watch, but the fee for entering the race starts at $75.

April

Toyota Grand Prix of Long Beach

888-827-7333, longbeachgp.com

The Lowdown: Southern California's most anticipated street race roars to life on the coast of Long Beach. The big races of this three-day motor-sporting tradition are held on Sunday, when the pros burn up a 1.97-mile course winding along Shoreline Drive. Saturday is when drivers like Clint Eastwood, Jay Leno, Cameron Diaz, and Ashley Judd take to the streets for the celebrity laps.

When and How Much: *Early to mid-April every year.* Tickets range from $45 for general admission up to $725 for special-access and multiday passes.

May

Cinco de Mayo Festival

213-628-1274, cityofla.org/elp

The Lowdown: May 5 marks not Mexico's Independence Day but its miraculous victory over French invaders during the Battle of Puebla (1862). The main event is held Downtown around historic Olvera Street, where mariachis, dancers, food stalls, and plenty of other festive offerings are in full swing, sometimes for three days straight. The nighttime, when the tequila flows freely, is the best for revelry.

When and How Much: *May 5.* Free.

Venice Art Walk
310-392-9255, venicefamilyclinic.org

The Lowdown: This annual art crawl, food fair, and local fundraiser is your two-day ticket to Venice's thriving art scene. More than 60 private studios open their doors to visitors, who can enjoy several one-time exhibits as well as meetings with emerging and famous painters, sculptors, photographers, cartoonists, and graphic artists. Don't miss the silent auction, where bids are placed for hundreds of contemporary works.

When and How Much: *Third weekend in May.* Prices start at $50 for walking tours or art auctions.

June

Playboy Jazz Festival
310-449-1173, festivalproductions.net/events.php

The Lowdown: Hugh Hefner puts on a respectable two-day show at the Hollywood Bowl featuring an eclectic range of fully clothed jazz legends, international musicians, and hot newcomers usually hosted by longtime Master of Ceremonies Bill Cosby. Past performers at this music event approaching its 30th year include the Blind Boys of Alabama, Dave Brubeck, Herbie Hancock, and Boz Scaggs.

When and How Much: *Father's Day weekend.* Ticket prices range from $30 for the bleachers up to $100 for box seats.

July

Festival of Arts and Pageant of the Masters
800-487-3378, foapom.com

The Lowdown: Laguna Beach hosts one of California's largest, longest-running, and—at times—oddest summer art shows during the months of July and August. Works from more than 140 artists in this six-acre canyon setting near the coast run the gamut from paintings, sculpture, and photographs to hand-crafted furniture, musical instruments, and scrimshaw. Several workshops, hands-on demonstrations, and docent-led tours are offered throughout the day. Evening guests can enjoy the weirdly beautiful Pageant of the Masters, a surreal 90-minute tableaux series featuring real-life reenactments of classic works of art accompanied by live narration and an orchestral score.

When and How Much: *From early July to the beginning of September.* Ticket prices range from $20 to $80.

PRIME TIME

Honda U.S. Open of Surfing

310-473-0411, usopenofsurfing.com

The Lowdown: Huntington Beach is a surfer-dude hotbed any day of the summer, but during the annual U.S. Open of Surfing, it's ground zero, attracting many of the world's best big-wave riders and more than 200,000 tanned fans. Running alongside the main event are the Beach Games, with competitions in BMX biking and skateboarding. Women's surfing finals are usually held on Saturday, followed by the men's finals on Sunday. Food and entertainment are included.

When and How Much: *Last full week of July.* Free.

August

Long Beach Blues Festival

562-985-5566, jazzandblues.org

The Lowdown: This two-day blues fest, held on the Long Beach State University campus, is more than 25 years old. A thinning supply of old-school blues legends has forced the annual concert to widen its parameters, with recent "blues" headliners including Joe Cocker, Al Green, and the Allman Brothers. It's still the biggest and best blues festival in the West. Wine, beer, and food are served.

When and How Much: *Labor Day weekend.* Tickets start at about $45 (six acts per day).

Nisei Week Japanese Festival

213-687-7193, niseiweek.org

The Lowdown: One of the oldest Japanese-American celebrations has been held in Downtown's Little Tokyo district since the 1930s. The nine-day cultural festival includes art exhibits, Ondo dance performances, martial arts demonstrations, fashion shows, a parade, traditional tea ceremonies, the crowning of a kimono-clad queen, and some of the best karaoke this side of Honshu.

When and How Much: *Mid-August.* Most events are free.

September

Los Angeles County Fair

909-623-3111, fairplex.com

The Lowdown: Started in 1922, this 17-day happening set in Pomona, about 35 miles east of Downtown L.A., has grown into one of the world's largest events of its kind. Throughout most of September, the Fairplex grounds teem with livestock and agricultural displays, art exhibits, quilting and cooking competitions, entertainment stages, food stands, carnival rides, and live thoroughbred racing.

When and How Much: *Starts the second Friday of September (closed Mondays and Tuesdays).* Tickets are $10 for weekdays and $15 for weekends. (Rides cost about $1 each.)

Watts Towers Day of the Drum

213-847-4646, wattstowers.net

The Lowdown: Percussion traditions from around the world are celebrated at this full-day drum fest in the Watts Art Center Amphitheater—adjacent to the amazing towers built by folk art legend Simon Rodia. A jazz concert is hosted here on the following day.

When and How Much: *Toward the end of September.* Free.

October

Halloween Carnaval

800-368-6020, holloweenwesthollywood.com

The Lowdown: All persuasions except the overly timid are welcome to participate or gape at this flamboyant Halloween street party thrown by West Hollywood's gay community. The spectacle takes place, of course, on October 31 along a small portion of Route 66 where folks are definitely getting their kicks—Santa Monica Boulevard between La Cienega Boulevard and Doheny Boulevard. Various stages and booths line the cordoned-off blocks, but the night's best, spookiest draw is the parade of outrageous costumes.

When and How Much: *Every Halloween.* Free.

November

AFI Fest

866-234-3378, afi.com

The Lowdown: If you can't make it to Cannes or Sundance, this prestigious event hosted by the American Film Institute gives you a taste of Hollywood festival hype—right in Hollywood, of all places. More than 130 films from emerging filmmakers around the world are screened. Filmmaker and audience receptions, cultural events, and live entertainment are all part of the scene as well. And, yes, celebrities do come out for this one, particularly at gala showings held in the Arclight's Cinerama Dome. Book ahead.

When and How Much: *Starts first week in November.* Each screening is $11.

Catalina Island Triathlon

714-978-1528, pacificsportsllc.com

The Lowdown: L.A.'s favorite offshore escape is also one of the world's most beautifully situated triathlon sites. If you can bear the mid-60-degree water in Avalon Bay and the roads and hills of Catalina Island—or if you want to check into a charming inn and watch others stumble through this half-mile swim, 10-mile cycle, and 3.1-mile run—make your hotel reservations long in advance.

When and How Much: *Usually held the first Saturday in November.* Being a spectator is free, but entering the competition costs $125.

PRIME TIME

Doo Dah Parade

626-205-4029, pasadenadoodahparade.info

The Lowdown: Pasadena's most colorful event was inspired by the Rose Bowl Parade—in the most lampoonish sense. The Doo Dah Parade (aka "The Other Parade") is as wacky as its older sibling is wholesome. Offbeat participants include Johnny Neurotic, the Hairy Krishnas, and The Howlelujah Chorus. The parade usually starts at 11:30am, heading south on Raymond Avenue (from Holly Street), west out to Colorado Boulevard, and ending at Pasadena Avenue.

When and How Much: *Sunday before Thanksgiving.* Free.

Hollywood Christmas Parade

323-469-2337, hollywoodchristmasparade.org

The Lowdown: Back in the 1920s, the draw consisted of a few pine trees and a young starlet sitting with a guy dressed up as Santa Claus in a reindeer-pulled sleigh. Now, close to a million spectators come to see some 100 celebrities parading along the streets of Hollywood. Live performances, marching bands, equestrians, and a pageant of star-studded floats run east on Hollywood Boulevard and west on Sunset Boulevard between Highland Avenue and Vine Street. Santa Claus is somewhere in there too. The parade is at 5pm, but get there by 3pm if you want to see anything.

When and How Much: *Sunday after Thanksgiving.* Free.

L.A. Auto Show

213-741-1151, laautoshow.com

The Lowdown: Car culture was practically invented in Los Angeles, so it's no surprise that this city hosts one of the world's biggest and coolest auto expos. For ten days in November, the L.A. Convention Center is a car-, truck-, and SUV-lover's fantasy, featuring about 1,000 hot new rides including futuristic models and more than two dozen world and North American debuts. Keep an eye out for special guests like Mario Andretti. Avoid the mobs by attending a special sneak preview hosted the evening before the show.

When and How Much: *Usually the end of November.* Admission is $10.

December

Holiday Light Festivals

888-527-2757, laparks.org

The Lowdown: Griffith Park's holiday light show is one of the largest and most impressive of its kind on the West Coast. Cars and leisurely foot traffic are drawn nightly to this illuminated mile along Crystal Springs Drive—leading to large traffic jams, so go on a weeknight if possible. Another bright spot during the holiday season is on the coast at Marina del Rey, where boats of all shapes and sizes are adorned in strands of light.

When and How Much: *Starts in early December or late November.* Free.

HIT the GROUND RUNNING

If you've never been here before—or even if you live here—the Los Angeles area can seem overwhelming. Which freeway takes you where? Which mountains are those? And by the way, what season is it? If you want to make like a native, you need to know the basics. Here are most of the facts and figures, including our *Cheat Sheet*, a quick-reference countdown of vital information that'll help you feel like an instant Angeleno.

City Essentials

Getting to Los Angeles: By Air

Los Angeles International Airport (LAX)
1 World Way, Los Angeles, 310-646-5252, lawa.org/LAX

Better known as LAX, Los Angeles International Airport ranks among the world's five busiest airports, with 60 million passengers and more than 2 million tons of cargo passing through annually. Nine terminals are arranged in a double-tiered U-shape with curbside baggage check-in available on the upper (departure) level and baggage claim on the lower (arrival) level. Clearly marked shuttle and courtesy van stops are also on the lower level in front of each terminal. Amenities include a first-aid station in the Tom Bradley International Terminal, the 48-port Travel Right cyber cafe in Terminal 4, free shuttle service between terminals on LAX's "A" Shuttle, and plenty of food and beverage options ranging from McDonald's and Starbucks to California Pizza Kitchen and Wolfgang Puck. A franchise of the Brioche Dorée deli cafes in Terminal 4 has fresh salads and sandwiches, and the bread is baked on the premises. In Terminal 7 and Terminal 2, San Francisco sourdough bakery Boudin serves the same chowder in the same sourdough bowl you'll get on Fisherman's Wharf. LAX's grooviest venue is the Encounter Restaurant, perched in the historic Theme Building complex between the terminals. Travelers Aid Society of Los Angeles (310-646-2270) operates booths in every terminal on weekdays.

Located right on the coast between El Segundo and Marina del Rey, LAX is an easy commute to Santa Monica or the South Bay beach communities. Traffic allowing, Hollywood and Downtown are each about a 45-minute drive—however, traffic is rarely light.

Directions from LAX: To Santa Monica, follow Sepulveda Blvd./Hwy. 1 north to Lincoln Blvd./Hwy. 1. To Manhattan Beach and the South Bay, take Sepulveda Blvd./Hwy. 1 south. To Beverly Hills, West Hollywood, and Hollywood, take

Direct Flying Times to Los Angeles

Nonstop From	Airport Code	Time (hr.)
Chicago	ORD	4
Honolulu	HNL	5
Las Vegas	LAS	1
London	LHR	11
Miami	MIA	5
New York	JFK	6
San Francisco	SFO	1½
Seattle	SEA	2½
Tokyo	NRT	10
Washington, D.C.	IAD	5½

Airlines Serving Los Angeles (LAX) Airport

Airline	Website	800 Number	Terminal
Air Canada	aircanada.ca	888-247-2262	2
Air China	airchina.com	800-882-8122	2
Air France	airfrance.us	800-237-2747	2
Air Tran Airways	airtran.com	800-247-8726	3
Alaska Airlines	alaskaair.com	800-426-0333	TB Int./3
America West	americawest.com	800-235-9292	1
American Airlines	aa.com	800-433-7300	4
American Trans Air	ata.com	800-435-9282	3
British Airways	britishairways.com	800-247-9297	TB Int.
Cathay Pacific	cathaypacific.com	800-233-2742	TB Int.
China Airlines	china-airlines.com	800-227-5118	TB Int.
Continental Airlines	continental.com	800-525-0280	6
Delta Airlines	delta.com	800-221-1212	5
EVA Air	evaair.com	800-695-1188	TB Int.
Frontier Airlines	flyfrontier.com	800-432-1359	3
Horizon Air	horizonair.com	800-547-9308	3
Japan Airlines	japanair.com	800-525-3663	TB Int.
KLM Royal Dutch	klm.com	800-225-2525	2
Korean Air	koreanair.com	800-438-5000	TB Int.
Lufthansa	lufthansa.com	800-645-3880	TB Int.
Mexicana	mexicana.com	800-531-7921	TB Int.
Midwest Airlines	midwestairlines.com	800-452-2022	3
Northwest Airlines	nwa.com	800-225-2525	2
Qantas	qantas.com.au	800-227-4500	TB Int./4
Singapore Airlines	singaporeair.com	800-742-3333	TB Int.
Southwest Airlines	southwest.com	800-435-9792	1
United Airlines	united.com	800-241-6522	6, 7, 8
US Airways	usairways.com	800-428-4322	1
Virgin Atlantic	virgin-atlantic.com	800-862-8621	2

HIT THE GROUND

Century Blvd. west to I-405 north and exit Santa Monica Blvd. east. For an alternate route north (especially useful during rush hour), take La Cienega Blvd. To Downtown or Pasadena, take Sepulveda Blvd. south to I-105 east to I-110 north.

Into Town by Taxi: All taxis have a flat rate of $38 to Downtown from LAX. Approximate rates from LAX to other destinations are as follows:

Manhattan Beach: $15, West Hollywood: $30-$35, Santa Monica: $30-$35, Hollywood: $40. Except for Downtown, an additional $2.50 flat fee is added for all pickups from the airport.

Into Town by Airport Shuttle Service: Several shuttles offer 24-hour door-to-door service from LAX, making a few stops along the way. Fares are often cheaper than taxis, but for groups of three or more, taxis are a better bet. Typical shuttle fares from LAX start at: Downtown $15; Hollywood $25; Santa Monica $20; Pasadena $35. Add $10 for each additional passenger.

- Airport Express   310-645-8181   800-311-5466
- Metropolitan Express   310-417-5050   800-338-3898
- Prime Time Shuttle   310-536-7922   800-733-8267
- SuperShuttle   310-782-6600   800-258-3826

Into Town by Public Transit: The "C" shuttle on the arrivals level will take you to the Metro Bus Center, where a number of buses service the Greater Los Angeles area. There is also a FlyAway bus service that offers a nonstop express to Downtown (lawa.org/flyawayinfo2.cfm). It runs 5am-1am every half-hour, and every hour 1am-5am. It's $3 each way, and as a bonus, when taking it to the airport, you can check your bags when you board at Union Station. At LAX, find it at the arrivals level under the green signs.

Best Alternative to LAX

Bob Hope Airport
2627 N. Hollywood Way, Burbank, 818-840-8840, bobhopeairport.com

The Bob Hope Airport in Burbank, which is closer than LAX to many of the city's major destinations, including the Rose Bowl, Dodger Stadium, Downtown L.A., and Hollywood, has nonstop service to many West Coast cities, as well as New York. In addition, it has far less crowds and a valet parking service. Its facilities are limited, in terms of restaurants or shops. You won't find anything more than basic airport fare here. However, one perk is that this airport offers valet parking right at the terminal. Simply follow the signs, and when your flight lands upon return, you can call ahead to have your car waiting.

Directions from Bob Hope Airport: To reach Downtown, take the 5 South towards Los Angeles. Continue to the 110 Harbor Freeway. The 110 takes you through Downtown. To reach Santa Monica, continue just past Downtown on the 110, then exit 10 West.

Taxis: Taxis are an afterthought in Los Angeles. You'll find them at the airport, at stands throughout the city, or if you call, but don't expect to hail one from the street. Base fares usually start at $2.20 and cost about $2.20 per mile. Companies servicing the airport include:

Agency	Local Number	800 Number
Beverly Hills Cab	323-469-6611	800-273-6611
Independent Taxi	323-666-0050	800-521-8294
United Taxi	323-653-5050	800-411-0303
Yellow Cab	310-412-8000	800-200-1085

Into Town by Taxi: Taxis are not as abundant at Burbank as at LAX, but finding one still shouldn't be a problem—just look in front of the terminal or call (Yellow and Checker Cab 800-750-4400 or City Cab 818-848-1000). Burbank to Downtown averages about $40, depending on traffic.

Into Town by Airport Shuttle Service: Multiple companies run shuttles from Burbank airport, but they all require advance reservations. Burbank to Downtown is about $30, while service to Hollywood is about $35. The farther west your destination, the higher the fare.

• Express Shuttle	310-324-1222	800-427-7483
• Glendale Airport Van	818-243-9570	800-896-8645
• Karmel Shuttle	714-670-3480	888-995-7433
• Prime Time Shuttle	310-536-7922	800-733-8267
• Roadrunner Shuttle	805-389-8196	800-247-7919
• Super Shuttle	310-782-6600	800-660-6042

Into Town by Public Transport: Amtrak and Metrolink both share a station within walking distance of the airport, and also offer a free shuttle to this station. Tickets can be purchased at kiosks in the station, which take cash and credit cards. Burbank to Downtown is about $5.

Airlines Serving Bob Hope Airport

Airline	Website	800 Number	Terminal
Alaska Airlines	alaskaair.com	888-426-0333	2
American Airlines	aa.com	800-433-7300	2
America West Airlines	americawest.com	800-235-9292	2
Delta Airlines	delta.com	800-221-1212	2
Jetblue Airways	jetblue.com	800-538-2583	1
Southwest Airlines	southwest.com	800-435-9792	1
United Airlines	united.com	800-241-6522	2

HIT THE GROUND

Getting to Los Angeles: By Land

By Car: Los Angeles is accessed by several major highways.

From the North: I-5 is the straightest shot through central California's San Joaquin Valley, entering the San Fernando Valley and passing Downtown L.A. en route to San Diego. For a more scenic but longer drive, U.S. 101 winds along the coast ranges from San Jose, accessing San Luis Obispo and Santa Barbara before entering Ventura County, Hollywood, and the highway's terminus in Downtown L.A. The scenic Pacific Coast Highway (also known as PCH or Hwy. 1) traces the Big Sur Coast, entering L.A. through Malibu and connecting with I-10 East in Santa Monica.

Driving Times to Los Angeles

From	Distance (mi.)	Approx. Time (hr.)
Chicago	2,050	34
Las Vegas	270	4½
New York	2,790	47
Phoenix	370	6
Salt Lake City	690	10
San Diego	120	2
San Francisco	380	6½
Seattle	1,141	19

From the South: I-5 leads into Downtown L.A. from San Diego and Orange County. I-405 splits from I-5 at the southern end of Orange County, running through L.A.'s Westside before reconnecting with I-5 at the top of the San Fernando Valley.

From the East: I-10 passes through Downtown L.A., through the heart of the city, and curves north into PCH at the beach in Santa Monica.

By Train: Amtrak (800-USA-RAIL, amtrak.com) enters and leaves Los Angeles from Downtown's Union Station (800 N. Alameda St.). Trains pulling into this classic Mission-style building include the Coast Starlight, heading down the West Coast from Seattle through Portland and Oakland; the Pacific Surfliner, offering 11 daily round-trips from San Diego and carrying on to Santa Barbara in the north; the Southwest Chief, starting in Chicago and cutting through Kansas City and Albuquerque; the Sunset Limited, leaving from New Orleans to Orlando, Florida, on a two-day trip through the Southwest (until further notice, service is modified due to Hurricane Katrina).

Rental Cars: All major rental car companies offer complimentary shuttle service to offices just outside the airport. Courtesy phones are available in the arrival areas.

Agency	Website	Local Number	800 Number
Alamo	alamo.com	310-649-2242	800-327-9633
Avis	avis.com	310-646-5600	800-331-1212
Budget	budget.com	310-642-4555	800-527-0700
Dollar	dollar.com	310-274-0001	800-800-4000
Enterprise	enterprise.com	310-649-5400	800-325-8007
Hertz	hertz.com	310-568-5100	800-654-3131
National	nationalcar.com	310-338-8200	800-227-7368
Thrifty	thrifty.com	310-645-1880	800-367-2277

Luxury

• Beverly Hills Rent-A-Car	310-337-1400	800-479-5996

Independent

• Rent-A-Wreck	310-826-7555	800-995-0994

Los Angeles: Lay of the Land

Los Angeles is spread out like no other city. In theory, it's possible to get around without a car, but it can be incredibly time-consuming. A basic knowledge of the main freeways and streets (see later in this chapter) is invaluable. So is a Thomas Guide (a complete indexed street map) for Los Angeles and Orange Counties if you're planning on spending much time here. Speed limits, unless otherwise posted, are 35 mph on city streets and 65 mph on freeways. Rush hour is generally from 7-10am and 3-7pm. Accidents clogging up the freeways can be avoided by tuning into traffic updates reported every six to ten minutes on the AM stations KNX 1070 and KFWB 980. Freeway carpool lanes can be a huge time-saver, but don't risk a $341 fine if you're driving alone.

HIT THE GROUND

Getting Around Los Angeles

By Bus: Relying on the bus to see L.A. is a bit like relying on the breast stroke to tour Venice, Italy. That said, you can get around cheaply on one. A network of more than 200 bus lines covers L.A., mainly for car-less local commuters. Contact the Metropolitan Transportation Authority (MTA) for maps, timetables, and passes (213-626-4455, mta.net). The Cadillac of L.A. bus services is Santa Monica's Big Blue Bus (bigbluebus.com, 310-451-5444), which offers clean, efficient service throughout the Westside. DASH (808-2273, no area code needed, ladottransit.com) offers 25-cent rides all over the Downtown area from dawn to dusk.

By Taxi: Taxis are an afterthought in Los Angeles. You'll find them at the airport, at stands throughout the city, or if you call, but don't expect to hail one from the street. Fares start at $2.20 and cost $2.20 per additional mile. (See the taxi list in the previous section, "Into Town by Taxi.")

By Train: Metro Rail (213-626-4455 / 800-266-6883, mta.net) offers four lines connecting a large portion of Greater Los Angeles. The Blue Line runs north-south between Downtown and Long Beach. The Green Line runs east-west between Norwalk and Redondo Beach. The Red Line is L.A.'s subway, running northwest from Downtown through Hollywood to Universal City and North Hollywood. The Gold Line runs northeast from Downtown to Pasadena. The recently opened Orange Line is a bus that connects Metro Rail with the San Fernando Valley. Metrolink (800-371-5465, metrolinktrains.com) is a commuter train system connecting Downtown's Union Station with neighboring Orange, Riverside, San Bernardino, and Ventura Counties.

Parking: Street parking is easy and relatively safe in many areas of the city and far more difficult in congested parts of Downtown and permit-only neighborhoods close to all the action. Keep a stash of quarters and small bills handy. City-run lots in Beverly Hills, Santa Monica, and West Hollywood usually offer two free hours of parking during the day and low hourly rates thereafter. In the restaurant districts, valet parking is convenient, ubiquitous, and a service commonly used like a public lot in Los Angeles. Rates range anywhere from $3 to $12.

Parking Garages

Agency	Address
Brighton Parking Garage	9510 Brighton Way at Rodeo Dr., Beverly Hills
Central Parking Inc.	633 W. Fifth St. at Grand Ave., Downtown
Hollywood & Highland Parking Garage	6801 Hollywood Blvd. at Orange, Hollywood
Pacific Design Center Parking Lot	8687 Melrose Ave. at San Vicente Blvd., West Hollywood
Santa Monica Place Mall	Fourth & Broadway, Santa Monica

Other Practical Information

Money Matters (Currency, Taxes, Tipping, and Service Charges): It's dollars ($) and cents (100 to the dollar). For currency conversion rates, go to xe.com/ucc. There is no national sales (value-added) tax. However, the sales tax within the city of Los Angeles is 8.25 percent; it's 14 percent for hotels and is added onto the bill (not included in the price). Service charges are not included in prices but, depending on the venue, may be added to the bill. Hotels generally do not include breakfast in their prices. Tipping for taxis and restaurants and spas should be in the 15 to 20 percent range.

Metric Conversion

From	To	Multiply by
Inches	Centimeters	2.54
Yards	Meters	0.91
Miles	Kilometers	1.60
Gallons	Liters	3.79
Ounces	Grams	28.35
Pounds	Kilograms	0.45

HIT THE GROUND

Safety: Being so spread out can make Los Angeles a bit less safe in certain areas than other, more heavily trafficked metropolitan areas. But as in other big cities, caution is the rule of thumb. Avoid walking around alone at night, if possible. Other general rules of thumb apply: Lock up valuables in hotel safes, don't leave luggage or goods in parked cars, keep your wallets and handbags close to your side, and ask for directions before venturing into unfamiliar neighborhoods.

Gay and Lesbian Travel: When it comes to acceptance of gay rights, Los Angeles is right up there with San Francisco. West Hollywood (WeHo), the epicenter of L.A.'s gay scene, was the first city in the United States to have a gay-majority city council. The heart of "Boystown" stretches along Santa Monica Blvd. from La Cienega Boulevard to Robertson

Numbers to Know (Hotlines)

Emergency, police, fire department, ambulance, and paramedics	911
Poison Control	800-876-4766
Rape / Domestic Violence Crisis Line	213-626-3393
Los Angeles Suicide Crisis Line	310-391-1253
24-Hour Access Mental Health Helpline	800-789-2647

Along the highways, you'll find call boxes for emergency use.

Travelers Aid Society of Los Angeles (nonemergency medical conditions)	310-646-2270
The Dental Referral Service	800-336-8478

24-hour emergency rooms

• Cedars-Sinai Medical Center 8700 Beverly Blvd., L.A.	310-423-3277
• St. John's Health Center 1328 22nd St., Santa Monica	310-829-5511
• UCLA Medical Center 10833 Le Conte Ave., L.A.	310-825-9111

Late-night pharmacies

• CVS Pharmacy (24 hrs.) 3010 S. Sepulveda Blvd., West L.A.	310-478-9821
• Horton & Converse (until midnight) 11600 Wilshire Blvd., West L.A.	310-478-0801
• Rite Aid (until midnight) 1101 Westwood Blvd., Westwood	310-209-0708

Boulevard. West Hollywood's Halloween Carnaval, which sees some 350,000 attendees, is L.A.'s most flamboyant celebration.

Traveling with Disabilities: Check accessnca.com for the basics and icanonline.net for travel tips and ideas.

Print Media: *The Los Angeles Times* (latimes.com) is one of the most widely read and respected newspapers in the country. The thick-as-a-book Sunday edition includes "Calendar," a current city-wide entertainment and listings guide. *L.A. Weekly* (laweekly.com) is the city's largest free weekly entertainment publication, published every Thursday. *Los Angeles Magazine* (lamag.com) is L.A.'s monthly glossy, with a mini dining guide in the back of each issue.

Shopping Hours: Most department stores and shops are open 10am-6pm, with many shops extending hours on Saturday. Shops may open later on Sundays, and close a bit earlier.

Attire: This may be Southern California but it's also the high desert. Layering is key. Pack all the bathing suits, shorts, T-shirts, and sunglasses you want, but make sure to include a light jacket and some reasonably warm clothes for those cool summer evenings. Warmer clothing is required in the winter, when you can see your breath at night. Wear sunscreen. Even on the rare cloudy day, the rays are strong.

Radio Stations (a selection)

FM Stations

Freq	Call	Format
88.1	KKJZ	Jazz
89.3	KPCC	NPR
89.9	KCRW	NPR, Electric
91.5	KUSC	Classical
92.3	KHHT	Urban Contemporary
93.1	KCBS	Rock
93.9	KZLA	Country
94.7	KTWV	Smooth Jazz
95.5	KLOS	Rock
96.3	KXOL	Spanish
97.1	KLSX	Talk
98.7	KYSR	Mainstream Rock
100.3	KKBT	Urban Contemporary
101.1	KRTH	Oldies
102.7	KIIS	Top 40
104.3	KBIG	Adult Contemporary
105.1	KMZT	Classical
105.9	KPWR	Hip-Hop
106.7	KPOQ	Rock

AM Stations

Freq	Call	Format
570	KLAC	Sports
640	KFI	Talk
710	KSPN	ESPN Sports
790	KABC	News/Talk
980	KFWB	News/Traffic Reports
1070	KNX	News/Traffic Reports
1150	KXTA	Talk

HIT THE GROUND

Los Angeles is obsessively style conscious, but otherwise as relaxed or done-up as you want to make it. Casually hip is the usual dress code. Jeans and a funky shirt (and don't forget the right shoes) may be the uniform here, but they're the right sort of jeans and the right sort of shirt—and dry-cleaned just so. Jackets, ties, and traditional formal wear are rarely required, and will more likely stick out than blend in. Don't panic if you feel at all out of place—there's lots of shopping available.

Size Conversion

Dress Sizes

US	6	8	10	12	14	16
UK	8	10	12	14	16	18
France	36	38	40	42	44	46
Italy	38	40	42	44	46	48
Europe	34	36	38	40	42	44

Women's Shoes

US	6	6½	7	7½	8	8½
UK	4½	5	5½	6	6½	7
Europe	38	38	39	39	40	41

Men's Suits

US	36	38	40	42	44	46
UK	36	38	40	42	44	46
Europe	46	48	50	52	54	56

Men's Shirts

US	14½	15	15½	16	16½	17
UK	14½	15	15½	16	16½	17
Europe	38	39	40	41	42	43

Men's Shoes

US	8	8½	9½	10½	11½	12
UK	7	7½	8½	9½	10½	11
Europe	41	42	43	44	45	46

When Drinking Is Legal: The legal drinking age is 21.

Smoking: It's not quite illegal to smoke in L.A., but almost. It's prohibited in restaurants and bars (except on patios) and in virtually every other building. You are also prohibited from smoking within 20 feet of buildings where the public congregates (such as government buildings). There are even laws against lighting up on beaches, most notably in Santa Monica.

Drugs: California may be more liberal in some ways than most states, but drugs like cocaine, marijuana, and ecstasy are as illegal as they've ever been and can get you some serious time behind bars.

Additional Resources for Visitors

Los Angeles Convention and Visitors Bureau L.A.'s main visitors' hub offers city maps, calendars, TV taping listings, amusement park discounts, friendly advice, and round-the-clock information on the events hotline (same telephone number). *Mon-Fri 8am-5pm, Sat 8:30am-5pm.* 685 S. Figueroa St., Los Angeles, 213-689-8822, seemyla.com

Beverly Hills Convention and Visitors Bureau 239 S. Beverly Dr., Beverly Hills, 310-248-1015, lovebeverlyhills.org

Hollywood Chamber of Commerce 7018 Hollywood Blvd., Hollywood, 323-469-8311, hollywoodchamber.net

Pasadena Convention and Visitors Bureau 171 S. Los Robles Ave., Pasadena, 626-795-9311, pasadenacal.com

Santa Monica Convention and Visitors Bureau 1400 Ocean Ave, Santa Monica, 310-393-7593, santamonica.com

West Hollywood Convention and Visitors Bureau 8687 Melrose Ave., Suite M-38, West Hollywood, 310-289-2525, visitwesthollywood.com

Foreign Visitors

Foreign Embassies in the U.S.: state.gov/misc/10125.htm

Passport requirements: travel.state.gov/travel/tips/brochures /brochures_1229.html

Cell phones: North America operates on the 1,900MHz frequency. Cell phones may be used while driving. For buying or renting a phone go to telestial.com/instructions.htm

Toll-free numbers in the U.S.: 1-800, 1-866, 1-877, and 1-888

Telephone directory assistance in the U.S.: 411

Electrical: U.S. standard is AC, 110 volts/60 cycles, with a plug of two flat pins set parallel to one another.

The Latest-Info Websites

Go to laweekly.com and calendarlive.com for events and restaurant reviews, as well as the scoop on nightlife.
And, of course, **pulseguides.com.**

Time Zone: Los Angeles falls within the Pacific time zone. A note on daylight saving: Clocks are set ahead one hour at 2am on the first Sunday in April and set back one hour at 2am on the last Sunday in October.

HIT THE GROUND

Party Conversation—A Few Surprising Facts

- A state-wide smoking ban can get you fined $100 and booted out of a Los Angeles bar for lighting a cigarette.

- The Getty Center cost $275 million to build. Admission is free.

- Avoid rush hour on the 405 freeway. When heading north from LAX, take La Cienega Boulevard instead.

- The sports and entertainment complex L.A. Live is set to open next to the Staples Center in 2008. Will it really motivate people to go Downtown?

- At current growth rates, the population of Los Angeles County (currently 3,844,829) will triple by the year 2100.

- Griffith Park is the largest city park in the country, and is nearly five times the size of New York's Central Park. Spread across 4,107 acres, it has a zoo, a museum, an observatory, the historic Greek Theatre, three golf courses, and miles of hiking and horseback trails.

- The first two neon signs in the U.S. were purchased and hung at a Los Angeles car dealership in 1923.

- L.A.'s Red Line subway runs 17.4 miles and cost $4.5 billion, making it the most expensive subway per mile ever built—that's $49,000 per foot.

- Los Angeles, the country's second biggest sports market, hasn't had an NFL team since the Raiders and Rams bailed in 1995.

- In 2006, The Los Angeles Clippers won its first playoff series in more than 30 years. The last time that happened, the team was named the Buffalo Braves, and Gerald Ford was president.

- Migrating gray whales can be spotted off the L.A. coast between December and April.

- You can still be a contestant on *The Price Is Right*. Send a self-addressed, stamped envelope specifying dates to CBS Television City, 7800 Beverly Blvd., L.A., CA 90036. Or call 323-575-2458.

The Cheat Sheet
(The Very Least You Ought to Know
About Los Angeles)

If you're going to hang out here, you had better know something about the place. Here's a countdown of the ten most essential facts and factoids you need to avoid looking like a *turista*.

10 Neighborhoods and Suburbs

Beverly Hills has pretty much been home to the rich and famous since the coining of the term. Its Downtown fashion district, the Golden Triangle, is one of the world's easiest places to max out several platinum cards in one spree. Highlights include Rodeo Drive, the Museum of Television & Radio, and the Polo Lounge at the Beverly Hills Hotel.

Burbank's sedate east San Fernando Valley location is the unlikely headquarters for some of the world's largest studios and recording companies, including Walt Disney Productions, Warner Bros. Studios, and NBC Studios.

Downtown is where the whole L.A. thing got started a few centuries ago. Bursting with history and with history-in-the-making, it's home to the new Walt Disney Concert Hall, the Staples Center, Chinatown, the Museum of Contemporary Art—and, yes, that mandatory grove of bank towers.

Hollywood is simultaneously hip, seedy, and occasionally glamorous. You'll find old Tinseltown chestnuts here like the Egyptian and Chinese theaters, one of the world's most popular tourist traps (the Walk of Fame), newer additions like the Kodak Theatre, and enough bars to keep you hopping.

Malibu's 25 miles of sunny shoreline boasts some of the best surfing and sand-lazing spots in (and out of) the city. Backed by the rugged Santa Monica Mountains National Recreation Area (and fronted by its share of celebrity mansions), Malibu is home to several state parks and beaches, including Leo Carillo State Park and Zuma Beach.

Manhattan Beach is where the Beach Boys spent a few endless summers before the rents went up. Now a yuppified mecca for surfers, rollerbladers, volleyball studs and babes, and investment bankers, this South Bay charmer boasts a fine patch of sand and easy access to the area's party headquarters next door in Hermosa Beach.

Pasadena is L.A.'s influential neighbor to the north and the cultural center of the San Gabriel Valley. Its many famous sites include the Huntington Botanical Gardens, the Norton Simon Museum, the Pasadena Playhouse, and the Rose Bowl. Downtown Pasadena also has a hip small-town feel (if that's not an oxymoron) that can offer a nice break from the L.A. buzz.

Santa Monica is L.A.'s most time-honored (and televised) beach community—a thriving city in its own right offering first-class dining, shopping, and fun-seeking right on the coast. Highlights include the Third Street promenade, the Santa Monica Beach promenade, Montana Avenue, Bergamot Station, and its popular next-door-neighbor, Venice Beach.

Silver Lake is the place where—along with its flanking neighborhoods Los Feliz and Echo Park—L.A.'s hipper, artsier Eastside crowd distinguishes itself with alternative music venues, retro lounges, backroom galleries, out-of-the-way cafes, wacky stores, and a smattering of architectural masterpieces by big guns Frank Lloyd Wright and Richard Neutra.

Westwood, home of UCLA, is about as college-town as it gets in Los Angeles. While neighboring communities like Santa Monica and Beverly Hills may steal its thunder, Westwood boasts the city's most impressive supply of big, loud, and rambunctious movie theaters, which see their share of red carpets and celebrities during premiere nights.

Major Streets

Hollywood Boulevard runs east from Laurel Canyon through Downtown Hollywood, merging with Sunset Boulevard at Hillhurst Avenue in Los Feliz.

La Brea Avenue runs north from I-10 to Hollywood.

La Cienega Boulevard runs north from the LAX area to West Hollywood.

Mulholland Drive straddles the Hollywood Hills from Hollywood to I-405.

Santa Monica Boulevard runs west from Hollywood and Downtown to Ocean Avenue in Santa Monica.

Sunset Boulevard runs west from Silver Lake and Downtown to Pacific Coast Highway in Pacific Palisades.

Ventura Boulevard runs along the south end of the San Fernando Valley from Universal City to Woodland Hills.

Western Avenue bisects the city, running south from Hollywood and Griffith Park to San Pedro.

Wilshire Boulevard runs west from Downtown to Ocean Avenue in Santa Monica. It crosses Santa Monica Boulevard in Beverly Hills.

Performing Arts Venues

Ahmanson Theatre One of the city's most important playhouses. 135 N. Grand Ave., Downtown, 213-628-2772, taperahmanson.com

Dorothy Chandler Pavilion Home of the L.A. Opera and Music Center Dance. 135 N. Grand Ave., Downtown, 213-972-7211, musiccenter.org

Geffen Playhouse Westside staple for culture. 10886 Le Conte Ave., Los Angeles, 310-208-5454, geffenplayhouse.com

Hollywood Bowl Great outdoor concert venue. 2301 N. Highland Ave., Hollywood, 323-850-2000, hollywoodbowl.org .

Kodak Theatre Noted for the Academy Awards. 6801 Hollywood Blvd., (Highland), Hollywood, 323-308-6300, kodaktheatre.com

Mark Taper Forum Downtown hotbed of high-profile plays. 135 N. Grand Ave., Downtown, 213-628-2772, taperahmanson.com

Pantages Theater Broadway plays. 6233 Hollywood Blvd., Hollywood, 323-468-1700, broadwayla.org/pantages/box_office.asp

Walt Disney Concert Hall The Gehry-designed venue for the L.A. Philharmonic. 11 S. Grand Ave., Downtown, 213-628-2772, wdch.com

7 Sports Teams

Los Angeles Avengers Arena Football League, 310-788-7744, laavengers.com

Los Angeles Clippers National Basketball Association, 213-742-7555, clippers.com

Los Angeles Dodgers Major League Baseball, 866-363-4377, dodgers.com

Los Angeles Galaxy Major League Soccer, 310-630-2200, lagalaxy.com

Los Angeles Kings National Hockey League, 888-546-4752, lakings.com

Los Angeles Lakers National Basketball League, 310-426-6031, lakers.com

Los Angeles Sparks Women's National Basketball Association, 310-426-6031, lasparks.com

6 Notable Freeways

Highway 1 The Pacific Coast Highway (or PCH) hugs the Los Angeles (and California) coast, merging at various points with several roads and freeways.

I-5 The Golden State Freeway runs northwest from Downtown into the Valley; the Santa Ana Freeway runs southeast from Downtown into Orange County.

I-10 The Santa Monica Freeway runs west from Downtown to Santa Monica; the San Bernardino Freeway runs east from Downtown to San Bernardino.

I-110 The Harbor Freeway runs south from Downtown to San Pedro, and north from Downtown to Pasadena.

HIT THE GROUND

I-405 The San Diego Freeway runs north from the LAX area to I-5 in the Valley and south from LAX to I-5 in Orange County.

US-101 The Hollywood Freeway runs northwest from Downtown to North Hollywood; the Ventura Freeway continues northwest from North Hollywood to Santa Barbara.

Area Codes

213 Downtown L.A.

310 Beverly Hills to Santa Monica and the South Bay—L.A.'s most coveted area code.

323 Hollywood, Eastside, and West Hollywood east of La Cienega Boulevard.

626 Pasadena.

818 San Fernando Valley.

Retail Centers

The Beverly Center The city's trendiest mall. 8500 Beverly Blvd., Los Angeles, 310-854-0070, beverlycenter.com

The Grove Outdoor shopping, dining, and movies, near the Farmers' Market. 189 The Grove Dr., Los Angeles, 323-900-8000, thegrovela.com

Third Street Promenade An outdoor carnival of shopping and street performers. Third St. (Broadway to Wilshire), Santa Monica, 310-393-8355, thirdstreetpromenade.com

Westfield Century City Shopping Center UCLA students mix with Westsiders and occasional celebrities at these 140 stores. 10250 Santa Monica Blvd., Century City, 310-553-5300, westfield.com/centurycity

Theme Parks

Disneyland 1313 S. Harbor Blvd., Anaheim, 714-781-7290, disneyland.com

Six Flags California 26101 Magic Mountain Pkwy., Valencia, 661-255-4100, sixflags.com

Universal Studios Hollywood 100 Universal City Plaza, Universal City, 818-508-9600, universalstudios.com

Sports Stadiums

Dodger Stadium Home of the Los Angeles Dodgers. 1000 Elysian Park Ave., Los Angeles, 866-363-4377

Staples Center Home of the Lakers, Clippers, and Kings. 1111 S. Figueroa St., Downtown, 213-742-7340

Singular Sensation

Grauman's Chinese Theatre They say if you haven't been to the Chinese Theatre, you haven't been to Los Angeles. 6925 Hollywood Blvd., Hollywood, 323-464-8111

Coffee (quick stops for a java jolt)

Abbot's Habit Strong brew, deli sandwiches, and plenty of chilled-out Venetians. 1401 Abbot Kinney Blvd. (California St.), 310-399-1171

Bourgeois Pig Come for the pool table and an *Arabian Nights* room in back. 5931 Franklin Ave. (Bronson Ave.), 323-464-6008

Chango Coffee Service comes with some ironic detachment at this corner joint in Echo Park. 1559 Echo Park Ave. (Delta St.), 213-977-9161

Coffee Bean & Tea Leaf A little caffeine and some major celebrity-spotting along Sunset Blvd. 8789 Sunset Blvd. (Horn Ave.), 310-659-1890

The Coffee Table Great cappuccinos and lattes with a hearty Silver Lake breakfast on the patio. 2930 Rowena Ave. (Herkimer St.), 323-644-8111

Cow's End This slow-paced spot near the Venice boardwalk also serves smoothies. 34 Washington Blvd. (Pacific Ave.), 310-574-1080

Figaro Drink a cup of organic coffee at a sidewalk table while the hipsters stroll by. 1802 N. Vermont Ave. (Melbourne Ave.), 323-662-1587

The Green Room Get a mocha fix between Walk of Fame star sightings. 6752 Hollywood Blvd. (Highland Ave.), 323-860-0775

Highland Grounds A courtyard fire pit and live acoustic music are the draws. 742 N. Highland Ave. (Melrose Ave.), 323-466-1507

Insomnia Cafe True to its word, this very lively joint is open until 1:30am daily. 7286 Beverly Blvd. (N. Poinsettia Pl.), 323-931-4943

Literati Café Shade-grown coffee and equally organic food in the heart of Brentwood. 12081 Wilshire Blvd. (Bundy Dr.), 310-231-7484

Urth Caffe Valet parking, organic sweets, and a great patio for people-watching in West Hollywood. 8565 Melrose Ave. (Westmount Dr.), 310-659-0628

HIT THE GROUND

Just for Business and Conventions

Los Angeles is a polycentric city, with seemingly as many business centers as there are screenplays "in production." If all of your meetings and conferences are confined to one particular area, say, Century City or Downtown, you can stay there overnight and not even think about traffic. But if you have a morning meeting in Santa Monica and an afternoon appointment in Burbank, you can expect to spend a fair amount of time behind the wheel sipping a caffe latte and fumbling with your cell phone, like everyone else here does. The good news is that every city center has a slightly different vibe, and you can always find an excellent restaurant or bar for those afterwork meals and cocktails with colleagues.

Addresses to Know

Convention Center

- Los Angeles Convention Center
  1201 S. Figueroa, Downtown,
  213-741-1151, lacclink.com

City Information

- Los Angeles Convention and
  Visitors Bureau
  333 S. Hope Street, 18th Floor,
  Downtown, 213-624-7300 /
  800-228-2452, lacvb.com

- Official City of Los Angeles website,
  ci.la.ca.us

- Official Los Angeles County website,
  lacounty.info

Business and Convention Hotels

Big business hotels tend to be Downtown, off the tourist and hipster radar.

Figueroa Hotel Downtown hotel with Moroccan and Spanish interiors is a stone's throw from the Convention Center. $$ 939 S. Figueroa St., 213-627-8971 / 800-421-9092, figueroahotel.com

Hyatt Regency Century Plaza Century City hotel with world-class spa and lobby bar. $$$ 2025 Avenue of the Stars, 310-228-1234 / 800-233-1234, centuryplaza.hyatt.com

The Sheraton Gateway Hotel Fifty executive suites, 24-hour fitness center, near Los Angeles International Airport. $$ 6101 W. Century Blvd., 310-642-1111 / 800-325-3535, sheratonlosangeles.com

Westin Bonaventure Hotel & Suites Downtown's iconic, cylindrical building has 42 restaurants and shops. $$$ 404 S. Figueroa St., 213-624-1000 / 888-625-5144, starwoodhotels.com/westin

Business Entertaining

The following *Los Angeles Black Book* recommended restaurants provide a great atmosphere for deal making ... or just blowing off steam.

Chaya Venice* The Westside's ideal Asian-fusion restaurant for mixing work and play. $$ (p.65) 110 Navy St. (Main St.), 310-396-1179

Ciudad* Bond with colleagues over post-work caipirinhas and mojitos at this Pan-Latin restaurant. $$ (p.103) 445 S. Figueroa St. (Fifth St.), 213-486-5171

The Ivy Because you should experience a power lunch here once in your life. $$$ (p.136) 113 N. Robertson Blvd. (Alden Dr.), 310-274-8303

Water Grill When you need to hook a prospective client, do it with sublime seafood. $$$ (p.140) 544 S. Grand Ave. (Fifth St.), 213-891-0900

Also see: **Best Power Lunches** (p.35)
Best Seafood (p.38)
Best Wine List (p.47)

Ducking Out for a Half-Day

If you're all conventioned out, take a break at one of the following places.

Petersen Automotive Museum Drive your stale rental car to this four-floor showroom of 150-plus vintage automobiles and motorcycles. (p.122) 6060 Wilshire Blvd. (Fairfax Ave.), 323-930-2277

Runyon Canyon Park A run in the sunny Hollywood Hills and a few celebrity sightings to boot. (p.123) 2000 N. Fuller (Hillside Ave.), 213-485-5111

Wilson and Harding Golf Courses Play an early round in Griffith Park and make it back for your lunch meeting. (p.123) 4730 Crystal Springs Dr. (Griffith Park Dr.), 323-664-2255

Also see: **Best Beaches** (p.16)
Best Movie Theaters (p.31)
Best Spas (p.40)

Gifts to Bring Home

What fun is unpacking if you can't pull out a treasure or two to share with those at home? Get the goods here.

Backstage at the Chinese The Chinese Theatre's gift shop can put your handprints in cement (to take home). 6925 Hollywood Blvd., 323-467-4723

MOCA Store The museum's walk-in store in Santa Monica sells pop-culture galore, including books on the history of graffiti in Los Angeles. 2447 Main St. (Ocean Park Blvd.), 310-396-9833, moca-la.org/store

Soap Plant and WACKO Take home some "Island Babe" salt-and-pepper shakers, a Gene Simmons action figure, or a bowling bag handbag. 4633 Hollywood Blvd. (Rodney Dr.), 323-663-0122

HIT THE GROUND

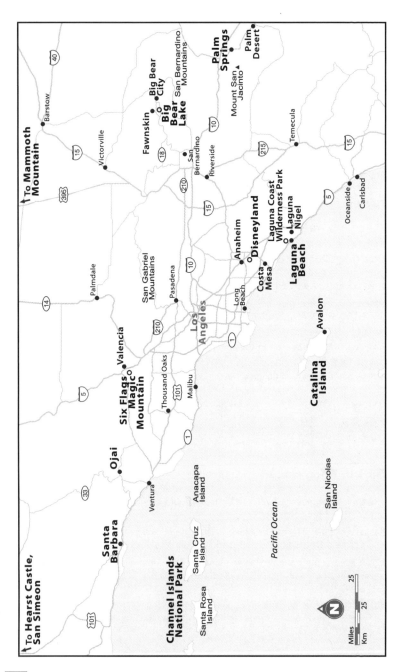

LEAVING LOS ANGELES

The best thing about Los Angeles is that it's smack-dab in the middle of one of the most beautiful and varied areas on God's green earth. In just a few hours you can be skiing at a top resort, golfing in a desert oasis, or flopping on a lonely beach. If you've got days to spare (or if you've seen enough of the scene and want a change of pace), take our advice and get out of town. Just because you've visited L.A. doesn't mean you've seen California.

Big Bear Lake

Hot Tip: Fill up your tank before you go and you shouldn't have to do it again until you return.

The Lowdown: It's L.A. cottage country up at this convenient mountain resort area a few hours east in the San Bernardino Mountains. Dotted with cabins, B&Bs, and a wide array of outdoor draws, this retreat has been reeling in weekenders since Gable and Lombard honeymooned here back in the '30s. Aspen it ain't, but unless you want to schlep up to Mammoth or—yeesh—to Tahoe, Big Bear is the city's most obvious alpine escape for a getaway crowd of skiers, hikers, bikers, anglers, and romantic-cabin-in-the-woods renters. The teddy-bearish village and its namesake lake are a merciful 7,000 feet above the neighboring Mojave Desert and the inland cities of Riverside and San Bernardino. Summer temperatures hang pleasantly in the low 70s during the day, dropping to the mid-40s at night. Winter brings around 120 inches of snowfall. Rates drop and crowds disappear midweek.

There are more than a dozen B&Bs in the Big Bear area, including Gold Mountain Manor (where Clark and Carole stayed), and several resorts, lodges, and cabins that range from bargain to luxury. Contact the Big Bear Lake Resort Association for a list. Skiers and snowboarders hit the slopes of the area's two alpine resorts, Bear Mountain and Snow Summit, and are followed by mountain bikers during the warmer months. Summer crowds are drawn to Big Bear Lake, an eight-mile-long freshwater oasis. Big Bear's forested slopes offer some of the best hiking trails south of the Sierras. Passes are required for parking at the trailheads. Contact the Big Bear Discovery Center for more information.

Best Attractions

Bear Mountain Twelve lifts, four peaks, 150-plus jumps, and Southern California's only superpipe. $$$ 43101 Goldmine Dr., Big Bear Lake, 909-585-2519, bearmountain.com

Big Bear Discovery Center This is the place to go for guided hiking adventures, Forest Service permits, and information on the best places to go four-wheeling, camping, or fishing. 40971 N. Shore Dr. (Hwy. 38), Fawnskin, 909-866-3437, bigbeardiscoverycenter.com

Snow Summit A total of 240 acres for skiing and more than 18 miles of trails make this the largest Southern California ski resort. $$$ 880 Summit Blvd., Big Bear Lake, 909-866-5766, snowsummit.com

Best Restaurants

Madlon's This gingerbread house of a restaurant serves a surprisingly sophisticated menu of pastas, seafood, and steak. $$ 829 W. Big Bear Blvd., Big Bear City, 909-585-3762, madlonsrestaurant.com

Old Country Inn Grab a hearty breakfast at this German restaurant before you hit the slopes or a gravy-heavy dinner before you hit the hay. $$ 41126 Big Bear Blvd., Big Bear Lake, 909-866-5600, oldcountryinn.net

Best Nightlife

Chad's Place Loud and packed to the gills during the ski season, this is the "place" to dance or play pool … if you have energy left over. 40740 Village Dr., Big Bear Lake, 909-866-2161, chads-place.com

Murray's Saloon & Eatery A friendly atmosphere awaits at this village bar and grill. 672 College Ln., Big Bear, 909-866-1444

The Pub Big Bear Village nightspot filled with a cast of characters, not to mention a fireside lounge. 664 Pine Knot Ave., Big Bear, 909-866-5755

Best Hotels

Gold Mountain Manor Chilled-out log-cabin lodge sits right on the Pacific Crest Trail passing through the San Bernardino National Forest. $$ 1117 Anita Ave., Big Bear City, 909-585-6997, goldmountainmanor.com

Windy Point Inn At this retreat on the north side of the lake, every room has a fireplace and your very own deck. $$ 39015 N. Shore Dr. (Hwy. 38), Big Bear Lake, 909-866-2746, windypointinn.com

Contacts

Big Bear Lake Resort Association 800-424-4232, bigbearinfo.com

LEAVING

Getting There: Take I-10 East. Exit at Hwy. 30 North and continue north on Hwy. 330, which turns into Hwy. 18. Follow Hwy. 18 East and turn right.

Catalina Island

Hot Tip: Check the calendar, because this small island town gets really crowded during events like JazzTrax (October) or the triathlon (November).

The Lowdown: Southern California may not have a Martha's Vineyard, but there's always Catalina. Officially part of the remote Channel Islands chain, this very accessible offshore resort got off the ground when chewing gum baron William Wrigley Jr. purchased the land in 1919 and built a hilltop mansion here. By the 1940s, Cecil B. DeMille and Winston Churchill were pulling into Avalon Bay to go fishing and Glenn Miller was performing in the landmark Casino Ballroom. Mediterranean-style Avalon, Catalina's single port town, is now sprinkled with hotels, B&Bs, restaurants, boutiques, spas, and dive shops catering to a slightly broader clientele, albeit with a whiff of family money still in the air. The rest of the island is largely a wilderness preserve overseen by the Santa Catalina Island Conservancy. Crowds thin and rates drop midweek and outside the summer peak season.

Catalina is as restful as you want to make it. Avalon boasts some of Southern California's most romantic retreats, including the Inn on Mount Ada (the old Wrigley Mansion) and an assortment of private villas and cottages managed by Catalina Island Vacation Rentals. The island's many activities include scuba diving, snorkeling, deep-sea fishing, and even mini-submarining through the rich marine world of Catalina's surrounding reefs. On land, there's a scenic nine-hole golf course (the oldest in Southern California), a heritage museum, botanical gardens, and hiking, horseback riding, and bus touring opportunities through the island's wild interior.

Best Attractions

Catalina Adventure Tours A submersible tour takes you through the marine-life–rich Avalon Bay. $$$$ 310-510-2888, catalinaadventuretours.com

Catalina Island Conservancy The island's caretakers hand out hiking and mountain biking permits, offer nature classes, and conduct tours of the island. 125 Claressa Ave., Avalon, 310-510-2595, catalinaconservancy.org

Jeep Eco-Tours This three-hour tour of the island literally takes you where the buffalo roam. $$$$ 310-510-2595, catalina.com/jeeptours

Wrigley Memorial and Botanical Garden A memorial tower and gardens feature stunning views of the bay below. 1400 Avalon Canyon Rd., Avalon, 310-510-2595, catalina.com/memorial.html

Best Restaurants

Armstrong's Fish Market and Seafood Restaurant The island's best seafood restaurant is located right on the water. $$ 306 Crescent Ave., Avalon, 310-510-0113, armstrongseafood.com.

Clubhouse Bar & Grill The Catalina Country Club hosts the island's premier restaurant. $$$ 1 Country Club Dr., Avalon, 310-510-7404

The Landing Order everything from Mexican food to gourmet pizzas on a deck overlooking the harbor. $ 101 Marilla Ave., Avalon, 310-510-1474, catalina.com/landing

Best Nightlife

Chi Chi Club The island's only dance club goes off on the weekends. 105 Sumner, Avalon, 310-510-2828, www.chichiclub.net

Luau Larry's This is the tacky tiki bar every city should have. Against your better judgment, order the Wiki Wacker. 509 Crescent Ave., Avalon, 310-510-1919, luaularrys.com

Best Hotels

The Avalon Hotel Many of the rooms in this new, Craftsman-style hotel have sweeping views of the harbor. $$$ 124 Whittley Ave., Avalon, 310-510-7070, theavalonhotel.com

Hotel Metropole and Market Place Posh, recently updated hotel resembles something out of New Orleans' French Quarter. $$$ 205 Crescent Ave., Avalon, 310-510-1884 / 800-300-8528 (Calif.) / 800-541-8528, hotel-metropole.com

Inn on Mount Ada The former summer home of William Wrigley Jr. has sumptuous rooms and spectacular views. $$$ 398 Wrigley Rd., 310-510-2030 / 800-608-7669, innonmtada.com

Snug Harbor This Cape Cod–style inn close to the water has just six rooms, each named after one of the Channel Islands. $$$ 108 Sumner Ave., Catalina, 310-510-8400, snugharbor-inn.com

Contacts

Catalina Island Chamber of Commerce 1 Green Pier, Avalon, 310-510-1520, visitcatalina.org

Catalina Island Vacation Rentals 310-510-2276, catalinavacations.com

Catalina Express 800-481-3470, catalinaexpress.com

Getting There: Four ferry lines serve Catalina Island with several daily departures leaving from San Pedro, Long Beach, Newport Beach, and Dana Point. Catalina Express makes the trip in about an hour from San Pedro or Long Beach. Island Express Helicopter Service lifts off from the boat terminals in Long Beach and San Pedro, getting you there in about 15 minutes.

LEAVING

Hearst Castle, San Simeon

Hot Tip: In spring and fall, night tours are led by period actors playing 1930s dress-up.

The Lowdown: Built over a span of nearly 30 years (and never quite finished), Hearst Castle exemplifies the power of the almighty dollar, the effects of unchecked megalomania, and the total inadequacy of the phrase "it's big" when describing certain real estate properties. Hearst and architect Julia Morgan began work on this amazing Mediterranean Revival compound looming above the village of San Simeon at the south end of Big Sur in 1919, stuffing it over the years with more priceless acquisitions than this 165-room pad could ever fully assimilate. And that's not even counting the pools and gardens and grounds. Deeded to the state after the family could no longer keep it up, Hearst Castle is now one of California's busiest tourist attractions, annually hosting more than a million visitors—none of whom will ever have it quite this good. Several small hotels, motels, and B&Bs serve Hearst Castle in neighboring coastal villages just south of San Simeon. For something wildly different, check into the Madonna Inn, a famous kitsch castle in San Luis Obispo featuring more than a hundred uniquely themed quarters. From there, it's a 40-mile drive north to Hearst Castle, where four separate two-hour walking tours are offered several times daily between 8:20am and 3:20pm during the winter (with slightly longer summer hours). Reservations are strongly recommended for all of them.

Best Attractions

Hearst Castle Perhaps the best-known residence in the United States outside of the White House, Hearst Castle was donated to the State of California in 1957 and includes a main home (Casa Grande) that has 38 bedrooms and 41 bathrooms in more than 60,000 square feet of space. $ 750 Hearst Castle Rd., San Simeon, 800-444-4445, hearstcastle.com

Pacific Coast Highway This isn't just a way to get to Hearst Castle, it's one of the most picturesque drives in world, skirting as it does the rocky coast of Central California. Most people take their sweet time driving to San Simeon, with a mandated stop or two along the way for pictures.

Best Restaurants

Mo's Smokehouse BBQ This Virginia-style barbecue joint is a big hit with the locals. $ 970 Higera St., San Luis Obispo, 805-544-6193, mosbbq.com

Novo Restaurant & Bakery Set in a brick building that used to be a cigar factory, Novo has an international wine list and an international menu that includes both tapas and traditional plates. $ 726 Higuera St., San Luis Obispo, 805-543-3986, novorestaurant.com

The Park Restaurant A fine-dining spot with organic California cuisine, a large wine list, and a seasonal patio—in other words, the quintessential Central Coast restaurant. $$$ 1819 Osos St., San Luis Obispo, 805-545-0000

The Sea Chest The wait is worth it for some of the best seafood on the Central Coast, the stars of the show here being oysters on the half shell. $$ 6216 Moonstone Beach Dr., Cambria, 805-927-4514

Best Nightlife

The Graduate The biggest dance floor on the Central Coast attracts a younger crowd most nights. 990 Industrial Way, San Luis Obispo, 805-541-0969, slograd.com

Mother's Tavern Beer American cuisine and live music are on tap at this urbane, centrally located nightspot. 725 Higuera St., San Luis Obispo, 805-541-8733, motherstavern.com

Best Hotels

Cambria Pines Lodge Take your pick between rustic cabins or suites on 25 wooded acres in the artist's colony of Cambria, which is just down the road (Highway 1) from Hearst Castle. $$ 2905 Burton Dr., Cambria, 805-927-4200, cambriapineslodge.com

Madonna Inn It's guaranteed you've never stayed in a hotel quite like this one, which has 109 rooms, all with different themes like Old Mexico, Pioneer America, and Traveler's Yacht. This is overnight kitsch at its finest. $$ 100 Madonna Rd., San Luis Obispo, 805-543-3000 / 800-543-9666, madonnainn.com

Ragged Point Inn Views of the ocean from this hotel about 15 miles north of San Simeon are sublime, particularly through the floor-to-ceiling glass of the hotel's dining room. $$$ 19019 Hwy. 1, Ragged Point, 805-927-4502, raggedpointinn.com

Contacts

San Luis Obispo County Visitors & Conference Bureau 805-541-8000 / 800-634-1414, sanluisobispocounty.com

LEAVING

Getting There: Follow U.S. 101 North about 200 miles from Los Angeles to San Luis Obispo. Then take the Pacific Coast Highway (Hwy. 1) another 40 miles north to San Simeon and Hearst Castle. Parking is in the visitor-center lot. Five miles up the hill is the Hearst estate, accessible only by tour buses.

Laguna Beach

Hot Tip: Laguna's beaches are part of a marine reserve that has sublime snorkeling and diving.

The Lowdown: Southern California's "Riviera" finds its nucleus in this prosperous seaside village lined with galleries, beaches, a boardwalk, and a half-dozen miles of premium ocean-facing property. The plein-air painters who founded Laguna's thriving artist colony back in the early 20th century would be appalled by today's summer weekend traffic inching into town along the coast. Otherwise, the same balmy postcard setting that inspired them is still basking in the sun here—but on four-star hotel balconies, leafy restaurant patios, and a squeaky-clean beach in the heart of Downtown. Most of the action in Laguna is concentrated in the Village, a quarter-mile stretch of cafes, bars, antique shops, boutiques, and art studios huddled on the north side of the Pacific Coast Highway (PCH). Directly across the street is Main Beach, the most central of Laguna's 30 beaches and coves running north and south. Among Laguna's many renowned events is the summer's biggest draw, the Festival of Arts and Pageant of the Masters (see *Calendar* section).

For a list of hotels, inns, and cottage rental companies serving Laguna Beach, contact the Visitors and Conference Bureau. Or simply check into the Surf & Sand Resort and Spa, the town's most elegant beach property, with balconies right above the waves. Top landmarks include the Laguna Art Museum and the award-winning Laguna Playhouse, the oldest continuously operating theater company on the West Coast. Beyond the Village's cluster of shops and galleries, Laguna boasts about 17,000 acres of coastal wilderness and marine preserves. Several local tour operators show hikers, horseback riders, divers, kayakers, and whale-watchers a good time in Laguna's great outdoors.

Best Attractions

Laguna Art Museum The creative soul of the city coordinates with local galleries to put on the First Thursday Art Walk (first Thursday of the month). $ 307 Cliff Dr., Laguna Beach, 949-494-8971, lagunaartmuseum.org

Laguna Coast Wilderness Park Hikers, bikers, horseback riders, and artists share this 19-acre parcel replete with coastal canyons, natural lakes, and indigenous foliage. Laguna Canyon Rd. (Fwy. 133), 949-497-8324, lagunacanyon.org

Laguna Playhouse This playhouse is one of the premier spots in Southern California for live theater. 606 Laguna Canyon Rd., Laguna Beach, 949-497-2787, lagunaplayhouse.com

Best Restaurants

Five Feet Nouvelle Chinese cuisine with a casual, social atmosphere that makes it one of the city's most popular. $$ 328 Glenneyre St., Laguna Beach, 949-497-4955, fivefeetrestaurants.com

Hush Beverly Hills–type attention to detail mixed with laid-back Laguna Beach–type service and contemporary American cuisine. $$ 858 S. Coast Hwy., Laguna Beach, 949-497-3616, hushrestaurant.com

Javier's Cantina & Grill Authentic Mexican food, a fun atmosphere, and great people-watching. $ 480 S. Coast Hwy., Laguna Beach, 949-494-1239, javiers-cantina.com

Studio A swank culinary experience involving California-Mediterranean cuisine and 280-degree views of the ocean. $$ Montage Resort and Spa, 30801 S. Coast Hwy., Laguna Beach, 949-715-6420, studiolagunabeach.com

Best Nightlife

Mosun After sampling some Pacific Rim offerings, head upstairs to this sushi bar's two-story Club M, suitable for dancing or lounging around. 680 S. Coast Hwy., Laguna Beach, 949-497-5646, mosunclubm.com

Rooftop Lounge at the Casa del Camino Hypnotic ocean views and fancy cocktails to match. 1287 S. Coast Hwy., Laguna Beach, 949-376-9718

White House The oldest, hottest nightclub in Laguna Beach with a patio overlooking the ocean. 340 S. Coast Hwy., Laguna Beach, 949-494-8088, whitehouserestaurant.com

Best Hotels

Casa del Camino Historic, Mediterranean-style hotel near the beach with a huge sunset terrace. $$$ 1289 S. Coast Hwy., Laguna Beach, 949-497-2446 / 888-367-5232, casacamino.com

Hotel Laguna Laguna's oldest hotel has a private beach with food and cocktail service. $$$ 425 S. Coast Hwy., Laguna Beach, 949-494-1151 / 800-524-2927, hotellaguna.com

Montage Resort & Spa Waterside spa has three swimming pools and more than 20 treatment rooms. $$$ 30803 S. Coast Hwy., Laguna Beach, 949-715-6000 / 866-271-6953, montagelagunabeach.com, spamontage.com

Ritz-Carlton Laguna Niguel Thanks to a recent $40 million renovation, the sleek interiors of this classic seaside hotel are more reflective of the ocean it overlooks. $$$$ 1 Ritz-Carlton Dr., Laguna Niguel, 949-240-2000 / 800-241-3333, ritzcarlton.com

Surf & Sand Resort Within walking distance of the active, artsy Downtown area, this bluffside resort precludes the need for a rental car. $$$ 1555 S. Coast Hwy., Laguna Beach, 949-497-4477, surfandsandresort.com

Contacts

Laguna Beach Visitors and Conference Bureau 949-497-9229 / 800-877-1115, lagunabeachinfo.org

LEAVING

Getting There: Take I-405 South to Hwy. 133 South and follow it to the Pacific Coast Highway and Laguna Beach. Turn left on PCH into the Village.

325 miles N

Mammoth Mountain

Hot Tip: Mammoth is often open for skiing right up to and including July 4th, since its elevation keeps it cool.

The Lowdown: This one's a drive, but well worth it if you can afford to spend a few days at a top alpine resort in the Sierra Nevada mountains. Just 30 miles south of Yosemite National Park and five miles from the tourism-fed town of Mammoth Lakes, Mammoth Mountain's 11,053-foot summit and 3,500 acres of ski terrain have opened up considerably since the first chairlift was built more than 50 years ago. Mammoth now boasts 28 state-of-the-art lifts, including two gondolas, and a surge of lodges, condos, restaurants, and shops sprouting around its brand-new Village at the base of the mountain. Also part of the Mammoth operation is June Mountain, a smaller boutique resort about 20 miles to the north. Perched above 7,000 feet, Mammoth enjoys a mild summer climate in the mid-70s during the day and rarely dips below 40 degrees at night. Sunny winters range from 10 to 40 degrees. The mountain gets an average of 385 inches of snow per year.

A wide range of hotels, B&Bs, and cabins serve Mammoth Mountain, including several luxury options right in the Village. Contact Mammoth Resort or the Mammoth Lakes Visitors Bureau for a full list of options. Primarily known as a major ski destination, Mammoth draws all forms of outdoors enthusiasts during the warmer months too, including fly-fishermen, hikers, mountain bikers, and golfers flocking to the Sierra Star Golf Club's stunning 18-hole championship course, at 8,000 feet the highest in California. Mountain bikes can be rented in the Village from the Adventure Center, where a U.S. Forest Service window provides information and shuttle service to backcountry trails.

Best Attractions

Adventure Center/U.S. Forest Service Rent a bike during the summer and head down the mountain a completely different way. $ Main Lodge, 760-934-0706

June Mountain Mammoth's little sister has seven lifts, including two quad chairs. $$$ 3819 Hwy. 158, 760-648-7733 / 888-586-3686, junemountain.com

Sierra Star Golf Club The 8,000-foot altitude helps the ball soar at California's highest golf course. $$$ 2001 Sierra Star Pkwy., Mammoth Lakes, 760-924-4653

Best Restaurants

Nevados A high-end favorite of locals, many of whom just order a prix-fixe three-course meal. $$$ Main St. at Minaret Rd., Mammoth Lakes, 760-934-4466

Restaurant at Convict Lake It's worth the ten-minute drive south of town to feast on game and fish in a rustic setting replete with a *Wine Spectator*–lauded wine selection. $$$ Convict Lake Rd. off U.S. 395, Mammoth Lakes, 760-934-3803, convictlake.com/restaurant.html

Skadi An eclectic menu and a decidedly non-rustic dining experience. $$ 587 Old Mammoth Rd., Suite B, Mammoth Lakes, 760-934-3902

Best Nightlife

Clocktower Cellar Beers and pool in a "basement bar" setting. The wine bar upstairs, Petra's, has a more sophisticated scene. 6080 Minaret Rd., Mammoth Lakes, 760-934-6330

Lakanuki During ski season, forget about the cold at this tiki-themed bar in the Village at Mammoth. 6201 Minaret Rd., Suite 200, Mammoth Lakes, 760-934-7447, lakanuki.com

Whiskey Creek Live music, a wild nightlife scene ... and it's a restaurant too. 24 Lake Mary Rd., Mammoth Lakes, 760-934-2555

Best Hotels

Double Eagle Resort and Spa *Forbes* called this mountain getaway at the base of Carson Peak "one of the world's ten best spas." $$$$ 5587 Hwy. 158, June Lake, 760-648-7004 / 877-648-7004, doubleeagleresort.com

Mammoth Mountain Inn You can walk to the Main Lodge from here. $$$ Minaret Rd., Mammoth Lakes, 760-934-2581 / 800-626-6684, mammothmountain.com

Tamarack Lodge Resort Set in rustic splendor along the John Muir Wilderness Area, this is a place for romance. $$$ Lake Mary Rd. (off Hwy. 203), Mammoth Lakes, 760-934-2442 / 800-626-6684, tamaracklodge.com

The Village at Mammoth In the winter, a gondola takes you straight to the mountain. $$$ 1111 Forest Trail, Mammoth Lakes, 760-934-1982 / 800-626-6684, mammothmountain.com

Contacts

Mammoth Lakes Visitors Bureau 2520 Main St. (Hwy. 203), Mammoth Lakes, 760-934-2712 / 888-466-2666, visitmammoth.com

Mammoth Mountain Ski Information 760-934-2571, mammothmountain.com

LEAVING

Getting There: Take I-5 North. Exit onto Hwy. 14 North, pass through the town of Mojave, and continue to Hwy. 395 North. Head west on Hwy. 203 (Mammoth Lakes Junction) and into the town of Mammoth Lakes.

Ojai

Hot Tip: One weekend every October, Ojai artists open their studios to the general public, but that's not the only time you can see where they work. Contact the Chamber of Commerce (see number below) for a list of artists who are open to a visit at other times of the year.

The Lowdown: Back in the 1930s, Frank Capra chose this lovely hideaway to represent mythical Shangri-La in the movie *Lost Horizon*. Generations of artists, Hollywood recluses, spiritual leaders, environmentalists, and ardently community-oriented folks have all had a hand in preserving the tiny town of Ojai and its surrounding valley on the edge of Los Padres National Forest. A quick, pleasant drive from L.A., Ojai's unflashy five square miles remain the smallest and slowest-growing city in Ventura County—by choice—sprinkled with galleries, spas, New Agey shops, cafes, and spiritual retreats. Best known for its arts events held throughout the year, including the very popular two-day Studio Artists Tour in October, Ojai has a small-town feel and serene woodland surroundings that are still the best draw of all.

Guests of Ojai can choose from B&Bs, vacation houses, meditation compounds, and a pair of time-honored resorts: The distinguished Ojai Valley Inn & Spa features an 18-hole championship golf course and horseback riding; The Oaks at Ojai is a down-to-earth health retreat offering a wealth of treatments and fitness classes. Antiquing, gallery-hopping, and latte-sipping are among the more popular activities in and around the Arcade, the town's Mission Revival–style nerve center. Outdoor recreation in the surrounding Ojai Valley includes long walks or bicycle rides along the Ojai Valley Trail leading into the coastal town of Ventura; camping, boating, and bass fishing at nearby Lake Casitas; and hiking in the backcountry trails of the vast Los Padres National Forest. Contact the Ojai Ranger Station (805-646-4348, 1190 E. Ojai Ave.) for maps, guidebooks, brochures, and wilderness permits.

Best Attractions

The Oaks at Ojai Stay the night or just get a massage and a sauna ... but either way, prepare to eat very healthy food. $$$ 122 E. Ojai Ave., 805-646-5573 / 800-753-6257, oaksspa.com

Ojai Valley Trail This picturesque 18-mile trail stretches from Ojai's Soule Park all the way to the ocean. 805-654-3951, ojaichamber.org

Best Restaurants

Boccali's A local favorite where pizza or lasagna is followed by the must-have strawberry shortcake. $$ 3277 Ojai-Santa Paula Rd., 805-646-6116, boccalis.com

L'Auberge Decadent French-Belgian cuisine in a recently remodeled Victorian home. $$$ 314 El Paseo, 805-646-2288, laubergeojai.com

The Ranch House Brunch in the lush garden is a great way to spend a Sunday. $$ South Lomita Ave., 805-646-2360, theranchhouse.com

Suzanne's French-influenced menu runs the gamut from penne to bouillabaisse to roasted quail. $$$ 502 W. Ojai Avenue, 805-640-1961, suzannescuisine.com

Best Nightlife

Movino Wine Bar & Gallery In a town devoid of nightlife, Movino has live music and is open until 1am on weekend nights. 308 E. Ojai Ave, 805-646-1555, movinowinebar.com

Best Hotels

Blue Iguana Inn A charming, artist-run Southwestern-style hotel a couple miles west of the town center. $$ 11794 N. Ventura Ave., 805-646-5277, blueiguanainn.com

Su Nido Inn Private patios and privacy are the hallmarks of this boutique hotel in Ojai Village. $$ 301 N. Montgomery St., 805-646-7080, sunidoinn.com

Ojai Valley Inn & Spa A recent renovation has maintained the Spanish Colonial integrity of this historic 220-acre resort. $$$ 905 Country Club Rd., 805-646-1111, ojairesort.com

Contacts

Ojai Valley Chamber of Commerce and Visitor's Bureau 201 S. Signal St., 805-646-8126, ojaichamber.org

LEAVING

Getting There: Take I-5 North past Valencia to Hwy. 126 West. Head north on Rt. 150 to Ojai. Or take U.S. 101 North to Ventura; exit onto Hwy. 33 East and follow the signs into Ojai.

Palm Springs

Hot Tip: With buildings by Richard Neutra and Albert Frey, among many other noted architects, Palm Springs is a design-lover's mecca. The visitor center (see below) has a map of significant architecture, created by the Palm Springs Modern Committee.

The Lowdown: The rehabilitation of Palm Springs from a washed-up desert convention site to a hot retro playground for college kids, gays, gamblers, golfers, hipsters, retired folks, and spirituality seekers is one of the more remarkable recoveries in the resort world. This arid strand of leisure communities (collectively known as Palm Springs Desert Resorts) hugging chocolate-brown mountains in the Coachella Valley is back in a major way. And why not? It's Palm Springs, which means perfect weather (when you're not boiling or freezing) and as wild, restful, or enlightening a scene as you want.

Nearly 7,000 hotel rooms and 150 hotels serve greater Palm Springs, ranging from bargain bungalows and quaint desert inns to full-service luxury resort and spa retreats. The Palm Springs Visitor Information Center offers a free hotel reservation service and can also assist in finding the right place. Besides shopping, lounging at the pool, and beelining to top local spas like Two Bunch Palms for a heavenly soak and a 90-minute rub, a wide array of outdoor recreation activities includes hiking and horseback riding through the desert outback, exploring the cleaned-up Tahquitz Canyon and other sacred Indian sites just south of town, and even taking a guided tour of the area's vast windmill fields. Golf fanaticism is palpable here, with more than 110 courses gracing the valley. When blistering summer days are breaking the thermometer, cool off at 8,500 feet by riding the Palm Springs Aerial Tramway up Mount San Jacinto for some great views aboard the world's largest rotating tramcars. Top draws in town include the Fabulous Palm Springs Follies (featuring seasoned showgirls over the age of 50) and the Cahuilla Indian–run Spa Resort Casino.

Best Attractions

Palm Springs Aerial Tramway Rotating tramcars make sure you don't miss the spectacular views during the 2.5-mile ride. $ 1 Tramway Rd., 760-325-1391 / 888-515-8726, pstramway.com

Safari Trax Tour a Serengeti-like 80-acre reserve, where tigers, leopards, lynx, and other animals roam about for your (safe) viewing pleasure. $$ 760-318-1200 / 800-514-4866, elitelandtours.com

Spa Resort Casino Full-service resort with 900 slot machines and some 30 gaming tables. 401 E. Amado Rd., 760-325-1461, sparesortcasino.com

Tahquitz Canyon The rangers who patrol these cleaned-up sacred tribal lands also act as free guides. 500 W. Mesquite, 760-416-7044, tahquitzcanyon.com

Best Restaurants

Edgardo's Café Veracruz Tasty Mexican food and a small but festive patio perfect for people-watching. $ 787 N. Palm Canyon, 760-320-3558

Le Vallauris This French restaurant's patio is one of the area's most romantic spots. $$ 385 W. Tahquitz Canyon Way, 760-325-5059, levallauris.com

Norma's Breakfast dishes at this Parker Palm Springs eatery are over the top and loaded with calories. $ 4200 E. Palm Canyon Dr., 760-321-4630, theparkerpalmsprings.com

St. James A unique blend of Mediterranean and California cuisines in a Moorish setting. $$ 265 S. Palm Canyon Dr., 760-320-8041, stjamesrestaurant.com

Nightlife

Blue Guitar This intimate, second-story blues bar has the best music in town. 120 S. Palm Canyon Dr., 760-327-1549, blueguitarpalmsprings.com

Citron Bar The Viceroy Hotel's answer to 1940s Palm Springs, cocktail-style. 415 S. Belardo Rd., 760-318-3005, viceroypalmsprings.com

Las Casuelas Terrazza Drink monstrous top-shelf margaritas on the terrace and enjoy some stellar people-watching. 222 S. Palm Canyon Dr., 760-325-2794, lascasuelas.com

Best Hotels

La Quinta Resort & Club This Mission-style luxury property has five golf courses to choose from. $$$ 49499 Eisenhower Dr., Palm Desert, 760-564-4111 / 800-598-3828, laquintaresort.com

Movie Colony Hotel Designed by Albert Frey, this modernist hotel resembling a cruise ship is for the aesthete in you. $$ 726 N. Indian Canyon Dr., 760-320-6340 / 888-953-5700, moviecolonyhotel.com

Parker Palm Springs Merv Griffin's former Givenchy Resort and Spa has been given designer Jonathan Adler's Regency Moderne touch. $$$ 4200 E. Palm Canyon Dr., 760-770-5000 / 800-543-4300, theparkerpalmsprings.com

Two Bunch Palms Resort and Spa A quiet, secluded resort for adults only has clothing-optional areas and two pools of hot, natural mineral water. $$$ 67425 Two Bunch Palms Trail, Desert Hot Springs, 760-329-8791 / 800-472-4334, twobunchpalms.com

Viceroy Palm Springs Everything you've come to expect from Viceroy's cool, hip hotels. $$$ 415 S. Belardo Rd., 760-320-4117 / 800-670-6184, viceroypalmsprings.com

Contacts

Palm Springs Visitor Information Center 2901 N. Palm Canyon Dr., 760-778-8418, palm-springs.org

LEAVING

> **Getting There:** Take I-10 East. Exit at Hwy. 111 exit, which leads into Palm Springs along North Palm Canyon Drive.

Santa Barbara

Hot Tip: Go carless for a day and explore Downtown, Stearns Wharf, and the harbor, all within walking distance of each other.

The Lowdown: This moneyed city of fewer than 100,000 people holds its own as the easy seaside choice for weary Angelenos who need to get away but don't have the time or cash to do Napa or Hawaii. If red-tiled roofs, cute shops, and Spanish heritage properties are your passion, you'll find Downtown Santa Barbara very exciting. The rest of us will be happy to give State Street a few slow laps before heading to more than a dozen high-quality beaches lining the shore, exploring the satellite coastal communities of Carpinteria, Goleta, and Montecito, or wine-tasting in the neighboring Santa Ynez and Santa Maria Valleys. Originally settled by Chumash Indians and redecorated by Spanish missionaries, Mexican ranchers, American robber barons, and Hollywood celebs, this relaxed place has a draw that's easy to see with its artsy undertones and perfect Mediterranean climate.

Accommodation options include historic B&Bs, family-run inns, guest ranches, cottage rentals, and palatial beachside resorts like the Four Seasons Biltmore in celebrity-studded Montecito. Santa Barbara's architectural heritage can be best experienced along Downtown's Red Tile Walking Tour, covering five square blocks of landmarks. Sailing, kayaking, windsurfing, deep-sea fishing, beach-bumming, and day-tripping out to Channel Islands National Park are all popular activities around the coast. On land, the area boasts eight championship golf courses and more than 100 vineyards in the city's neighboring wine country. Hikers can escape even farther, along miles of trails in the surrounding Santa Ynez Mountains.

Best Attractions

Mission Santa Barbara The "Queen of the Missions" was originally built ten years after America declared its independence. 2201 Laguna St., 805-682-4149

Santa Barbara Botanic Garden This 78-acre wilderness of local flora and fauna hosts more than 120 species of birds every year. $ 1212 Mission Canyon Rd., 805-682-4726, sbbg.org

Stearns Wharf The oldest working wharf in California serves up some of the city's freshest seafood. Cabrillo Blvd. at State St., stearnswharf.org

Best Restaurants

Arigato Sushi This local legend was open before sushi became a fad. $$ 1225 State St., 805-965-6074

Brophy Brothers The seafood makes the inevitably long wait for a table at this harborside restaurant worth it. $$ 119 Harbor Way, 805-966-4418, brophybros.com

La Superica The late Julia Child was a devoted fan of this decidedly modest Mexican restaurant. $ 622 N. Milpas St., 805-963-4940

Nu Grab a seat in the courtyard for weekend jazz and some sublime California cuisine. $$$ 1129 State St., 805-965-1500, restaurantnu.com

Wine Cask True to its name, this popular, upscale California-Italian restaurant in the historic El Paseo arcade has an amazing wine list. $$$ 813 Anacapa St., 805-966-9463, winecask.com

Best Nightlife

Cooney's Order a brew, watch the game, then hit the largest dance floor in the city. 500 Anacapa St., 805-564-2040

Indochine Order a martini or a glass of champagne at this stylish, energetic Southeast Asian–style lounge. 434 State St., 805-962-0154, indochinebar.com

Q's Sushi A Go-Go Supermodel waitstaff, four bars, three levels, and strong drinks make this one of the most happening spots in the city. 409 State St., 805-966-9177, qs-pasadena.com/santabarbara

Best Hotels

Casa del Mar Spanish-Colonial inn situated midway between Stearns Wharf and the harbor. $$$ 18 Bath St., 805-963-4418 / 800-433-3097, casadelmar.com

Four Seasons Biltmore This historic red-tile–roofed resort fronting the ocean in tony Montecito has a legendary Sunday brunch. $$$ 1260 Channel Dr., 805-969-2261 / 800-819-5053, fourseasons.com/santabarbara

Contacts

Santa Barbara Chamber of Commerce Visitor Information Center 1 Garden St., 805-965-3021, sbchamber.org

Santa Barbara Conference & Visitors Bureau 1601 Anacapa St., 805-966-9222, santabarbaraca.com

LEAVING

Getting There: Take U.S. 101 North from Los Angeles straight into Downtown Santa Barbara. For a more scenic drive along the coast, take Hwy. 1 North through Malibu, which hooks up with U.S. 101 in Oxnard.

Channel Islands National Park

Hot Tip: The waters on the leeward side of the islands provide some of the best diving and snorkeling along the Southern California coast.

The Lowdown: Floating off the coast of Southern California like a Club Med for pinnipeds, sea birds, and more than 2,000 species of plants and animals (including 150 found nowhere else on the planet), Channel Islands National Park has been called America's Galapagos. Five islands—Anacapa, San Miguel, Santa Barbara, Santa Cruz, and Santa Rosa—comprise this scattered offshore preserve, which is believed to have risen out of the Pacific as a result of volcanic activity some 14 million years ago.

All five islands are accessible by boat from Ventura and Santa Barbara harbors year-round, offering unique offshore hiking, kayaking, tide-pooling, diving, and camping opportunities. Summer is the most popular time to visit the park, but the times to see migrating gray whales and the best wildflower shows are in the winter and spring, respectively. Anacapa is the most accessible island and is a good introduction to the park, featuring dramatic cliffs, hundreds of birds, barking sea lions, hiking trails, a picnic area and lighthouse, excellent diving sites, and remote caves once frequented by Chumash Indians. The largest of the islands, Santa Cruz, did time as a Mexican penal colony and cattle ranch before joining the park. Tours here are offered by the Nature Conservancy and provide some of the most varied hiking, beachcombing, and wildlife-spotting opportunities in the island group. Allow a full day and bring all your own food and water supplies, plus a hat, sunscreen, and sturdy hiking shoes.

Contacts

Channel Islands Aviation 305 Durley Ave., Camarillo, 805-987-1301, flycia.com
Channel Islands National Park Visitors Center 1991 Spinnaker Dr., Ventura, 805-658-5730, nps.gov/chis
Island Packers Ventura Harbor, 1691 Spinnaker Dr., Ventura, or Channel Islands Harbor, Oxnard, 3600 S. Harbor, 805-642-1393, islandpackers.com
Truth Aquatics 301 W. Cabrillo Blvd., Santa Barbara, 805-962-1127, truthaquatics.com

Getting There: Follow U.S. 101 North to Ventura. Take the Victoria Ave. exit, turning left onto Victoria Ave., then right onto Olivas Park Dr. to Harbor Blvd., where Olivas Park Dr. runs straight into Spinnaker Drive. The Channel Islands National Park Visitors Center (free parking at the beach parking lot) is located at the very end of Spinnaker Drive. Island Packers provides boat service to all of the Channel Islands from Ventura Harbor, offering a variety of half-day and multiday trips. Truth Aquatics is the park's concessionaire for boat travel to the islands from Santa Barbara Harbor (90 miles north of L.A. on U.S. 101). Trips to the islands take anywhere from 90 minutes to 5 hours.

20
miles
S

Disneyland

Hot Tip: The park is the least crowded from the end of August to early November, when school is back in session.

The Lowdown: Having celebrated its 50th anniversary in 2005 and, before that, a $1.5 billion expansion that included the opening of Disney's California Adventure, the world's most famous theme park has more to see and do—and buy—than ever before. The Disneyland Resort Hopper ticket includes back-and-forth admission to both parks all day. Disneyland is divvied up into eight theme lands teeming with rides, shows, and all those happy, fuzzy creatures smiling on the outside and suffering heatstroke on the inside. Honorable mentions include Adventureland, home of the popular Indiana Jones Adventure thrill ride, an audio-animatronic-enhanced Jungle Cruise, the Polynesian-themed Enchanted Tiki Room, and the straight-out-of-Africa attraction, Tarzan's Treehouse. Disney's California Adventure Park honors its home state—and the natives, explorers, immigrants, aviators, entrepreneurs, and entertainers who built it—with three separate theme lands: the Golden State, the Hollywood Pictures Backlot, and Paradise Pier. The Hollywood Pictures Backlot celebrates movie culture with its 2,000-seat Hyperion Theater, which presents live stage versions of classic Disney animated features. Also here is Jim Henson's MuppetVision 3-D spectacle and the Twilight Zone Tower of Terror, where passengers plunge 13 stories in a hotel elevator that moves faster than gravity.

Best Restaurants

Carnation Cafe Big portions of classic dishes, serving three meals a day. $$$ Main St., Disneyland, 714-781-3463

Blue Bayou This Creole favorite is considered one of the park's best dining spots, but it's reservation only, so call ahead. $$$ New Orleans Square, Disneyland, 714-781-3463

Gibson Girl Ice Cream Parlour Cool treats with Disney-themed flavors. $ Main St., Disneyland, 714-781-3463

Contacts

Anaheim/Orange County Visitor and Convention Bureau 800 W. Katella Ave., Anaheim, 714-765-8888, anaheimoc.org

Disneyland Customer Service 714-781-7290

Disneyland Recorded Information 714-781-4565

Disneyland Tickets and Reservations 714-781-4400

Disneyland Website disneyland.com

LEAVING

Getting There: Take I-5 South to Anaheim in Orange County. Exit at Disneyland Drive and turn left.

Six Flags Magic Mountain

Hot Tip: The earlier you get there, the lighter the lines for all 17 thrill rides will be.

The Lowdown: Southern California's hair-raising branch of the Six Flags empire has come a long way from its humble beginnings in the early 1970s. It now features more than 100 rides, games, and attractions, and—if you can ignore all the Valley youths and the odd street-gang daytrip here—several are unlike anything you've ever experienced. Once just a one-roller-coaster stop, the 260-acre theme park is now an Xtreme coaster nirvana, with 16 of them (the most in any park in the world) looping, corkscrewing, and cobra-rolling their way into several world titles. There's the world's second tallest roller coaster (Superman: The Escape at 415 feet), the world's tallest and fastest stand-up roller-coaster (The Riddler's Revenge at 156 feet, 65 mph), and the world's tallest and fastest suspended looping boomerang coaster (Déjà Vu at 196 feet, 65 mph), among others. Magic Mountain's nine themed lands offer several more lunch-churners with names like Freefall, Goliath, and Colossus (the tallest wooden coaster west of the Rockies). The latest addition is Scream, an aptly named floorless coaster with more than seven 360-degree inversions. Right next door to Magic Mountain is Six Flags' tropical-themed aqua park, Hurricane Harbor.

A General Use Admission ticket ($44.99) includes all rides, shows, and attractions at Magic Mountain. Combo tickets also get you into Hurricane Harbor on the day of your visit or on any other day during the season. Magic Mountain is open daily between April and early September, Fridays and weekends through September and October, and weekends and holidays the rest of the year.

Contacts

Six Flags Mountain and Hurricane Harbor 26101 Magic Mountain Pkwy. (The Old Rd.), Valencia, 661-255-4100, sixflags.com

Getting There: Take I-5 North (or I-405 North to I-5 North) to the Magic Mountain Parkway exit just past Valencia.

LOS ANGELES BLACK BOOK

You're solo in the city–where's a singles-friendly place to eat? Is there a good lunch spot near the museum? Will the bar be too loud for easy conversation? Get the answers fast in the *Black Book*, a condensed version of every listing in our guide that puts all the essential information at your fingertips. A quick glance down the page and you'll find the type of food, nightlife, or attractions you are looking for, the phone numbers, and which pages to turn to for more detailed information. How did you ever survive without this?

Los Angeles Black Book

Hotels

NAME TYPE (ROOMS)	ADDRESS (CROSS STREET) WEBSITE	AREA PRICE	PHONE 800 NUMBER	EXPERIENCE 99 BEST	PAGE PAGE
Avalon Hotel Trendy (84)	9400 W. Olympic Blvd. (Canon Dr.) avalonbeverlyhills.com	BH $$	310-277-5221 800-535-4715	Hip	98
Beach House at Hermosa Modern (96)	1300 The Strand (14th St.) beach-house.com	SB $$$	310-374-3001 888-895-4559	Hot & Cool	58
Beverly Hills Hotel & Bungalows Timeless (204)	9641 Sunset Blvd. (Cresent Dr.) beverlyhillshotel.com	BH $$$$	310-276-2251 800-283-8885	Classic Hotel Pools	131 28
Beverly Wilshire Four Seasons Hotel Timeless (395)	9500 Wilshire Blvd. (El Camino Dr.) fourseasons.com/beverlywilshire	BH $$$$	310-275-5200 800-332-3442	Classic Presidential Suites	131 36
Casa del Mar Timeless (131)	1910 Ocean Way (Pico Blvd.) hotelcasadelmar.com	SM $$$$	310-581-5533 800-898-6999	Hot & Cool	*52*, 58
Chateau Marmont Timeless (63)	8221 W. Sunset Blvd. (Marmont Ln.) chateaumarmont.com	WH $$$	323-656-1010	Hot & Cool	58
Four Seasons Hotel Timeless (285)	300 S. Doheny Dr. (Burton Way) fourseasons.com	BH $$$$	310-273-2222 800-332-3442	Hot & Cool	59
Hollywood Roosevelt Hotel Timeless (300)	7000 Hollywood Blvd. (N. Orange Dr.) hollywoodroosevelt.com	HW $$	323-466-7000 800-950-7667	Hip Hotel Pools	98 28
Hotel Bel-Air Timeless (92)	701 Stone Canyon Rd. (Sunset Blvd.) hotelbelair.com	BA $$$$	310-472-1211 800-648-4097	Classic	131
Inn at Playa del Rey Timeless (21)	435 Culver Blvd. (Pershing Dr.) innatplayadelrey.com	VA · $$	310-574-1920	Hip	98
Luxe Hotel Rodeo Drive Modern (86)	360 N. Rodeo Dr. (Brighton Way) luxehotels.com	BH $$$	310-273-0300 866-589-3411	Hot & Cool	59
Maison 140 Timeless (43)	140 S. Lasky Dr. (S. Santa Monica Blvd.) maison140beverlyhills.com	BH $$$	310-281-4000 800-432-5444	Classic	132
Malibu Beach Inn Modern (47)	22878 Pacific Coast Hwy. (Sweetwater Canyon Dr.) malibubeachinn.com	MB $$$	310-456-6444 800-462-5428	Hot & Cool	59
Millennium Biltmore Hotel Grand (683)	506 S. Grand Ave. (W. Fifth St.) millenniumhotels.com	DT $$	213-624-1011 800-245-8673	Classic	132
Mondrian Trendy (237)	8440 W. Sunset Blvd. (Olive Dr.) mondrianhotel.com	WH $$$$	323-650-8999 800-525-8029	Hip Hotel Pools	99 28
The Peninsula Beverly Hills Timeless (196)	9882 S. Santa Monica Blvd. (Wilshire Blvd.) peninsula.com	BH $$$$	310-551-2888 866-382-8388	Classic Presidential Suites	133 36
Raffles L'Ermitage Beverly Hills Modern (121)	9291 Burton Way (Foothill Rd.) raffleshotels.com	BH $$$$	310-278-3344 800-800-2113	Hot & Cool	60

Neighborhood (Area) Key

BA =	Bel-Air	**LF** =	Los Feliz	**SB** =	South Bay
BH =	Beverly Hills	**MB** =	Malibu	**VA** =	Various
DT =	Downtown	**PD** =	Pasadena	**VB** =	Venice Beach
HW =	Hollywood	**SM** =	Santa Monica	**WH** =	West Hollywood
LA =	Los Angeles (Central)	**SL** =	Silver Lake		

NAME TYPE (ROOMS)	ADDRESS (CROSS STREET) WEBSITE	AREA PRICE	PHONE 800 NUMBER	EXPERIENCE 99 BEST	PAGE PAGE
Shade Hotel Trendy (38)	1221 N. Valley Dr. (Manhattan Beach Blvd.) shadehotel.com	SB $$$	310-546-4995 866-987-4233	Hot & Cool	61
Shutters on the Beach Timeless (198)	1 Pico Blvd. (Ocean Way) shuttersonthebeach.com	SM $$$$	310-458-0030 800-334-9000	Hot & Cool Presidential Suites	61 36
The Standard Downtown Trendy (207)	550 S. Flower St. (Sixth St.) standardhotel.com	DT $$$	213-892-8080	Hip	99
The Standard Hollywood Trendy (129)	8300 W. Sunset Blvd. (N. Sweetzer Ave.) standardhotel.com	WH $$$	323-650-9090	Hip	100
Sunset Marquis Hotel & Villas Timeless (115)	1200 N. Alta Loma Rd. (Holloway Dr.) sunsetmarquishotel.com	WH $$$$	310-657-1333 800-858-9758	Hip	100
Sunset Tower Timeless (74)	8358 Sunset Blvd (N. Sweetzer Ave.) sunsettowerhotel.com	WH $$$	323-654-7100 800-225-2637	Classic	133
Viceroy Modern (162)	1819 Ocean Ave. (Pico Blvd.) viceroysantamonica.com	SM $$$	310-260-7500 800-670-6185	Hip	100
W Los Angeles Westwood Modern (258)	930 Hilgard Ave. (Le Conte Ave.) whotels.com	VA $$$	310-208-8765 888-625-4988	Hip	101

Restaurants

NAME TYPE	ADDRESS (CROSS STREET) WEBSITE	AREA PRICE	PHONE SINGLES/NOISE		EXPERIENCE 99 BEST	PAGE PAGE
A.O.C. Mediterranean	8022 W. Third St. (S. Laurel Ave.) aocwinebar.com	LA $$	323-653-6359 Ⓑ	⩵	Hot & Cool Wine List	54, 62 47
Ago Italian	8478 Melrose Ave. (Crescent Heights Blvd.) agorestaurant.com	WH $$$	323-655-6333 -	⩵	Hot & Cool Celebrity Rests.	53, 62 18
Alcove Cafe & Bakery American	1929 Hillhurst Ave. (Franklin Ave.) alcovecafe.com	LF $	323-644-0100 -	⩵	Hip	92, 102
Alegria on Sunset Mexican	3510 W. Sunset Blvd (Golden Gate Ave.) alegriaonsunset.com	LF $	323-913-1422 -	⩵	Hip	102
Angelini Osteria Italian	7313 Beverly Blvd. (Poinsettia Pl.) angeliniosteria.com	LA $$$	323-297-0070 Ⓑ	≣	Hot & Cool	62

Restaurant and Nightlife Symbols		
Restaurants Singles Friendly (eat and/or meet) ⬚ = Communal table Ⓑ = Food served at bar (G) = Gourmet destination	**Nightlife** Price Warning Ⓒ = Cover or ticket charge	**Restaurant + Nightlife** Prime time noise levels ⌣ = Quiet ⩵ = A buzz, but still conversational ≣ = Loud
Venues followed by an * are those we recommend as both a restaurant and a destination bar.		

Note regarding page numbers: Italic = itinerary listing; Roman = description in theme chapter listing.

BLACK BOOK

Restaurants (cont.)

NAME TYPE	ADDRESS (CROSS STREET) WEBSITE	AREA PRICE	PHONE SINGLES/NOISE	EXPERIENCE 99 BEST	PAGE PAGE
Apple Pan American	10801 W. Pico Blvd. (Glendon Ave.)	VA $	310-475-3585 - ⊟	Classic	134
Arnie Morton's of Chicago Steakhouse	735 S. Figueroa St (W. Seventh St.) mortons.com	DT $$$	213-553-4566 - ⊟	Classic	134
Asia de Cuba Asian Fusion	8440 W. Sunset Blvd. (La Cienega Blvd.) mondrianhotel.com	WH $$$	323-848-6000 Ⓑ ☰	Hot & Cool	63
Avenue American	1141 Manhattan Ave. (Manhattan Beach Blvd.) avenuemb.com	SB $$	310-802-1973 Ⓑ ⊟	Hot & Cool	63
Barney Greengrass Deli	9570 Wilshire Blvd., 5th Floor (Rodeo Dr.) barneys.com	BH $	310-777-5877 - ⊟	Hot & Cool Power Lunches	51, 63 35
Beacon Asian Fusion	3280 Helms Ave. (Washington Blvd.) beacon-la.com	VA $	310-838-7500 Ⓑ ⊟	Hip	102
BlackSteel* French/Japanese	6683 Hollywood Blvd. (Las Palmas Ave.) blacksteel.tv	HW $$$	323-469-3456 Ⓑ ☰	Hot & Cool	63
BLD American	7450 Beverly Blvd. (Vista St.) bldrestaurant.com	LA $$	323-930-9744 Ⓑ ⊟	Hip	91, 102
The Bowery* Fusion	6268 Sunset Blvd. (Vine St.) theboweryhollywood.com	HW $	323-465-3400 - ⊟	Hip Date Spots	103 21
Brandywine American	22757 Ventura Blvd. (Fallbrook Ave.)	VA $$	818-225-9114 - ⊟	Hot & Cool	64
Breadbar American	8718 W. Third St. (Arnaz Dr.)	LA $	310-205-0124 - ⊟	Hot & Cool	54, 64
Bridge Restaurant and Lounge* Italian	755 N. La Cienega Blvd. (Waring Ave.) bridgela.com	WH $$$$	310-659-3535 - ☰	Hot & Cool Trendy Tables	53, 64 45
Brighton Coffee Shop American	9600 Brighton Way (Camden Dr.)	BH $	310-276-7732 - ⊟	Classic	126, 134
Busby's* American	3110 Santa Monica Blvd. (Berkely St.) busbysonline.com	SM $$	310-828-4567 - ⊟	Hot & Cool	64
Cabo Cantina* Mexican	8301 W. Sunset Blvd. (Sweetzer Ave.)	LA $	323-822-7820 Ⓑ ⊟	Classic	134
La Cachette French (G)	10506 Santa Monica Blvd. (Thayer Ave.) lacachetterestaurant.com	VA $$$	310-470-4992 - ⊟	Hot & Cool	64
Café Pinot Cal-French	700 W. Fifth St. (S. Flower St.) patinagroup.com/cafePinot	DT $$	213-239-6500 - ⊟	Hot & Cool	65
Campanile Cal-Med	624 S. La Brea Ave. (Sixth St.) campanilerestaurant.com	LA $$$$	323-938-1447 Ⓑ ⊟	Classic	128, 134
Canter's American	419 N. Fairfax Ave. (Oakwood Ave.) cantersdeli.com	LA $	323-651-2030 - ☰	Classic Late-Night Eats	126, 134 29
Capo Italian (G)	1810 Ocean Ave. (Pico Blvd.) caporestaurant.com	SM $$$$	310-394-5550 - ⊟	Hot & Cool	65
Cha Cha Cha Cuban	7953 Santa Monica Blvd (N. Hayworth Ave.) theoriginalchachacha.com	WH $	323-848-7700 - ⊟	Hip	103
Chaya Venice* Asian Fusion	110 Navy St. (Pacific Ave.) thechaya.com	VB $$	310-396-1179 Ⓑ ☰	Hot & Cool	65

NAME TYPE	ADDRESS (CROSS STREET) WEBSITE	AREA PRICE	PHONE SINGLES/NOISE	EXPERIENCE 99 BEST	PAGE PAGE
Chinois on Main Fusion	2709 Main St. (Hill St.) wolfgangpuck.com	SM $$$	310-392-9025 - ≣	Hot & Cool	66
Cicada Italian	617 S. Olive St. (Sixth St.) cicadarestaurant.com	DT $$$	213-488-9488 - ≈	Hot & Cool	66
Cinespace* American	6356 Hollywood Blvd., 2nd Floor (Ivar St.) cinespace.info	HW $$	323-817-3456 - ≣	Hot & Cool Date Spots	66 21
Citizen Smith* American	1602 N. Cahuenga Blvd. (Selma Ave.) citizensmith.com	HW $$	323-461-5001 - ≈	Hot & Cool Date Spots	66 21
Ciudad* Latin	445 S. Figueroa St. (Fifth St.) ciudad-la.com	DT $$	213-486-5171 - ≣	Hip	*92*, 103
Clafoutis French	8630 W. Sunset Blvd. (Sunset Plaza Dr.) le-clafoutis.com	WH $	310-659-5233 - ≣	Hot & Cool	*52*, 66
Cobras & Matadors Spanish	4655 Hollywood Blvd. (N. Vermont Ave.)	LF $	323-669-3922 Ⓑ ≈	Hip	*93*, 103
Crustacean Seafood	9646 Little Santa Monica Blvd. (N. Bedford Dr.) anfamily.com	BH $$$	310-205-8990 - ≈	Hot & Cool	67
Cut Steakhouse	9500 Wilshire Blvd. (Beverly Dr.) wolfgangpuck.com	BH $$$	310-276-8500 - ≈	Hot & Cool Trendy Tables	67 45
Dakota Steakhouse	7000 Hollywood Blvd. (Orange Dr.) dakota-restaurant.com	HW $$$	323-769-8888 Ⓑ ≈	Hot & Cool	67
Dan Tana's Steakhouse	9071 Santa Monica Blvd. (Doherty Dr.) dantanasrestaurant.com	WH $$$$	310-275-9444 Ⓑ ≈	Classic Steakhouses	*128*, 135 41
Dar Maghreb Moroccan	7651 W. Sunset Blvd. (Stanley Ave.) darmaghrebrestaurant.com	HW $$	323-876-7651 - ≈	Classic	135
Derek's Bistro Cal-French	181 E. Glenarm St. (S. Marengo Ave.) dereks.com	PD $$	626-799-5252 - ≈	Hot & Cool	67
Dolce Enoteca e Ristorante* Italian	8284 Melrose Ave. (Sweetzer Ave.) dolceenoteca.com	WH $$$	323-852-7174 Ⓑ ≣	Hot & Cool	68
Du-Pars American	6333 W. Third St. (Fairfax Ave.) dupars.com	VA $	323-933-8446 - ≣	Classic	135
Duke's Malibu* American	21150 Pacific Coast Hwy. (Las Flores Canyon Rd.) dukesmalibu.com	MB $$	310-317-0777 Ⓑ ≈	Hip	103
Dusty's Bistro American	3200 W. Sunset Blvd. (Descanso Dr.) dustysbistro.com	SL $$$	323-906-1018 Ⓑ ≈	Hip	*93*, 104
El Guapo Mexican Cantina* Mexican	7250 Melrose Ave. (Alta Vista Blvd.) elguapocantina.com	LA $	323-297-0471 - ◻	Hip	104
Empress Pavilion Chinese	Bamboo Plaza, 988 N. Hill St. (Bamboo Ln.) empresspavilion.com	VA $	213-617-9898 - ≣	Classic	135
Falcon* American	7213 Sunset Blvd. (Pointsettia Pl.) falconslair.com	HW $$	323-850-5350 - ≈	Hot & Cool	68
Father's Office* American	1018 Montana Ave. (10th St.) fathersoffice.com	SM $$	310-393-2337 - ≣	Hip	104
Ford's Filling Station American	9531 Culver Blvd. (Washington Blvd.) fordsfillingstation.net	CC $$	310-202-1470 Ⓑ ≈	Hip	*93*, 104

Restaurants (cont.)

NAME TYPE	ADDRESS (CROSS STREET) WEBSITE	AREA PRICE	PHONE SINGLES/NOISE	EXPERIENCE 99 BEST	PAGE PAGE
410 Boyd American	410 Boyd St. (San Pedro St.)	DT $$	213-617-2491 B ⬚	Hip	92, 105
Fred 62 American	1850 N. Vermont Ave. (Russell St.) fred62.com	LF $	323-667-0062 - ⬚	Hip	92, 105
Geisha House* Japanese	6633 Hollywood Blvd. (Cherokee Ave.) geishahousehollywood.com	HW $$$	323-460-6300 B ≡	Hot & Cool Celebrity-Own Rests.	68 18
Geoffrey's American	27400 Pacific Coast Hwy. (Meadows Ct.) geoffreysmalibu.com	MB $$$	310-457-1519 - ⬚	Hot & Cool	54, 68
Gingergrass Vietnamese	2396 Glendale Blvd. (Brier Ave.) gingergrass.com	SL $$	323-644-1600 - ≡	Hip	105
Grace American	7360 Beverly Blvd. (N. Fuller Ave.) gracerestaurant.com	LA $$$	323-934-4400 ⬚	Hot & Cool	68
The Grill on the Alley Steakhouse	9560 Dayton Way (Wilshire Blvd.) thegrill.com	BH $$$	310-276-0615 B ≡	Hot & Cool Power Lunches	51, 69 35
HamaSaku Japanese	11043 Santa Monica Blvd. (Sepulveda Blvd.) hamasakula.com	VA $$	310-479-7636 - ⬚	Hot & Cool	69
Hotel Bel-Air Restaurant Cal-French (G)	701 Stone Canyon Rd. (Chalon Rd.) hotelbelair.com/terrace.html	BA $$$	310-472-5234 - ⬚	Classic Patio Dining	126, 136 33
House of Blues* Southern	8430 Sunset Blvd. (Kings Rd.) hob.com	LA $$	323-848-5100 ≡	Hip	94, 105
The Hungry Cat Seafood	1535 N. Vine St. (Sunset Blvd.) thehungrycat.com	HW $$	323-462-2155 B ⬚	Hip Seafood	105 38
Il Cielo Italian	9018 Burton Way (Wetherley Dr.) ilcielo.com	BH $$$	310-276-9990 - ⬚	Classic Romantic Dining	126, 136 37
Inn of the Seventh Ray American/Vegetarian	128 Old Topanga Canyon Rd. (Topanga Canyon Blvd.) innoftheseventhray.com	VA $$$$	310-455-1311 - ⬚	Hot & Cool Romantic Dining	69 37
The Ivy American	113 N. Robertson Blvd. (Alden Dr.)	BH $$$	310-274-8303 - ⬚	Classic Celebrity-Spot Rests.	126, 136 19
Ivy at the Shore American	1535 Ocean Ave. (Broadway St.)	SM $$$	310-393-3113 B ≡	Hot & Cool	70
Jar American	8225 Beverly Blvd. (Harper Ave.) thejar.com	LA $$$	323-655-6566 B ⬚	Hip	94, 106
Jer-ne Fusion	4375 Admiralty Way (Promenade Way) ritzcarlton.com	SB $$$$	310-574-4333 - ⬚	Hot & Cool	54, 70
JiRaffe Cal-French	502 Santa Monica Blvd. (Fifth St.) jirafferestaurant.com	SM $$	310-917-6671 - ⬚	Hot & Cool	52, 70
Joe's Restaurant American	1023 Abbot Kinney Blvd. (Broadway St.) joesrestaurant.com	VB $$	310-399-5811 B ⬚	Hip	93, 106
Jones Hollywood* Italian	7205 Santa Monica Blvd. (Formosa Ave.)	WH $	323-850-1726 B ≡	Hip	106
Josie American (G)	2424 Pico Blvd. (25th St.) josierestaurant.com	SM $$	310-581-9888 - ⬚	Hot & Cool	70
Katana Japanese	8439 W. Sunset Blvd. (La Cienega Blvd.) katanarobata.com	WH $$	323-650-8585 - ≡	Hot & Cool Patio Dining	70 33

NAME TYPE	ADDRESS (CROSS STREET) WEBSITE	AREA PRICE	PHONE SINGLES/NOISE	EXPERIENCE 99 BEST	PAGE PAGE
Kate Mantilini American	9101 Wilshire Blvd. (Doheny Dr.)	BH $$	310-278-3699 Ⓑ ≡	Hip	106
King's Road Cafe American	8361 Beverly Blvd. (Kings Rd.) kingsroadcafe.com	LA $	323-655-9044 - ≈	Hip	94, 106
Koi Japanese	730 N. La Cienega Blvd. (Melrose Ave.) koirestaurant.com	LA $	310-659-9449 Ⓑ ≡	Hot & Cool	53, 71
Le Velvet Margarita Cantina* Mexican	1612 Cahuenga Blvd. (Hollywood Blvd.) velvetmargarita.com	HW $$	323-469-2000 - ≈	Hip	107
The Little Door Mediterranean	8164 W. Third St. (La Jolla Ave.) thelittledoor.com	LA $$$	323-951-1210 - ≈	Hot & Cool	71
The Lobster Seafood	1602 Ocean Ave. (Colorado Ave.) thelobster.com	SM $$	310-458-9294 - ≈	Hot & Cool	71
Lucques California-French (G)	8474 Melrose Ave (La Cienega Blvd.) lucques.com	WH $$$	323-655-6277 Ⓑ ≈	Hot & Cool	54, 71
Ma'Kai* Tapas	101 Broadway Ave. (Ocean Ave.) makailounge.com	SM $	310-434-1511 Ⓑ ≈	Hot & Cool	72
Madame Matisse French	3536 W. Sunset Blvd. (Maltman Ave.)	SL $	323-662-4862 - ≈	Hip	107
Magnolia* American	6266½ W. Sunset Blvd. (Argyle Ave.) magnoliahollywood.com	HW $$	323-467-0660 Ⓑ ≡	Hip	107
Maison Akira Fusion (G)	713 E. Green St. (Oak Knoll Ave.) maisonakira.com	PD $$	626-796-9501 ⊡	Hot & Cool	72
Martha's 22nd Street Grill American	25 22nd St. (Hermosa Ave.)	SB $	310-376-7786 - ≈	Hot & Cool	53, 72
Matsuhisa Sushi (G)	129 N. La Cienega Blvd. (Wilshire Blvd.) nobumatsuhisa.com	LA $$	310-659-9639 - ≈	Hot & Cool Sushi	72 43
Melisse French (G)	1104 Wilshire Blvd. (11th St.) melisse.com	SM $$$	310-395-0881 - ≈	Hot & Cool Wine List	52, 73 47
Memphis* Southern	6541 Hollywood Blvd. (Hudson Ave.) memphishollywood.com	HW $$	323-465-8600 Ⓑ ≡	Hip	91, 107
Michael's Californian (G)	1147 Third St. (Wilshire Blvd.) michaelssantamonica.com	SM $$$	310-451-0843 - ≈	Classic Patio Dining	136 33
Michelangelo's Pizzeria Ristorante Italian	1637 Silverlake Blvd. (Effie St.)	SL $	323-660-4843 - ≈	Hip	93, 107
Morton's Steakhouse	8764 Melrose Ave. (Robertson Blvd.) mortons.com	WH $$$	310-276-5205 - ≈	Classic	128, 137
Mr. Chow Chinese	344 N. Camden Dr. (Wilshire Blvd.) mrchow.com	BH $$$	310-278-9911 - ≈	Classic Celebrity-Spot Rests.	125, 137 19
Musso & Frank Grill* American	6667 Hollywood Blvd. (Highland Ave.)	HW $$	323-467-7788 - ≈	Classic Steakhouses	125, 137 41
Newsroom Café American/Vegetarian	120 N. Robertson Blvd. (Beverly Blvd.)	WH $	310-652-4444 Ⓑ ≈	Hip	94, 108
Nobu Malibu Japanese (G)	3835 Cross Creek Rd. (Pacific Coast Hwy.) nobumatsuhisa.com	MB $$$	310-317-9140 Ⓑ ≡	Hot & Cool	73

Restaurants (cont.)

NAME TYPE	ADDRESS (CROSS STREET) WEBSITE	AREA PRICE	PHONE SINGLES/NOISE	EXPERIENCE 99 BEST	PAGE PAGE
Norman's American	8570 Sunset Blvd. (Alta Loma Rd.) normans.com	WH $$	310-657-2400 B ▤	Hot & Cool	73
Nyala Ethiopian	1076 S. Fairfax Ave. (Whitworth Dr.) nyala-la.com	LA $	323-936-5918 B ▤	Hip	108
One Pico American	1 Pico Blvd. (Ocean Ave.) shuttersonthebeach.com	SM $$	310-587-1717 - ▤	Hot & Cool	73
Original Pantry Café American	877 S. Figueroa St. (Ninth St.) pantrycafe.com	DT $	213-972-9279 - ▤	Classic	127, 137
Ortolan French (G)	8338 W. Third St. (Kings Rd.) ortolanrestaurant.com	LA $$$	323-653-3300 B🗋 ▤	Hot & Cool Celebrity-Own Rests.	54, 73 18
Pacific Dining Car Steakhouse	1310 W. Sixth St. (Whitmer St.) pacificdiningcar.com	DT $$$$	213-483-6000 - ▤	Classic Steakhouses	137 41
Palms Thai Thai	5900 Hollywood Blvd., Suite B (Bronson St.) palmsthai.com	HW $	323-462-5073 🗋 ▤	Hip	94, 108
Patina Cal-French (G)	Walt Disney Concert Hall, 141 S. Grand Ave. (First St.) patinagroup.com/patina	DT $$$	213-972-3331 B ▤	Hot & Cool	52, 74
Patrick's Roadhouse American	106 Entrada Dr. (Pacific Coast Hwy.)	VA $	310-459-4544 - ▤	Classic	125, 138
Pedals American	1 Pico Blvd. (Ocean Ave.) shuttersonthebeach.com	SM $	310-587-1707 B ▤	Hot & Cool	74
Philippe the Original American	1001 N. Alameda St. (Ord St.) philippes.com	DT $-	213-628-3781 - ▤	Classic	138
Pie 'n Burger Diner	913 E. California Blvd. (S. Lake Ave.) pienburger.com	PD $-	626-795-1123 - ▤	Classic	127, 138
Pig 'n Whistle* American	6714 Hollywood Blvd. (Las Palmas Ave.) pignwhistle.com	HW $	323-463-0000 - ▤	Classic	138
Pink's American	709 N. La Brea Ave. (Melrose Ave.) pinkshollywood.com	HW $	323-931-4223 - ▤	Classic Late-Night Eats	126, 138 29
Polo Lounge* American	9641 Sunset Blvd. (Beverly Dr.) beverlyhillshotel.com	BH $$$	310-887-2777 B ▤	Classic	139
Primitivo Wine Bistro Spanish	1025 Abbot Kinney Blvd. (Broadway St.) primitivowinebistro.com	VB $$	310-396-5353 B ▤	Hip	108
Providence Seafood (G)	5955 Melrose Ave. (Cole Ave.) providencela.com	LA $$$$	323-460-4170 - ▤	Hot & Cool Seafood	53, 74 38
R-23 Japanese	923 E. Second St (Alameda St.) r23.com	DT $$	213-687-7178 - ▤	Hip	92, 109
The Raymond American	1250 S. Fair Oaks Ave. (Columbia St.) theraymond.com	PD $$$	626-441-3136 - ▤	Classic	127, 139
Il Ristorante di Giorgio Baldi Italian	114 W. Channel Rd. (Pacific Coast Hwy.) giorgiobaldi.com	SM $$$	310-573-1660 - ▤	Classic Celebrity-Spot Rests.	127, 139 19
Saddle Ranch Chop House* American	8371 W. Sunset Blvd. (La Cienega Blvd.) srrestaurants.com	LA $	323-656-2007 - ⊟	Hot & Cool	74
Sanamluang Café Thai	5176 Hollywood Blvd. (Kingsley Dr.) 	HW $	323-660-8006 - ▤	Hip Late-Night Eats	92, 109 29

NAME	ADDRESS (CROSS STREET)	AREA	PHONE	EXPERIENCE	PAGE
TYPE	WEBSITE	PRICE	SINGLES/NOISE	99 BEST	PAGE
La Scala Italian	434 N. Canon Dr. (Brighton Way)	BH $$	310-275-0579 - ⊟	Classic	139
Smoke House Steakhouse	4420 Lakeside Dr. (Olive Ave.) smokehouse1946.com	VA $$	818-845-3731 - ⊟	Classic	139
Social Hollywood* Moroccan	6525 W. Sunset Blvd. (Schrader Blvd.) socialhollywood.com	HW $$$	323-462-5222 - ⊟	Hip Trendy Tables	94, 109 45
Sona French (G)	401 N. La Cienega Blvd. (Melrose Ave.) sonarestaurant.com	WH $$$	310-659-7708 Ⓑ ⊟	Hot & Cool	75
Soot Bull Jeep Korean	3136 W. Eighth St. (S. Catalina St.)	VA $$$	213-387-3865 - ⊟	Hip	91, 109
Spago Californian	176 N. Cañon Dr. (Wilshire Blvd.) wolfgangpuck.com	BH $$$	310-385-0880 - ⊟	Classic Power Lunches	126, 139 35
Sunset Trocadero* Tapas	8280 Sunset Blvd. (Sweetzer Ave.)	LA $	323-656-7161 - ⊟	Classic	128, 140
Sushi Katsu-ya Japanese	11680 Ventura Blvd. (Colfax Ave.)	VA $$$	818-985-6976 - ⊟	Hip Sushi	110 43
Sushi Sasabune Japanese	12400 Wilshire Blvd. (S. Carmelina Ave.)	VA $$$$	310-820-3596 Ⓑ ⊟	Hip	110
Table 8 American	7661 Melrose Ave. (Stanley Ave.) table8la.com	LA $$$	323-782-8258 Ⓑ ⊟	Hot & Cool	75
Toast American	8221 W. Third St. (Harper Ave.) toastbakerycafe.net	LA $	323-655-5018 - ⊟	Hip	93, 110
Tower Bar American	8358 W. Sunset Blvd. (Sweetzer Ave.) sunsettowerhotel.com/tower-bar.html	WH $$$	323-848-6677 Ⓑ ⊟	Hot & Cool	75
25 Degrees American	7000 Hollywood Blvd. (Orange Dr.) 25degreesrestaurant.com	HW $	323-785-7244 Ⓑ ⊟	Hip	94, 110
24/7 Restaurant at The Standard American	8300 W. Sunset Blvd. (N. Sweetzer Ave.) standardhotel.com	WH $$	323-650-9090 - ⊟	Hip	54, 111
Urasawa Japanese (G)	218 N. Rodeo Dr. (Wilshire Blvd.)	BH $$$$	310-247-8939 - ▭	Hot & Cool Sushi	75 43
Valentino Italian (G)	3115 Pico Blvd. (31st St.) valentinosm.com	SM $$$$	310-829-4313 - ▭	Classic Wine List	140 47
Vermont American	1714 N. Vermont Ave. (Prospect Ave.) vermontrestaurantonline.com	LF $$	323-661-6163 Ⓑ	Hip	111
Water Grill Seafood (G)	544 S. Grand Ave. (Fifth St.) watergrill.com	DT $$$	213-891-0900 Ⓑ ⊟	Classic Seafood	127, 140 38
White Lotus* Asian Fusion	1743 Cahuenga Blvd. (Hollywood Blvd.) whitelotushollywood.com	HW $$	323-463-0060 - ⊟	Hot & Cool	76
Wilshire Restaurant* Californian	2454 Wilshire Blvd. (26th St.) wilshirerestaurant.com	SM $$$$	310-586-1707 - ⊟	Hot & Cool	52, 76
Yamashiro* Japanese	1999 N. Sycamore Ave. (Franklin Ave.) yamashirorestaurant.com	HW $$$$	323-466-5125 ⊟	Classic Romantic Dining	128, 140 37
Zucca Italian	801 S. Figueroa St. (W. Eighth St.) patinagroup.com/zucca	DT $$	213-614-7800 - ⊟	Hot & Cool	76

BLACK BOOK

Nightlife

NAME TYPE	ADDRESS (CROSS STREET) WEBSITE	AREA COVER	PHONE FOOD/NOISE	EXPERIENCE 99 BEST	PAGE PAGE
Acme Comedy Theatre Comedy	135 N. La Brea Ave. (First St.) acmecomedy.com	LA C	323-525-0202 - ▣	Hip	91, 112
Actor's Gang Theater Theater	9070 Venice Blvd. (Culver) theactorsgang.com	CC C	310-838-4264 - ▣	Hip	112
Ahmanson Theatre Theater	135 N. Grand Ave. (Temple St.) taperahmanson.com	DT C	213-628-2772 - ▤	Hip	112
The Bar Dive Bar	5851 Sunset Blvd. (Bronson St.)	HW -	323-468-9154 - ▣	Hip Dive Bars	94, 112 23
The Bar at Hotel Bel-Air Lounge	701 Stone Canyon (Tortuoso Way) hotelbelair.com	BA -	310-472-1211 - �	Classic	141
Bar Marmont Bar/Lounge	8171 W. Sunset Blvd. (Marmont Ln.) chateaumarmont.com	WH -	323-650-0575 - ▣	Classic	141
Basque Nightclub	1707 N. Vine St. (Hollywood Blvd.) basquehollywood.com	HW C	323-464-1654 - ▤	Hot & Cool Nightclubs	53, 77 32
Beauty Bar Theme Bar	1638 N. Cahuenga Ave. (Hollywood Blvd.) beautybar.com	HW -	323-464-7676 - ▣	Hip	112
BlackSteel* Ultra Lounge	6683 Hollywood Blvd. (Las Palmas Ave.) blacksteel.tv	HW C	323-469-3456 Ⓑ ▤	Hot & Cool	77
The Bigfoot Lodge Dive Bar	3172 Los Feliz Blvd. (Glen Feliz Blvd.) bigfootlodge.com	VA -	323-662-9227 - ▤	Hip	93, 113
The Bowery* Restaurant/Bar	6268 Sunset Blvd. (Vine St.) theboweryhollywood.com	HW -	323-465-3400 - ▣	Hip Date Spots	94, 113 21
Bridge Restaurant & Lounge* Lounge	755 N. La Cienega Blvd. (Waring Ave.) bridgela.com	WH -	323-659-3535 - ▣	Hot & Cool	77
The Brig Bar	1515 Abbot Kinney Blvd. (Palms Blvd.) thebrig.com	VB -	310-399-7537 - ▣	Hip	113
The Burgundy Room Dive Bar	1621½ N. Cahuenga Blvd. (Selma Ave.)	HW -	323-465-7530 - ▤	Classic Dive Bars	126, 141 23
Busby's* Sports Bar	3110 Santa Monica Blvd. (Berkely St.) busbysonline.com	SM C	310-828-4567 - ▣	Hot & Cool	77
Cabana Club Nightclub	1439 N. Ivar Ave. (Hollywood Blvd.) cabanaclubhollywood.com	HW C	323-463-0005 - ▣	Hot & Cool Nightclubs	54, 77 32
Cabo Cantina* Restaurant/Bar	8301 W. Sunset Blvd. (Sweetzer Ave.)	LA -	323-822-7820 - ▣	Classic Daytime Drink Spots	126, 141 22
Cameo Bar at the Viceroy Hotel Bar	1819 Ocean Ave. (Pico Blvd.) viceroysantamonica.com	SM -	310-260-7500 - �	Hot & Cool Hotel Bars	51, 78 27
Chaya Venice* Lounge	110 Navy St. (Main St.) thechaya.com	VB -	310-396-1179 Ⓑ ▣	Hot & Cool	54, 78
Cinespace* Restaurant/Nightclub	6356 Hollywood Blvd., 2nd Floor (Ivar St.) cinespace.info	HW C	323-817-3456 - ▤	Hot & Cool Date Spots	53, 78 21
Circle Bar Bar/Nightclub	2926 Main St. (Kinney St.) thecirclebar.com	SM C	310-450-0508 - ▣	Hot & Cool Singles Scenes	52, 78 39
Citizen Smith* Restaurant/Bar	1602 N. Cahuenga Blvd. (Selma Ave.) citizensmith.com	HW -	323-461-5001 - ▣	Hot & Cool Date Spots	54, 78 21

NAME TYPE	ADDRESS (CROSS STREET) WEBSITE	AREA COVER	PHONE FOOD/NOISE	EXPERIENCE 99 BEST	PAGE PAGE
Ciudad* Restaurant/Bar	445 S. Figueroa St. (Fifth St.) ciudad-la.com	DT -	213-486-5171 - ≡	Hip	93, 113
Club Bar at the Peninsula Beverly Hills Bar/Lounge	9882 S. Santa Monica Blvd. (Charleville Blvd.) peninsula.com	BH -	310-551-2888 - ⌐	Classic	126, 142
The Derby Restaurant/Lounge	4500 Los Feliz Blvd. (Hillhurst Ave.) clubderby.com	LF Ⓒ	323-663-8979 - ≡	Hip	113
Dolce Enoteca e Ristorante* Lounge	8284 Melrose Ave. (Sweetzer Ave.) dolceenoteca.com	WH -	323-852-7174 Ⓑ ≡	Hot & Cool	79
The Dresden Room Restaurant/Lounge	1760 N. Vermont Ave. (Melbourne Ave.) thedresden.com	LF Ⓒ	323-665-4294 - ≡	Hip	92, 114
Duke's Malibu* Bar	21150 Pacific Coast Hwy. (Las Flores Canyon Rd.) dukesmalibu.com	MB	310-317-0777 - ≡	Hip	114
El Carmen Lounge	8138 W. Third St. (Crescent Heights Blvd.) committedinc.com	LA Ⓒ	323-852-1552 - ≡	Hip	114
El Coyote Mexican Cafe Restaurant/Bar	7312 Beverly Blvd. (La Brea Ave.) elcoyotecafe.com	LA -	323-939-2255 - ⌐	Hip	114
El Guapo Mexican Cantina* Restaurant/Bar	7250 Melrose Ave. (Alta Vista Blvd.) elguapocantina.com	LA -	323-297-0471 - ⌐	Hip	114
Falcon* Restaurant/Bar	7213 Sunset Blvd. (N. Alta Vista Blvd.) falconslair.com	HW -	323-850-5350 - ⌐	Hot & Cool	53, 79
Father's Office* Restaurant/Bar	1018 Montana Ave. (Tenth St.) fathersoffice.com	SM -	310-393-2337 - ≡	Hip	115
Formosa Café Restaurant/Bar	7156 Santa Monica Blvd. (N. Formosa Ave.) formosacafe.com	HW -	323-850-9050 - ⌐	Classic	126, 142
4100 Bar Bar	4100 W. Sunset Blvd. (Manzanita St.)	SL Ⓒ	323-666-4460 - ≡	Hip	92, 115
Geisha House* Ultra Lounge	6633 Hollywood Blvd. (Cherokee Ave.) geishahousehollywood.com	HW -	323-460-6300 Ⓑ ≡	Hot & Cool	54, 79
Golden Gopher Lounge	417 W. Eighth St. (Olive St.) goldengopherbar.com	DT -	213-614-8001 - ⌐	Hip	93, 115
Good Luck Bar Bar	1514 Hillhurst Ave. (Hollywood Blvd.)	LF Ⓒ	323-666-3524 - ≡	Hip	93, 115
Greek Theatre Live Music	2700 N. Vermont Ave. (Los Feliz Blvd.) greektheatrela.com	VA Ⓒ	323-665-5857 - ≡	Classic	142
Guy's Nightclub	8713 Beverly Blvd. (La Cienega Blvd.)	WH Ⓒ	310-729-4031 - ≡	Hot & Cool	79
Holly's Ultra Lounge	1651 Wilcox Ave. (Hollywood Blvd.)	HW Ⓒ	323-461-1400 - ≡	Hot & Cool Celebrity Hangouts	53, 79 17
Hollywood Bowl Live Music	2301 N. Highland Ave. (S. Dixie Way) hollywoodbowl.com	HW Ⓒ	323-850-2000 - ≡	Classic	128, 142
House of Blues* Live Music	8430 W. Sunset Blvd. (Kings Rd.) hob.com	LA Ⓒ	323-848-5100 - ≡	Hip	115
Ivan Kane's Forty Deuce Theme Bar	5574 Melrose Ave. (Gower St.) fortydeuce.com	LA Ⓒ	323-466-6263 - ≡	Hip Theme Bars	94, 116 44

BLACK BOOK

Nightlife (cont.)

NAME TYPE	ADDRESS (CROSS STREET) WEBSITE	AREA COVER	PHONE FOOD/NOISE	EXPERIENCE 99 BEST	PAGE PAGE
Ivar Nightclub	6356 Hollywood Blvd. (Ivar Ave.) ivar.cc	HW C	323-465-4827 - ☰	Classic	128, 142
Jones Hollywood* Restaurant/Bar	7205 Santa Monica Blvd. (Formosa Ave.)	WH -	323-850-1726 - ☰	Hip	91, 116
L'Scorpion Theme Bar	6679 Hollywood Blvd. (Las Palmas Ave.) lscorpion.com	HW -	323-464-3026 - ▭	Hip Theme Bars	94, 116 44
Laugh Factory Comedy	8001 Sunset Blvd. (Crescent Heights Blvd.) laughfactory.com	LA C	323-656-1336 - ▭	Classic	128, 143
LAX Nightclub	1714 N. Las Palmas Ave. (Hollywood Blvd.) laxhollywood.com	HW C	323-464-0171 - ☰	Hot & Cool Celebrity Hangouts	53, 80 17
Le Velvet Margarita Cantina* Restaurant/Lounge	1612 Cahuenga Blvd. (Hollywood Blvd.) velvetmargarita.com	HW -	323-469-2000 - ☰	Hip Theme Bars	94, 116 44
Lobby Bar at the Four Seasons Bar/Lounge	300 S. Doheny Dr. (Gregory Way) fourseasons.com	BH -	310-273-2222 - ▭	Hot & Cool	80
Lobby Lounge, the Standard Hollywood Ultra Lounge	8300 W. Sunset Blvd. (Sweetzer Ave.) standardhotel.com	WH -	323-650-9090 - ☰	Hot & Cool Daytime Drink Spots	54, 80 22
Lola's Bar	945 N. Fairfax Ave. (Romaine St.) lolasla.com	WH -	213-736-5652 - ☰	Classic	128, 143
Los Angeles Neon Tour Tour	Museum of Neon Art, 501 W. Olympic Blvd. (Grand Ave.) neonmona.org	DT C	213-489-9918 - -	Hip Guided Tours	94, 117 25
Lucky Strike Lanes Bowling Alley	6801 Hollywood Blvd. (Highland Ave.) bowlluckystrike.com	HW -	323-467-7776 - ☰	Hip	94, 117
Magnolia* Restaurant/Lounge	6226½ W. Sunset Blvd. (Argyle Ave.) magnoliahollywood.com	HW -	323-467-0660 - ☰	Hip	92, 117
Ma'Kai* Restaurant/Nightclub	101 Broadway Ave. (Ocean Ave.) makailounge.com	SM C	310-434-1511 - ▭	Hot & Cool	52, 80
Mark Taper Forum Theater	135 W. Grand Ave. (First St.) taperahmanson.com	DT C	213-628-2772 - ▭	Hip	117
Memphis* Restaurant/Lounge	6541 Hollywood Blvd. (Hudson Ave.) memphishollywood.com	HW -	323-465-8600 - ☰	Hip	117
Mood Nightclub	6623 Hollywood Blvd. (Cherokee Ave.) moodla.com	HW C	323-464-6663 - ☰	Hip Singles Scenes	91, 117 39
Mor Bar Nightclub	2941 Main St. (Kinney St.) themorbar.com	SM C	310-396-6678 - ☰	Hot & Cool	52, 81
The Music Box @ The Henry Fonda Theatre Live Music	6126 Hollywood Blvd. (Gower St.)	DT C	323-464-0808 - ☰	Classic Live Music Venues	143 30
Musso & Frank Grill* Restaurant/Bar	6667 Hollywood Blvd. (Highland Ave.)	HW -	323-467-7788 - ☰	Classic	125, 143
Nacional Nightclub	1645 Wilcox Ave. (Hollywood Blvd.) nacional.cc	HW C	323-962-7712 - ☰	Hot & Cool	81
Pantages Theatre Theater	6233 Hollywood Blvd. (Argyle Ave.) broadwayla.org	HW C	323-468-1700 - ☰	Classic	144
Pig 'n Whistle* Restaurant/Bar	6714 Hollywood Blvd. (Las Palmas Ave.) pignwhistle.com	HW -	323-463-0000 - ☰	Classic	125, 144

NAME	ADDRESS (CROSS STREET)	AREA	PHONE	EXPERIENCE	PAGE
TYPE	WEBSITE	COVER	FOOD/NOISE	99 BEST	PAGE
Polo Lounge*	9641 Sunset Blvd. (Beverly Dr.)	BH	310-887-2777	Classic	126, 144
Restaurant/Lounge	beverlyhillshotel.com		- ▣		
Privilege	8117 Sunset Blvd. (Crescent	WH	323-654-0030	Hot & Cool	52, 81
Nightclub	Heights Blvd.) sbeent.com	C	- ▦	Nightclubs	32
Renee's Courtyard Café	522 Wilshire Blvd. (Fifth St.)	SM	310-451-9341	Hot & Cool	52, 81
Bar		-	- ▭		
Rokbar	1710 N. Las Palmas Ave. (Hollywood	HW	323-461-5600	Hot & Cool	52, 82
Nightclub	Blvd.) rokbaronline.com	-	- ▦		
Rooftop Bar at the	550 S. Flower St. (Fifth St.)	DT	213-892-8080	Hot & Cool	82
Standard Downtown					
Hotel Bar	standardhotel.com	C	- ▭	Hotel Bars	27
The Roost	3100 Los Feliz Blvd.	VA	323-664-7272	Hip	118
Bar	(Edenhurst St.)				
Saddle Ranch Chop House*	8371 W. Sunset Blvd. (La Cienega	LA	323-656-2007	Hot & Cool	53, 82
Restaurant/Bar	Blvd.) srrestaurants.com	-	- ▦	Daytime Drink Spots 22	
Skybar	8440 W. Sunset Blvd. (La Cienega	WH	323-848-6025	Hot & Cool	54, 82
Hotel Bar	Blvd.) mondrianhotel.com	-	- ▭	Hotel Bars	27
Social Hollywood*	6525 W. Sunset Blvd. (Schrader	HW	323-462-5222	Hip	94, 118
Restaurant/Lounge	Blvd.) socialhollywood.com	-	- ▦		
Spaceland	1717 Silver Lake Blvd. (Effie St.)	SL	323-661-4380	Hip	93, 118
Live Music	clubspaceland.com	C	- ▦		
Spider Club	1737 N. Vine St. (Hollywood Blvd.)	HW	323-462-8900	Hot & Cool	83
Nightclub	avalonhollywood.com/spider.html	C	- ▦	Singles Scenes	39
Sunset Trocadero*	8280 Sunset Blvd. (Sweetzer Ave.)	LA	323-656-7161	Classic	144
Restaurant/Bar		-	- ▭		
Temple Bar	1026 Wilshire Blvd. (Eleventh St.)	SM	310-393-6611	Hip	118
Live Music	templebarlive.com	C	- ▦		
Tiki Ti	4427 W. Sunset Blvd. (Virgil Pl.)	LF	323-669-9381	Classic	144
Dive Bar	tiki-ti.com	-	- ▦	Dive Bars	23
Tropicana Bar at the	7000 Hollywood Blvd. (Orange Dr.)	HW	323-466-7000	Hip	91, 118
Roosevelt Hotel Bar	hollywoodroosevelt.com	-	- ▭	Celebrity Hangouts 17	
Troubadour	9081 Santa Monica Blvd.	LA	310-276-6168	Classic	128, 144
Live Music	(Doheny St.) troubadour.com	-	B ▦	Live Music Venues 30	
The Well	6255 W. Sunset Blvd. (Argyle)	HW	323-467-9355	Hip	93, 119
Bar		-	- ▦		
White Lotus*	1743 Cahuenga Blvd. (Hollywood	HW	323-463-0060	Hot & Cool	83
Restaurant/Nightclub	Blvd.) whitelotushollywood.com	C	- ▦		
Wilshire Restaurant*	2454 Wilshire Blvd. (26th St.)	SM	310-586-1707	Hot & Cool	83
Restaurant/Bar	wilshirerestaurant.com	C	- ▦		
The Wiltern LG	3790 Wilshire Blvd. (Western Ave.)	LA	213-380-5005	Classic	145
Live Music	thewiltern.com	C	- ▦	Live Music Venues 30	
Yamashiro*	1999 N. Sycamore Ave. (Franklin	HW	323-466-5125	Classic	128, 145
Restaurant/Lounge	Ave.) yamashirorestaurant.com	-	- ▭		
Ye Rustic Inn	1831 Hillhurst Ave.	LF	323-662-5757	Hip	93, 119
Bar	(Melbourne St.)	-	- ▦		

Nightlife (cont.)

NAME	ADDRESS (CROSS STREET)	AREA	PHONE	EXPERIENCE	PAGE
TYPE	WEBSITE	COVER	FOOD/NOISE	99 BEST	PAGE
Zanzibar	1301 Fifth St. (Arizona Ave.)	SM	310-451-2221	Hip	119
Lounge	zanzibarlive.com	C	- ⩳		

Attractions

NAME	ADDRESS (CROSS STREET)	AREA	PHONE	EXPERIENCE	PAGE
TYPE	WEBSITE	PRICE		99 BEST	PAGE
Arclight Cinemas	6360 W. Sunset Blvd. (Vine)	HW	323-464-4226	Hip	*94*, 120
Movie Theater	arclightcinemas.com	$$		Movie Theaters	31
Bergamot Station	2525 Michigan Ave. (Cloverfield	SM	310-829-5854	Hip	*93*, 120
Site/Shopping	Blvd.) bergamotstation.com	-			
Beverly Hills Trolley Tours	Rodeo Dr. and Dayton Way	BH	310-285-2438	Classic	146
Tour	beverlyhills.org	$			
Beverly Hot Springs	308 N. Oxford Ave. (Beverly Blvd.)	LA	323-734-7000	Hot & Cool	84
Spa	beverlyhotsprings.com	$$$$			
Bliss	930 Hilgard Ave. (Weyburn Ave.)	VA	323-930-0330	Hip	120
Spa	blissworld.com/spa/location/la	$$$$		Spas	40
Bradbury Building	304 S. Broadway (Third St.)	DT	213-626-1893	Classic	146
Site	bradburybuilding.info	-			
Briles Wing & Helicopter	16303 Waterman Dr.	VA	877-863-5952	Hot & Cool	84
Tour	(Roscoe Blvd.) toflyla.com	$$$$		Views of L.A.	46
Brookside Golf Course	1133 Rosemont Ave. (Rose Bowl Dr.)	PD	626-796-0177	Classic	*127*, 146
Golf	brooksidemensgolfclub.com	$$$$			
Chinatown		VA	213-680-0243	Classic	146
Site	chinatownla.com	-			
Crunch Fitness	8000 W. Sunset Blvd. (Crescent	WH	323-654-4550	Hip	120
Gym	Heights Blvd.) crunch.com	$		Workouts	48
Dtox Day Spa	3206 Los Feliz Blvd. (Glenfeliz	LF	323-665-3869	Hip	*92*, 120
Spa	Blvd.) dtoxdayspa.com	$$$$			
Egyptian Theatre	6712 Hollywood Blvd. (Las Palmas	HW	323-466-3456	Classic	*127*, 147
Movie Theater	Ave.) egyptiantheatre.com	$		Movie Theaters	31
Epicurean School of	8500 Melrose Ave. (La Cienega	WH	310-659-5990	Classic	147
Culinary Arts Activity	Blvd.) epicureanschool.com	$$$$			
Farmers Market	6333 W. Third St. (Fairfax Ave.)	LA	323-933-9211	Classic	*126*, 147
Market	farmersmarketla.com	-			
The Geffen Contemporary	152 N. Central Ave. (First St.)	DT	213-621-2766	Hip	*93*, 121
Art Museum	moca.org	$			
The Getty Center	1200 Getty Center Dr.	LA	310-440-7300	Hot & Cool	*51*, 84
Museum	(Sepulveda Blvd.) getty.edu	-			
Getty Villa	17985 Pacific Coast Hwy.	VA	310-440-7300	Classic	*125*, 147
Art Museum	(Sunset Blvd.) getty.edu/visit	-		Cool Museums	20

NAME TYPE	ADDRESS (CROSS STREET) WEBSITE	AREA PRICE	PHONE	EXPERIENCE 99 BEST	PAGE PAGE
Gold's Gym Gym	360 Hampton Dr. (Rose Ave.) goldsgym.com	VB $$	310-392-6004	Classic Workouts	148 48
Grand Central Market Market	317 S. Broadway (Fourth St.) grandcentralsquare.com	DT -	213-624-2378	Classic	148
Grauman's Chinese Theatre Movie Theater	6925 Hollywood Blvd. (Orange Dr.) manntheatres.com/chinese	HW $	323-461-3331	Classic	127, 148
Greystone Park and Mansion Park/Site	905 Loma Vista Dr. (Robert Ln.) greystonemansion.org	BH -	310-550-4796	Classic	148
Griffith Park Observatory Park/Site	Griffith Park griffithobs.org	LF $-	888-695-0888	Classic	92, 148
Hollywood & Highland Shopping	6801 Hollywood Blvd. (Highland Ave.) hollywoodandhighland.com	HW -	323-467-6412	Hot & Cool	127, 84
Hollywood Entertainment Museum Museum	7021 Hollywood Blvd. (Orange Dr.) hollywoodmuseum.com	HW $	323-465-7900	Classic	127, 149
Hollywood Forever Cemetery Cemetery	6000 Santa Monica Blvd. (Gower St.) hollywoodforever.com	HW -	323-469-1181	Classic Graveyards of Stars	128, 149 24
Hollywood Walk of Fame Site	Hollywood Blvd. (Vine St.) hollywoodchamber.net	HW -	-	Classic	127, 149
Holy Cross Cemetery Cemetery	5835 W. Slauson Ave. (Bristol Pkwy.)	CC -	310-670-7697	Classic Graveyards of Stars	149 24
Huntington Botanical Gardens Garden	1151 Oxford Rd. (E. Union St.) huntington.org	PD $-	626-405-2100	Classic	127, 150
Jet Rag Shop	825 N. La Brea Ave. (Waring Ave.)	LA -	323-939-0528	Hip	121
Kiehl's Shop	100 N. Robertson Blvd. (Beverly Blvd.) kiehls.com	LA -	310-860-0028	Hot & Cool	85
Kinara Spa Spa	656 N. Robertson Blvd. (Melrose Ave.) kinaraspa.com	WH $$$$	310-657-9188	Hot & Cool Spas	53, 85 40
Kitson Shop	115 S. Robertson Blvd. (Third St.) shopkitson.com	BH -	-	Hot & Cool	85
Kodak Theatre Site	6801 Hollywood Blvd. (Highland Ave.) kodaktheatre.com	HW -	323-308-6300	Hot & Cool	127, 85
Leo Carillo State Beach Beach	35000 Pacific Coast Hwy. (Mulholland Hwy.)	MB -	818-880-0350	Classic	150
Little Tokyo Site	- -	VA -	-	Hip	121
Los Angeles Conservancy Walking Tours Tour	523 W. Sixth St., Suite 826 (Olive St.) laconservancy.org	DT $	213-623-2489	Classic Guided Tours	150 25
Los Angeles County Museum of Art (LACMA) Museum	5905 Wilshire Blvd. (Fairfax Ave.) lacma.org	LA $	323-857-6000	Classic Cool Museums	126, 150 20
Los Angeles Horseback Riding Tour	2623 Old Topanga Canyon Rd. (Pinehurst Rd.) losangeleshorsebackriding.com	VA $$$$	818-591-2032	Hot & Cool	54, 85
Los Feliz Municipal Golf Course Golf	3207 Los Feliz Blvd. (Glenfeliz Blvd.)	LF $	323-663-7758	Hip	121

Attractions (cont.)

NAME TYPE	ADDRESS (CROSS STREET) WEBSITE	AREA PRICE	PHONE	EXPERIENCE 99 BEST	PAGE PAGE
Madison Shop	9630 Brighton Way (Bedford Dr.) madisonstyle.com	BH -	310-273-4787	Classic	150
Malibu Country Club Golf	901 Encinal Canyon Rd. (Mulholland Hwy.) malibucountryclub.com	MB $$$$	818-889-6680	Classic	*54*, 151
Malibu Country Mart Shopping	3835 Cross Creek Rd. (Civic Center Way) malibucountrymart.com	MB	-	Hot & Cool	86
Manhattan Beach Beach	End of Manhattan Beach Blvd.	SB -	-	Classic Beaches	151 16
Mann's Village Theatre Movie Theater	961 Broxton Ave. (Weyburn Ave.) manntheaters.com	VA $	310-248-6266	Classic Movie Theaters	151 31
Marina del Rey Sportfishing Sport	Dock 52, Fiji Way (Admiralty Way) mdrsf.com	VA $$$	310-822-3625	Hot & Cool	86
Marina Sailing Sport	13441 Mindanao Way (Admiralty Way) marinasailing.com	VA $$$$	800-262-7245	Hot & Cool	86
Mulholland Highway Site	Hwy. 1 West	VA -	-	Hip	121
Museum of Contemporary Art (MOCA) Art Museum	250 S. Grand Ave. (First St.) moca.org	DT $	213-626-6222	Hip	*92*, 122
Museum of Neon Art (MONA) Art Museum	501 W. Olympic Blvd. (Grand Ave.) neonmona.org	DT $	213-489-9918	Hip	*93*, 122
Museum of Television & Radio Cultural Museum	465 N. Beverly Dr. (Little Santa Monica Blvd.) mtr.org	BH -	310-786-1000	Hot & Cool	*53*, 86
Museum of the American West Cultural Museum	4700 Western Heritage Way (Zoo Dr.) autrynationalcenter.org	LF $	323-667-2000	Hip	122
Museum of Tolerance Cultural Museum	9786 W. Pico Blvd. (Roxbury Dr.) museumoftolerance.com	LA $	310-553-8403	Classic	*126*, 151
NBC Studios Site/Tour	3000 W. Alameda Ave. (W. Olive Ave.) nbc.com	VA $	818-840-3537	Hot & Cool Studio Tours	86 42
Norton Simon Museum Art Museum	411 W. Colorado Blvd. (Orange Grove Blvd.) nortonsimon.org	PD $	626-449-6840	Classic Cool Museums	*127*, 151 20
Ole Henriksen Face/Body Spa	8622-A W. Sunset Blvd. (Sunset Plaza Dr.) olehenriksen.com	WH $$$$	310-854-7700	Hot & Cool Spas	*52*, 87 40
Paradise Bound Yacht Charters Tour	4375 Admiralty Way (Bali Way) aaparadiseboundyacht.com	VA $$$$	310-578-7963	Hot & Cool	87
Paramount Pictures Tour/Site	5555 Melrose Ave. (Van Ness Ave.) paramount.com	HW $$$	323-956-5000	Classic	152
Paramount Ranch Site	Paramount Ranch Rd. (Cornell Rd.) paramount.com	VA -	818-597-9192	Classic	152
Petersen Automotive Museum Cultural Museum	6060 Wilshire Blvd. (Fairfax Ave.) petersen.org	LA $	323-930-2277	Hip	*94*, 122
The Pierce Bros. Westwood Village Memorial Park Site	1218 Glendon Ave. (Wilshire Blvd.)	VA -	310-474-1579	Hot & Cool Graveyards of Stars	*51*, 87 24
Point Mugu State Park Hike	9000 Pacific Coast Hwy. (Sycamore Canyon Rd.) parks.ca.gov	MB -	818-880-0350	Hot & Cool Hikes	*54*, 87 26

NAME	ADDRESS (CROSS STREET)	AREA	PHONE	EXPERIENCE	PAGE
TYPE	WEBSITE	PRICE		99 BEST	PAGE
Polkadots & Moonbeams	8367 W. Third St. (Kings Rd.)	LA	323-651-1746	Hip	122
Shop	polkadotsandmoonbeams.com	-			
Pure Surfing Experience	Parking lot at 40th St.	SB	310-374-5902	Hip	123
Sport	(Rosecrans Ave.) campsurf.com	$$$$			
Rancho Park Golf Course	10460 W. Pico Blvd. (Patricia	LA	310-838-7373	Hot & Cool	87
Golf	Ave.) lagolfclubs.com/clubs	$$			
Red Line Tours	6773 Hollywood Blvd.	HW	323-402-1074	Classic	152
Tour	(Highland Ave.) redlinetours.com	$		Guided Tours	25
Rose Bowl Flea Market	1001 Rose Bowl Dr.	PD	323-560-7469	Classic	152
Market	(N. Arroyo Blvd.) rgcshows.com	-			
Runyon Canyon Park	2000 N. Fuller Ave. (Franklin Ave.)	HW	213-644-6661	Hip	94, 123
Park	runyon-canyon.com	-		Hikes	26
Satine	8117 W. Third St. (Crescent	LA	323-655-2142	Hip	123
Shop	Heights Blvd.) satineboutique.com	-			
Silent Movie Theatre	611 N. Fairfax Ave. (Melrose Ave.)	HW	323-655-2520	Classic	152
Movie Theater	silentmovietheatre.com	$			
South Bay Bicycle Trail	From Will Rogers to Torrence Beaches			Hot & Cool	88
Sport	coastalconservancy.ca.gov	VA	-		
Southwest Museum of the American Indian					
	234 Museum Dr. (Marmion Way)	LA	323-221-2163	Classic	153
Cultural Museum	southwestmuseum.com				
The Sports Club / LA	1835 Sepulveda Blvd. (Olympic	LA	310-473-1447	Hot & Cool	88
Gym	Blvd.) thesportsclubla.com	$$		Workouts	48
Sunset Strip	Sunset Blvd. (La Cienega Blvd.)	WH	-	Classic	153
Site		-			
Temescal Gateway Park	15601 W. Sunset Blvd. (Temescal	VA	310-454-1395	Classic	153
Park	Canyon Rd.) lamountains.com	-		Hikes	26
3rd Street Dance	8558 W. Third St. (San Vicente	LA	310-275-4683	Classic	153
Activity	Blvd.) 3rdstreetdance.com	$$$$			
Third Street Promenade	Third St. (btwn Broadway and	SM	310-393-8355	Hot & Cool	51, 88
Shopping	Wilshire Blvd.) downtownsm.com	-			
Tracey Ross	8595 W. Sunset Blvd.	WH	310-854-1996	Classic	153
Shop	(Sunset Plaza Dr.) traceyross.com	-			
Universal Studios	100 Universal City Plaza	VA	800-864-8377	Hot & Cool	52, 88
Hollywood	(Universal Studios Blvd.)				
Site/Tour	themeparks.universalstudios.com	$$$$		Studio Tours	42
Venice Beach/Ocean Front	Ocean Front Walk from Rose Ave.	VB	-	Hip	93, 123
Walk Beach/Walk	to Washington St.	-		Beaches	16
Walt Disney Concert Hall	111 S. Grand Ave. (Second St.)	DT	213-972-7211	Hot & Cool	52, 89
Concert Venue/Site	musiccenter.org/wdch	$			
Warner Brothers Studios	4000 Warner Blvd. (Avon St.)	VA	818-972-8687	Classic	126, 154
Site/Tour	wbsf.warnerbros.com	$$$$	818-954-1744	Studio Tours	42
Will Rogers State Historic	1501 Will Rogers State Park Rd.	VA	310-454-8212	Classic	154
Park Activity	(Sunset Blvd.) parks.ca.gov	$			

NAME	ADDRESS (CROSS STREET)	AREA	PHONE	EXPERIENCE	PAGE
TYPE	WEBSITE	PRICE		99 BEST	PAGE
Williams-Sonoma Home	8772 Beverly Blvd. (Robertson)	BH	310-289-2420	Hot & Cool	89
Shop	wshome.com	-			
Wilson/Harding Golf	4730 Crystal Springs Dr.	LF	323-664-2255	Hip	92, 123
Courses	(Griffith Park Dr.)				
Golf	laparks.org/dos/sports/golf.htm	$$			
Zuma Beach	30050 Pacific Coast Hwy.	MB	-	Classic	154
Beach	(Morning View Dr.)	-		Beaches	16

Los Angeles Black Book By Neighborhood

Bel-Air (BA)

H	Hotel Bel-Air	131
R	Hotel Bel-Air Restaurant	33 136
N	The Bar at Hotel Bel-Air	141

Beverly Hills (BH)

H	Avalon Hotel	98
	Beverly Hills Hotel & Bungalows	28 131
	Beverly Wilshire Four Seasons Hotel	36 131
	Four Seasons Hotel	59
	Luxe Hotel Rodeo Drive	59
	Maison 140	132
	The Peninsula Beverly Hills	36 133
	Raffles L'Ermitage Beverly Hills	60
R	Barney Greengrass	35 63
	Brighton Coffee Shop	134
	Crustacean	67
	Cut	45 67
	The Grill on the Alley	35 69
	Il Cielo	37 136
	The Ivy	19 136
R	Kate Mantilini	106
	Mr. Chow	19 137
	Polo Lounge*	139
	La Scala	139
	Spago	35 139
	Urasawa	43 75
N	Club Bar at the Peninsula Beverly Hills	142
	Lobby Bar at the Four Seasons	80
	Polo Lounge*	144
A	Beverly Hills Trolley Tours	146
	Greystone Park and Mansion	148
	Kitson	85
	Madison	150
	Museum of Television & Radio	86
	Williams-Sonoma Home	89

Downtown (DT)

H	Millennium Biltmore Hotel	132
	The Standard Downtown	99
R	Arnie Morton's of Chicago	134
	Café Pinot	65
	Cicada	66

Code: H-Hotels; R-Restaurants; N-Nightlife; A-Attractions. Blue page numbers denote listings in 99 Best. Black page numbers denote listings in theme chapters. The Los Angeles Neighborhoods Map is on p.232.

BLACK BOOK

Los Angeles Unique Shopping Index

For Neighborhood (Area) Key, see p.208

BLACK BOOK

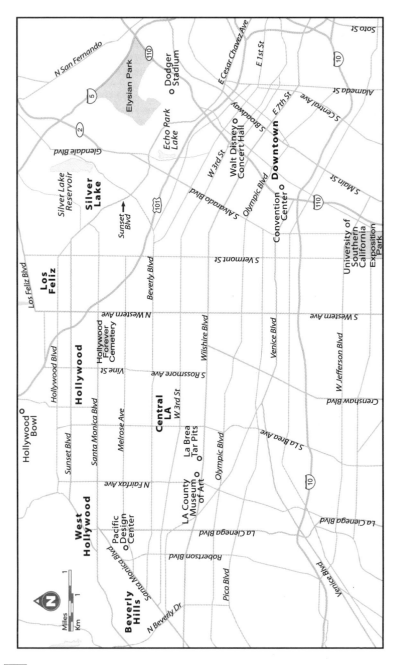

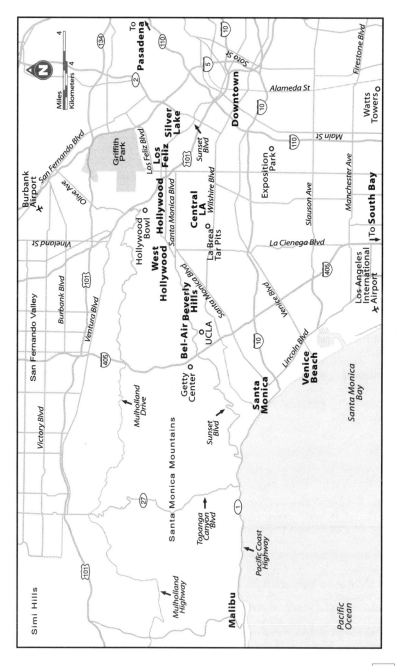

It's New. It's You.
Night+Day online
@ pulseguides.com

a travel web site designed to
complement your lifestyle

Today's urbane, sophisticated traveler knows
how fast things change in the world. What's hot,
and what's not? Now you have access to the
insider information you need, whenever you
need it—**Night+Day**—at pulseguides.com.

We're committed to providing the latest, most
accurate information on the hottest, hippest,
coolest and classiest venues around the world,
which means keeping our listings current—
even after you've purchased one of our
Night+Day guides.

Visit pulseguides.com and browse your way to any
destination to view or download the most recent
updates to the **Night+Day** guide of your choice.

Online and in print, **Night+Day** offers independent travel advice tailored to suit your lifestyle,
capturing the unique personality of each city.
From uptown chic to downtown cool, our guides
are packed with opinionated tips, and selective,
richly detailed descriptions geared toward the
discerning traveler.

Enhance your travel experience online:
- Zero in on hot restaurants, classic
  attractions and hip nightlife
- Print out your favorite itinerary to keep
  in your purse or pocket as you travel
- Update your **Night+Day** guide with
  what's new
- Read news and tips from around the world
- Get great deals on all the titles in our Cool
  Cities series

Night+Day—online now at pulseguides.com.